The Grasinski Girls

Ohio University Press Polish and Polish-American Studies Series

Series Editor: John J. Bukowczyk, Wayne State University

Framing the Polish Home: Postwar Cultural Constructions of Hearth, Nation, and Self, edited by Bożena Shallcross

Traitors and True Poles: Narrating a Polish-American Identity, 1880–1939, by Karen Majewski

Auschwitz, Poland, and the Politics of Commemoration, 1945–1979, by Jonathan Huener

The Exile Mission: The Polish Political Diaspora and Polish-Americans, 1939–1956, by Anna D. Jaroszyńska-Kirchmann

The Grasinski Girls: The Choices They Had and the Choices They Made, by Mary Patrice Erdmans

The Grasinski Girls

*The Choices They Had and
the Choices They Made*

Mary Patrice Erdmans

With the Grasinski Girls

OHIO UNIVERSITY PRESS

ATHENS

Ohio University Press, Athens, Ohio 45701
© 2004 by Ohio University Press

Ohio University Press books are printed on acid-free paper ∞

11 10 09 08   5 4 3

Vignette photograph of Angela Helen Grasinski Erdmans and figure 7 by Andrew Erdmans.

Cover: *Top, left to right:* Angel, Gene, and Mary at their home, Christmas 1956. *Bottom, left to right:* Fran, Caroline, Mari, Nadine, Angel, and Elaine (widow of Joe Grasinski), 1990.

Library of Congress Cataloging-in-Publication Data

Erdmans, Mary Patrice.
  The Grasinski girls : the choices they had and the choices they made / Mary Patrice Erdmans.— 1st ed.
       p.   cm.   —   (Ohio University Press Polish and Polish-American studies series)
  Includes bibliographical references and index.
  ISBN 0-8214-1581-6 (cloth : alk. paper) — ISBN 0-8214-1582-4 (pbk. : alk. paper)
    1. Polish American families—Michigan—Case studies. 2. Women, White—Michigan—Case studies. 3. Grasinski family. 4. Erdmans, Mary Patrice—Family. 5. Michigan—Social life and customs—20th century. I. Title. II. Series.
  F575.P7E73 2004
  305.8′9185′073—dc22

                                                    2004015018

Publication of books in the Polish and Polish-American Studies Series has been made possible in part by the generous support of the following organizations:

Polish American Historical Association, New Britain, Connecticut

Stanislaus A. Blejwas Endowed Chair in Polish and Polish American Studies, Central Connecticut State University, New Britain, Connecticut

Madonna University, Livonia, Michigan

The Polish Institute of Arts and Sciences of America, Inc., New York, New York

The Piast Institute: An Institute for Polish and Polish American Affairs, Detroit, Michigan

To Nathan Frances
I pray you learn to sing

Contents

Illustrations

Series Editor's Preface

HISTORIANS AND SOCIAL SCIENTISTS have studied the male-dominated public side of Polish immigrant and ethnic life that took place in the churches and organizations, in the shops and the factories, on the picket line, and at the ballot box. But few studies have peered into the homes to examine the hidden, inner social world of white ethnic families and communities like those of Polish America and, more specifically, the private lives of the white ethnic women of modest, working-class backgrounds who lived therein.

Through extensive interviews and interactions with five Polish-American sisters—the author's own aunts and mother—sociologist Mary Patrice Erdmans enters this secret yet signally important world to tell the story of a generation of women who, for the most part, have remained voiceless in both the ethnic and women's history narratives. In *The Grasinski Girls: The Choices They Had and the Choices They Made,* Erdmans describes this world as seen through the women's own eyes, a world of small victories, silent hurts, ordinary pleasures, and, above all, the triumph of survival. Their world, to be sure, was bounded by the structures and strictures of patriarchal relations with their father, their husbands, and their employers, but men remain mostly offstage in this volume. This is, instead, the story of five women and the personal engagement of one Polish-American daughter and sociologist with the lives of these women, who, perhaps without their knowing it, nurtured her own professional ambitions and feminist consciousness.

Professor Erdmans, associate professor of sociology at Central Connecticut State University, also is the author of *Opposite Poles: Immigrants and Ethnics in Polish Chicago, 1976–1990.* In *The Grasinski Girls,* Erdmans has written a unique and pathbreaking study of gender, ethnicity, and class that will enlighten scholars, students, and general readers interested in women's studies, ethnic studies, and the Polish-American experience.

The Grasinski Girls: The Choices They Had and the Choices They Made is the fifth volume in the Ohio University Press Polish and Polish-American Studies Series. The series revisits the historical and contemporary experience of one of America's largest European ethnic groups and the history of a European homeland that has played a disproportionately important role in twentieth-century and contemporary world affairs. The series aims to publish innovative monographs and more general works that investigate under- or unexplored topics or themes that offer new, critical, revisionist, or comparative perspectives in the area of Polish and Polish-American Studies. Interdisciplinary or multidisciplinary in profile, the series seeks manuscripts on Polish immigration and ethnic communities, the country of origin, and its various peoples in history, anthropology, cultural studies, political economy, current politics, and related fields.

Publication of the Ohio University Press Polish and Polish-American Studies Series marks a milestone in the maturation of the Polish Studies field and stands as a fitting tribute to the scholars and organizations whose efforts have brought it to fruition. Supported by a series advisory board of accomplished Polonists and Polish-Americanists, the Polish and Polish-American Studies Series has been made possible through generous financial assistance from the Polish American Historical Association, the Polish Institute of Arts and Sciences of America, the Stanislaus A. Blejwas Endowed Chair in Polish and Polish American Studies at Central Connecticut State University, Madonna University, and the Piast Institute, and through institutional support from Wayne State University and Ohio University Press. The series meanwhile has benefited from the warm encouragement of a number of persons, including Gillian Berchowitz, M. B. B. Biskupski, the late Stanislaus A. Blejwas, Thomas Gladsky, Thaddeus Gromada, Sister Rose Marie Kujawa, CSSF, James S. Pula, Thaddeus Radzilowski, and David Sanders. The moral and material support from all of these institutions and individuals is gratefully acknowledged.

John J. Bukowczyk

Guide to Pronunciation

THE FOLLOWING KEY provides a guide to the pronunciation of Polish words and names.

a is pronounced as in *father*

c as ts in *cats*

ch like a guttural h

cz as hard ch in *church*

g always hard, as in *get*

i as ee

j as y in *yellow*

rz like French j in *jardin*

sz as sh in *ship*

szcz as shch, enunciating both sounds, as in *fresh cheese*

u as oo in *boot*

w as v

ć as soft ch

ś as sh

ż, ź both as zh, the latter higher in pitch than the former

ó as oo in boot

ą as French *on*

ę as French *en*

ł as w

ń changes the combinations -in to -ine, -en to -ene, and -on to -oyne

The accent in Polish words always falls on the penultimate syllable.

The Grasinski Girls

THEY HAVE BEAUTIFUL NAMES: Caroline Clarice, Genevieve Irene, Frances Ann, Mary Nadine née Patricia Marie, Angela Helen, Mary Marcelia. These are the Grasinski Girls. They are the daughters of Helen Frances Grasinski, and I am her granddaughter.

What I remember about my grandma Helen is that she was tall and she stood tall. She kept her shoulders back and chin high. I remember her as a wanderer. I have images of her getting on and off buses, in and out of cars, with a small suitcase that was actually just a big purse, as she traveled from house to house, one-bedroom apartment to one-bedroom apartment, daughter's house to daughter's house. Caroline, her eldest daughter, recalls, "Mom used to say, the minute she hears the freight train she wants to pack her suitcase and go. I really don't know if it's a thing, a place, or whether it's something inside you, this wandering and searching and looking for something." She moved eighteen times in her life. She was a good traveler, everything efficiently packed in that neat little bag, and she had an ability to make a place a home in a short period of time. Caroline continued, "She would be unpacked with all the pictures on the wall by the end of the day, and then she was sittin' there."

What I don't remember about my grandmother, but what I am often told, is that she had a beautiful voice. I don't remember her singing, but her daughters do. She sang arias while washing the dishes and folk songs while peeling potatoes; she sang Polish carols like "Lulajże Jezuniu" at Christmas and popular American songs like "Let the Rest of the World Go By" and "I'll See You Again and I'll Smile" while picking the grime out of the space between the floorboards with a safety pin. As a young farm girl she took voice lessons in Grand Rapids, riding twenty miles on the Interurban. She was a soprano, and if I close my eyes I can imagine a robust, resplendently piercing soprano, chin held high, neck straight, shoulders squared. At the age of sixteen she was given her chance. A professional impresario offered to take her to New York to become a concert singer. But her father said no. Instead, she married a local boy, Joe Grasinski, sang to her seven children, and spent the rest of her life moving here and there, around and about a sixty-mile ring of familial enclosure in southwestern Michigan.

Years later, Helen found her daughter—my mother—sitting in my bedroom listening to a scratchy Crosby, Stills, and Nash tape and crying, saddened by the fact that I had gone to live in Asia for a few years. She expressed little sympathy. "Why are you crying? You were the one who let her go." As if she had a choice. But it seems that it didn't matter if we were kept back or let go, both Grandma and I became wanderers and we both carry small bags. My orbit is a little wider than hers, but, like her, I keep returning home, never able to walk away and keep on walking.

|||

Today, Helen's daughters are called Caroline, Gene, Fran, Nadine, Angel, and Mari. Many of you will recognize the Grasinski Girls in your own mothers, aunts, sisters, and grandmothers. They are white, Christian Americans of European descent, and therefore represent the sociological and numerical majority of women in the United States. Born in the 1920s and 1930s, they created lives typical of women in their day: they went to high school, got married, had children, and, for the most part, stayed home to raise those children. And they were happy doing that. They took care of their appearance and married men who took care of them. Like most women in their cohort, they did not join the women's movement and today either reject or shy away from feminism. They do not identify with Betty Friedan's "problem that has no name," and they are on the pro-life side of the abortion debate.[1] They give both time and money to support charitable (usually religiously affiliated) organizations working to ease the suffering of those less fortunate.[2] Most of them go to church every Sunday and they read their morning prayers as faithfully and necessarily as I drink my morning coffee.

The Grasinski Girls' immigrant grandparents were farmers. Their father was a skilled factory worker, and their children have college degrees. Their

Polish ancestry is visible in their high cheekbones and wide hips, but otherwise hidden in the box of Christmas ornaments stored carefully in the attic. Theirs is a story of white working-class women.

Who are these women who sing in church pews, hum in hallways, and cry to sad songs about miseries they do not have? Do we see their curved backs tending gardens in the backyard, or bent over sewing machines or dining room tables cluttered with their latest craft project? When I read social science literature written before the 1970s, I read mostly about men—and mostly white men. Since then we have heard more women's voices, mostly the voices of white middle-class women. But again, that is changing, and now we hear from and about black women, Latinas and Chicanas, Asian women, and Native-American women, as well as low-income women, homeless women, and immigrant women. Traditional gender studies ignored class and race when they developed theories about all women based on the experiences of white middle-class women.[3] Contemporary gender studies are more likely to acknowledge race, but too often they obscure class by folding it into race. For example, Aida Hurtado states, "When I discuss feminists of Color I will treat them as members of the working class, unless I specifically mention otherwise. When I discuss white feminists, I will treat them as middle class."[4] When combined with those of white middle-class women, the voices (and disadvantages) of white working-class women are lost. A similar confusion occurs when white working-class women are grouped together with working-class racial minorities and immigrants. In this case, however, white native-born privilege gets overlooked.

When the voices of white working-class women are heard, they are more likely to be public and "classed" voices related to labor-market position. Social scientists generally examine social life in places where they can see it, that is, in the public sphere (e.g., the workplace, the neighborhood association, government offices). Public-sphere activity is also easier for scholars to grasp and write about because it is normative.[5] Donna Gabaccia found that immigrant community studies "do not ignore women but describe mainly those aspects of women's lives (wage-earning and labor activism) that most resemble men's. Distinctly female concerns—housework, marketing, pregnancy or child rearing—receive little or no attention."[6] As a result, we hear working-class women chanting protests in front of factories and challenging public officials at neighborhood meetings, but we seldom hear them praying in the early dark of morning or laughing with their sisters in the warmth of the kitchen.[7]

While the Grasinski Girls moved through the public sphere as secretaries, nurses, cooks, teachers, and den mothers, they constructed their identity mostly in the domestic sphere. To begin to understand their worldview, I visited with them in their kitchens, living rooms, dining rooms, bedrooms, and local parks. Over a period of four years (1998–2002), I listened to and recorded their stories. I then constructed their oral histories from these transcripts. Then, they reconstructed my construction. Together we hammered out a representation and an analysis of who I thought they were and who they wanted to be seen as.

|||

> Every phase of my life, just wonderful things have been there, I have to admit it. Well, there are some mistakes you always make, but basically, I mean I liked the way I live, what life has given me, what came from that little farm girl.
>
> Nadine

The Grasinski Girls tell stories of contented lives with abundant blessings, a God who loves and protects them, and children who are healthy. "I don't think there is anything I would have changed or say I regret. God has been good to all of us," Fran writes to me. They experienced no great tragedies but instead lived "ordinary" lives. Sure, there have been ups and downs, but they pretty much, in all categories, fall in the middle of the bell curve. They are "normal," and social scientists have not studied normal very much. Perhaps this is because the life of the average Jane is not as compelling as that of the exotic Jane. Perhaps it is because stories that are seductively sensational are easier to sell.[8] A less cynical reason that ordinary lives are not researched is that they do not present "social problems." Social scientists more often study populations and institutions that are troubling and cry out for solutions (e.g., drug addiction, suicide, domestic violence). But what are we missing when we focus on the extremes and ignore the more subtle ways that social structures constrain lives? And what are we missing when we focus on discrimination but not privilege?

When privilege is taken for granted, it is not placed under the microscope for examination, and the absence of problems becomes defined as normal rather than as privilege. When, instead, we focus on the normal, as Ashley Doane has done, privilege becomes visible and we can see those otherwise hidden ways that the political and economic structures relatively advantage certain populations.[9] Alternatively, when we focus on extreme oppression, we miss the subtlety of inequality. When we study horrific problems, we amplify social life so that we can hear it more clearly. Domestic violence shouts patriarchy. But where is the whisper of patriarchy that robs women of the opportunity to develop their full potential? In the same way, when we study social movements, we see individuals publicly working to change social institutions, but not the nudging of resistance in our private lives. How does resistance operate in the kitchen and the bedroom? How do people challenge structures of inequality in their everyday routines? And, conversely, how do their routines reproduce inequality?

In telling the stories of the Grasinski Girls, I try to make visible their privileges hidden under the cloak of normalcy as well as the nuances of oppression often overlooked. Their contented life stories made it easier for me to see their privilege than their oppression. Moreover, they construct narratives of happiness that undermine discussion of oppression. In fact, they do not even like the word *oppression* appearing in a book written about them. One of the sisters, commenting on a draft of the manuscript, said, "This oppression, this is the one thing that we didn't feel. It just seems like it's brought up so much. You see, it's very hard for you to go back in time to where we were. You're putting feelings into us that were not there. We didn't feel like we were oppressed. It wasn't that we didn't recognize it, it just wasn't there."

They have wonderful lives, they say. While there were some dark moments, they shied away from bruised areas and did not dwell in the valley of darkness. Have faith; be happy! That's their motto. Why? I wonder. Why do they insist on constructing happy narratives, and how do they go about achieving happiness? Happiness is not the absence of sadness but an ability to live with sadness and still see the beauty of the day. To breathe deeply and inhale the gray wetness of rain as nourishment, the white thickness of fog as misty backdrop. To be happy is to smile even when you don't get your way, to be grateful for the gifts you have been given. To be sure, happiness may be correlated with privilege—the more one's needs are met, the easier it is to be happy. But, for these women (and, I suspect, many others), happiness is also a modus operandi, and one of their life tasks is to figure out how to be happy.

While the sisters wanted me to present them as women who were happy, I wanted to present them as tough women who, even when things weren't going exactly right, figured out ways to live satisfying lives. Perhaps they didn't change the world, but they had the social competence to live in the world with dignity. They rejected many of my attempts to portray them, or their mother, as feisty, defiant, or discontented. They were not fighters, they said, but peacemakers; they were not wanderers, but homemakers. Even if they were less than happy at times, they did not see my point in focusing on *that* part of their lives.[10] As one sister said, "If you are going to say it, put it somewhere in a little corner, don't broadcast it and emphasize it," because the unhappy parts were not representative of their lives. They were privileged, they say ("blessed" is their term, because God, not social structure, is the prime mover in their worldview).

They were privileged by race and to some degree by class. They had, for the most part, economically stable and comfortable lives. As adults, some moved into the middle class, and even those in the working class lived well; they were certainly not poor, not even working poor, even if they were on tight budgets. And yet, growing up, they did not have the opportunities that the middle class offered—for example, the encouragement and means to continue their education. Moreover, they were not given (though some did acquire) the dispositions, routines, and linguistic styles of the professional middle class. They were also disadvantaged by their gender identities—at least my feminist perspective leads me to believe this. So do many of my colleagues, who shook their heads at these women's constructions of a "blessed" life, saying, "they have a revisionist history," "they are suffering from false consciousness," or the "opiate of their religion is really strong." You may also be suspicious. You may think that because I love and respect my aunts I won't tell their whole stories—warts and all. You are right. Weren't there more failures, sorrows, and ugliness? Yes. How complete is the story I am telling you? It is partial. How truthful is the story? There are sins of omission but not commission. There are no falsehoods or deliberate attempts to mislead you. I respected their right to construct their life stories as they wanted—if they wanted to leave out some parts, so be it. My question was, why did they construct their narratives in the way that they did?[11] Why do they want to present themselves as happy women—and how did they achieve, to varying degrees, their happiness?

Their happiness is partly a consequence of their position of relative privilege via race and class identities, but it also comes from their own actions, what sociologists call agency, their potential to construct the worlds within which they live. Their mother and their grandmother taught them how to sing and how to pray, how to plant flowers and how to suckle children. They also taught them how to be women: to depend on their selves and their Jesus to make them smile; to be strong, like the Blessed Virgin Mary, especially when things are bad; and to define their lives in the private sphere, in the family. The Grasinski Girls did not passively and blindly accept the insults of gender and relative class inequality. Instead, they resisted—not by joining social movements, but by planting gardens and listening to love songs, taking driver-training courses and using lawyers to help collect child support payments.

Black women writers like Patricia Hill Collins, Paula Giddings, and Audre Lorde taught me to look for resistance in places that no white male authority or traditional sociologist taught me to look: in the belly, in the backyard, in a late-afternoon conversation.[12] Even thought can be resistance. Refusing to engage in self-blame or refusing to believe negative messages of inferiority are ways of resisting oppressive cultures. These women claimed freedom by not embracing the competitive, alienating values of the public sphere; they claimed space in the house by taking over the kitchen table with their projects; they claimed power through generations by arguing for their daughters' right to move more freely in the worlds of work and love.

What I am calling resistance, some historians have called accommodation. Eugene Genovese, writing about slavery, defined accommodation as "a way of accepting what could not be helped without falling prey to the pressures for dehumanization, emasculation, and self-hatred" and suggested that accommodation "embraced its apparent opposite—resistance."[13] Accommodation is a non-insurrectionary form of resistance, a resistance that does not attempt to overthrow the system, but, at the same time, does not submit wholly to the humiliations of subordination. While it does not challenge the objective conditions of inequality, it does help prevent the internalization of inferiority. Even if the resistance takes place only in the mind, accommodation, as an adjustment to social conditions, implies action not docility, agency not resigned acceptance. This response to structural conditions offers both dignity and a modicum of happiness.

For the Grasinski Girls, the mind and the family were sites of resistance. Patricia Hill Collins argues that women often use existing structures to carve out spheres of influence rather than directly challenging "oppressive structures because, in many cases, direct confrontation is neither preferred nor possible."[14] The Grasinski Girls did not disrupt the balance of power, but they did create private worlds based somewhat on a set of values that ran counter to those that dominate public space. Whether conscious of it or not, their domestic routines and commitment to motherhood, while complementing men's work in the public sphere and thereby reproducing gendered status and capitalist relations of production, nonetheless tempered the arrant commercialization of the private sphere. Their moral careers as mothers, caretakers, and spiritual teachers valued affective rather then instrumental relations, placed people before profits, and embraced the nonmaterial and noncommidifiable forms of religious devotion.

|||

Once, I was sad about a problem I was having with a relationship that stemmed, I believed, from larger structures of gender inequalities. I was crying and wanted some female empathy, so I called home to my mother. I poured out my woes and feelings of anger, sadness, and depression and then asked, "Mom, haven't you ever felt this way?" She paused, coming up with nothing at first, but then said brightly, "Maybe you're pre-menopausal."

In trying to tackle these two tasks—explaining the lives of these ordinary women who represent the majority of women in America in their age cohort, and trying to understand their laughing personas—I landed in the middle of an epistemological funk. How do I step out of my worldview, my set of values, my matrix of perception, to see them as they see themselves, to understand them from *their* social location rather than from my location?[15]

The Grasinski Girls live in a world of colors, texture, shapes, and aromas; they live in an emotional world where sentences are punctuated by laughter and tears. They live in a caring world where the relationship comes before the self, and the self is found in the relationship. They live mostly at home. In contrast, I live in the public sphere, in an academic world made up of words and arguments, thoughts and books. I live in relationships, but my identity also is shaped by my profession. I live in a world of competition and ambition. My life is oriented toward seeing inequality with the purpose of changing it; their lives are oriented toward cultivating happiness in the social house into which they were born.

They live in a world very different from my own. At first I could not reconcile how my view of the world and their view of the world could be so different without one of us being wrong. And so I challenged their contentment, their belief that women have more power than men, their desire to stay in the private sphere. I challenged their playing dress-up with life; I challenged their days defined by how many pounds they have gained or lost and how good they still look. I challenged their "life is grand, cook him a good meal, believe in Jesus" brand of living. I wanted them to be feminists, to not be so concerned with diets and clothes, to understand gender and race and class inequality and to do something to fix it. I wanted them to stop coddling men and start thinking about themselves. I did not necessarily like the *way* they were women, and I think a part of me blamed gender inequality on women like them, women who throw like a girl and can't drink like a man.

In the end, they challenged me to see them without judging them by my standards, my values, my routines. Comparing their generation to my generation is different from judging their generation based on the values and beliefs of my generation. They struggle and resist, not in the way I do, which is to fight to join the man-made world. Instead, they fight to preserve their private, female world. My job as a sociologist was to try to understand their world. In some ways, it felt like going into foreign territory, in other ways, like I was coming home.

Our understanding is shaped by our position in the social order and embedded in the relation between the object (what we seek to know) and the subject (ourselves). Sociologist Karl Mannheim refers to this as relational knowledge.[16] Relational knowledge is not false knowledge, but partial knowledge. It is a view of the world from a particular social position or, as some feminist scholars refer to this, a particular standpoint.[17] The relevant epistemological and sociological questions are not about the veracity of knowledge but the social base of knowledge: Why do they think the way that they think? Why do they see the world the way that they see the world? What aspects of social structure shape how they perceive and understand their world?

Each generation has different opportunities, different perceptions of those opportunities, and, as a result, different choices. I want to both understand the world as they see it, and, with generational distance, frame their lives in historical-structural context. But when I use my frames—the frames of an educated professional woman who came of age in the 1970s—to understand the lives of these women, I am not hearing them, I am hearing myself. As is often the case, travel into foreign lands teaches us mostly about ourselves. And so, writing about their generation laid open my generation; trying to understand their lives, I could better see the value structure underlying my own standpoint.

Understanding knowledge as standpoints (theirs and mine) produced more egalitarian relations because the production of knowledge became the sharing of standpoints. I have tried to let you hear both their voices and mine, to give you their objections to my interpretations as well as my objections to their narrations.

‖‖

Dear Mary Patrice,

Sending you a few things. Upon seeing you last, I think the Grasinski Girls are wearing you out. It's difficult to write about people who see themselves one way, [different] than the way others see them.

I love you, Nadine

The Grasinski Girls guided this work. I would give them drafts and they would say, "No, that is not who I am!" "Where are my children? Put my children in the book!" "Tell them I love being a mother, did you say that, did you tell them I love being a mother?" One sister wrote to me early on that she was suspicious of my intentions: "We are not women with flabby arms flapping in the wind while we bake our apple pies." Don't insult us! I tried not to, and toward that end I gave them the right to edit the manuscript.

The participants in qualitative studies are always at least indirectly co-authors, in that they construct their story from which the social scientists construct *their* story. But this was a collaborative project in more explicit ways. The Grasinski Girls had ownership of their printed words. The collaborative, egalitarian structure of the project was a result of (1) the recognition of standpoints; (2) the fact that I was going to use their real names; and (3) the knowledge that I would always be going home for Christmas. Because of my intimate attachment to these women, I could not temporarily enter into their community, gather information, and then leave. There would be consequences to my writings in ways that mattered to me. I did not want to hurt them, so I could not go for the jugular. I could not reveal their deepest demons, their humiliations and unnamed fears—those were between them and Jesus. This is not a "tell-all" biography. I did not write this to expose them but to better understand the private worlds of white women in this generational cohort. Moreover, given my position as intimate insider, my mom and my aunts did not have the same privilege of withholding information as do strangers we encounter in the field. I know things about them that they could have kept hidden from outsiders. This ethically required a more restrictive reporting strategy. I had to allow them to edit out material that they felt made them vulnerable.

Some of my social science colleagues worried that I gave the Grasinski Girls too much control, and that their stories would be too "constructed" in a way that implied falsehood. But anthropologist Clifford James argues that ethnographies are always constructed truths shaped by the politics of the academy and the observer, and they are always partial, but not necessarily false. He writes, "All constructed truths are made possible by powerful 'lies' of exclusion and rhetoric. Even the best ethnographic texts—serious, true fictions—are systems, or economies, of truth. Power and history work through time in ways their authors cannot fully control."[18] Our understandings of the world are always shaped by paradigms and ideologies (hidden or visible), as well as taken-for-granted privileges and power. We are mistaken if we see only the paradigms and partial truths of the people of study, and not those that belong to the social scientist. We all look at some parts of the social world and ignore others. We manipulate data to argue a point or minimize conflicting data to emphasize analytical categories. We construct theoretical questions to fit with the methods that we know. We censor the solutions we propose according to the political ideologies we espouse.

In this study, the Grasinski Girls' life stories were constructed in the relationship between us, and in that relationship I was a niece and a daughter. As such, it felt odd and ineffectual to use only a traditional academic style of writing which, as Susan Krieger notes, "is designed to produce distance and to exclude emotion—to speak from above and outside experience, rather than from within."[19] Sociological language seemed too stark and sterile to be able to describe Aunt Caroline's wheat-colored baskets of overflowing dried flowers cascading from the tops of large wooden cabinets, or Aunt Nadine's rich desserts that are not too gooey, not too chocolaty, but have a lingering sweetness that makes me hold them on my tongue and groan, reluctant to swallow. When speaking from within, the complexity of the world is magnified by closeness. When we look at ourselves, or people who are close to us, the intimacy breathes contradictions and defies stark categorization: we can love and hate the same person, we resist and roll over in the face of oppression, we are both privileged and disadvantaged. The distant social scientist can more easily see individuals as social categories. But when I write about my aunts, I cannot see the categories for the faces.

What price did I pay for this closeness? While this insider knowledge made me privy to a lifetime of glances, nods, and stories that they do not want told to nonfamily outsiders, how does the fact that they are my mother and my aunts, for heaven's sake, interfere with my ability to "get it right?"[20] Sociologist Robert Merton notes that the problem of being an insider is that the myopic vision obscures the interpretation. "Dominated by the customs of the group, we maintain received opinions, distort our perceptions to have them accord with these opinions, and are thus held in ignorance and led into error which we parochially mistake for the truth."[21] But Merton also argues that in every situation researchers are both outsiders and insiders, and outsiders err by mistaking their own paradigms for the truth. Too close, we have distortions; too far, we have misunderstandings. The best we can do is work to correct our near- and farsighted visions.

My distortions come from a deep respect for the working class and my love for my family. Sharing my work with other academics helped adjust for this myopia. My misunderstandings are found in my feminist framework, which was critical of the Grasinski Girls' life worlds. I've tried to correct this by including in the text their responses to my interpretations as well as my objections to their responses. Ironically, the feminist stance that created the potential for misunderstanding also provided a corrective. Feminist inquiry rejects the methods of traditional science based on a positivist model which posits a duality between object and knower, and instead promotes methodologies that bring the researched into the research process to both minimize objectification and make evident the subjectivity of the researcher.[22] Allowing the Grasinski Girls to comment on and edit the manuscript helped correct the biases that arose from my outsider (academic and feminist) stance.

|||

I want this story not only to be about them but also to reflect them, to contain their affective, textured life of color, taste, sound, and light, to embody the warmth of thick breasts and fleshy arms. I want you, the reader, to meet them, giggling and jiggling and not finishing sentences, losing their selves in mixed pronouns, talking about "you" when they mean "I" and rearranging and reinventing the English language so that they can say what they want to say. I want you to see how they created space for themselves at their kitchen tables, found and lost their voices by talking and silencing each other, and maintained their happy faces by singing and praying and wearing lots of makeup.

To better hear them, I chose to use long passages from their oral histories, and to keep the words in their spoken form. Oral speech is less formal than written speech and captures their kitchen-table style of talking. To make the narrative more readable, I edited out many of the dead-end sentences and tried to tame the rambling, disjointed nature of conversation. I spliced sentences together, sometimes dialogue that was pages apart, because I wanted to keep intact the thread of the story. What I did not do, however, was "clean up" their language. I kept the rhythm of the oral speech, for example, the repetitions and partial sentences; I also kept the double negatives, the noun-verb disagreements, and a lot (but not all, or even most) of the filler phrases such as "you know," "like," "watchacallit," as well as the elided and blurred nature of oral speech (for example, "gonna," "wanna").

My intent from the beginning was to "give them voice." I wanted to empower them by letting them narrate their lives on their own terms in their own words.[23] But the stories told in their own words while sitting around their kitchen tables became "sort of funny looking" when "we see it on paper, and we don't like it"—especially when their informal, spoken words were placed next to my formal, written, professional language. Stuff that could be fixed, like poor grammar, they wanted me to fix. They wanted this for the same reason they put foundation on sallow skin or brighten their eyes with eyeliner. They didn't want a face lift, just some eyebrows. One sister said, "like, you always say 'gonna,' and I don't know if you did that purposely because you say that all along and it sounds like a hillbilly talking." As a result of exchanges such as this, I took most of the "gonna's" out of their text. As for the grammar mistakes, they all had a chance to edit their words. They did things like replace "kids" with "children," and "stuff" with "things." Some took out their double negatives. When they caught their own mistakes, I changed them. When one sister caught another sister's mistake, however, I did not fix it.

Some of them tried to rewrite their narratives, or at least large chunks of them, but I would not substitute written autobiographies for oral histories. I took some of their written comments and included them in different parts of the manuscript, but I always labeled them as written. For their life stories chapters, however, I pleaded with them to keep their animated, spirited style of oral speech, reassuring them that it did not sound "bad." I gave them pep talks about how the repetitions in spoken speech serve as emphasis, tone, mood, emotion, and that these are "typical" of spoken speech—they are "normal."

> ME: There's nothing wrong with your words. You can communicate very well. It's not about using fancy words.
>
> GG: You make me feel good because everyone always told me I didn't know too much.
>
> ME: Using big words—
>
> GG: —doesn't mean everything.

But using big words usually does mean something. It is one way that people signal their education as well as class position.

It is not just the content of their stories that describes what it is like being white working-class women. The form of their storytelling also shows us who they are, by making more evident their class location. This was another reason I used oral histories, and another reason they felt somewhat demeaned by this project. One sister said, "You shouldn't have left all those words like 'cuz' and 'watchacallit.' I know what you're trying to do. You're putting us in a class that you feel that we were in, kind of uneducated or kind of behind or something." Another said, "I didn't know you were going to take [us] word for word, I thought you were going to put it in your beautiful flowery writer's language. [laughs] And then again, I didn't really like the reason why you did it because you're like putting us with low poor-class people [laughs] and I didn't want to be portrayed like that."

I never intended to put them in a "low" or "poor" or "uneducated" class of people. All I said was that I wanted to show their working-class roots, and this was seen as denigrating them.

The Grasinski Girls do not identify themselves as working class, but as middle class. One sister continued to make notations in the margins whenever I mentioned that her father was a tool-and-die maker, writing, "He worked himself up . . . he got so he was wearing white shirts at work. He was the boss." In Mari's story, she talks about her reluctance to define herself as working class because it meant that she had not moved up in class from where she started. I asked Angel, the wife of a skilled auto laborer in Michigan, what she considered her "social class," and she said, "middle white class." I followed up: "Who is working class?" She answered, "That's all my friends. I think of all my friends as working class, people who work their whole life, nothing was ever given to them. Middle and working go together in my mind."

Class is one of the more unspoken oppressions in the United States. One way we avoid looking at class inequalities is by assuming we are all middle class (except the undeserving poor, the ideology of individualism argues, who could be middle class if they would only get a job). Lillian Rubin contends that the working class gets lost when it is "swallowed up in this large, amorphous and mythic middle class," which in 1990 was defined by the Congressional Budget Office as including any family of four with an annual income between $19,000 and $78,000.[24] Within these brackets the Grasinski Girls were all middle class.

Social class is a muddy category, as one's location is determined not only by income, but also by education and occupation (and this almost always refers to paid labor). For married women like most of the Grasinski Girls who are primarily engaged in unpaid domestic work, the social class of the household is determined largely by the husband's income and occupation.[25] Class also has ragged edges because democratic societies allow for some mobility over the generations, so that the class location of adulthood can differ from that of childhood. Moreover, classes bleed into each other, the working poor into the stable working class, into the lower-middle class, into the middle-middle class, and so on.

And yet, despite these complexities, ambiguities, and fluctuations, class differences are nonetheless real. While the economically stable working class and the lower-middle class may share the same income, neighborhoods, and schools, the skilled union worker has a different relation to production than the retail manager or small business owner.[26] While the sisters had different childhoods (e.g., some experienced the Depression, while others did not), they were raised by the same parents, whose level of education and cultural routines were shaped by their own class and ethnic background. Despite the fact that they have had different adult experiences (one needed food stamps, and another lives in a chateau; some have college educations, and others high school diplomas; some married men who have professional occupations, while others married tradesmen), their class background shaped their choices and their dispositions. The psychological dimension of class is "learned in childhood," Carolyn Steedman argues, and the emotions and scripts that we learn stay with us long into adulthood.[27]

Class provides cultural capital as well as material capital, and cultural capital (social skills, linguistic styles, tastes, preferences, and habits) is quite durable.[28] These repertoires of cultural and mental routines are taught to us by parents, teachers, and peers, and learned and practiced in institutions—in particular, the educational system. As such, our class backgrounds are encoded in linguistic and cultural practices. I left their language in the truest form possible so as to illustrate their class location and gendered personalities as encoded in the rhythms of their speech, their vocabularies, and their grammar. But they wanted their language changed for the same reason I wanted it preserved—it revealed class identity and education level.

With their speech kept as it was spoken, it felt as if their words had betrayed them, or that I had betrayed them.[29] But for what reason? In the 2001 National Basketball Association playoffs, Allen Iverson of the Philadelphia 76ers referred to something as "the most funnest." That grammar mistake was repeated in broadcasts numerous times over the following weeks. Why was it so necessary to repeat *that* phrase? What were they trying to do, show the world that his command of English was not as good as theirs? Was it a racist insinuation? Perhaps the Grasinski Girls thought I was doing the same thing, that I was looking for their class colors in order to insult them. But I don't show you these women to ridicule them. I reproduce their language in its original (sometimes grammatically incorrect) form because that is how they speak. I wanted to capture their class culture as manifest in their language styles and to be as true as possible to their experiences, and I didn't think that my professional speech alone could adequately reflect their everyday being.

Unfortunately, my naive attempts to produce egalitarian relations were derailed because I forced them to play my game—the academic game. Their spoken language is perfectly suitable for kitchen table discussion; it is the book context that makes it appear inadequate. I was trained to write, and that gives me power in this arena. As one sister said, "You write very nice. Of course you do, because that's what you do. I mean that's your education and that's what you do." Moreover, I can edit my formal language (and edit and edit and edit) and draw on my professional networks to make my written words read better—colleagues, publishers, copy editors all read the manuscript and cleaned up my language. I definitely have more power in this setting to shape my presentation of self than they do.

Given that I am a professional writer, I could have made them sound "better" than I did. And, given that I was family, maybe I should have. Yet, I thought that they looked damn good the way they were, and that in life, as in this book, they wear too much makeup. But then, they most likely think I don't wear enough.

| | |

In this book, I am interested in what C. Wright Mills calls the intersection of biography and history. I begin with the story of Frances Zulawski. Born in Chicago to Polish immigrant parents, she moved to a Polish farming parish in southwestern Michigan, where her father arranged her marriage. Her fourth child, Helen Frances, born in 1903, married Joseph Grasinski, and together they had seven children—six of whom were girls, the Grasinski Girls. The life grooves that were available to these Roman Catholic working-class American girls of Polish descent who came of age in the 1940s and 1950s started at the altar: marriage to God or marriage to a man. While the feminist frameworks in the 1970s challenged their ways of being in the world, they resisted *both* the negative patriarchal definitions of women and the feminist devaluation of the choices they made. These women struggled to assert their needs, carve out alternative life routes for their daughters, and retain dignity and pride within the worlds they actively constructed. They carried Christmas trees home on city buses, found open seats in crowded churches, and survived emotionally by developing a thick skin (something

Fig. 1. Caroline in front of her home, 1979

the next generation would require Prozac to accomplish).

While the Grasinski Girls represent a gender cohort (modified by class and race) and therefore share values and behaviors, the six women are also different, in part because their birth dates span twenty years, but also because of class mobility and educational achievements.

Caroline Clarice (Caroline), the oldest of the sisters, remains rooted in the family home in the ethnic farming parish that was the ancestral site of Polish immigrant settlement in Michigan. In 1942, at the age of nineteen, she married a Polish-American boy from the community who had just been drafted. Together they had three children. Her husband supported the family comfortably on wages from his skilled, unionized position in a subsidiary to the auto industry. She stayed home and cared for the children until her midfifties, when she

took a full-time position cooking school lunches at the local parochial school. Caroline lives with her hands: in the dirt growing hydrangeas and irises, weaving baskets, baking raisin-laced breads, sewing banners for the altar, and making crafts to sell at church bazaars.

The next daughter, Genevieve Irene (Gene), died of a cerebral hemorrhage in 1962 when she was thirty-six years old. She never married and never had children. Gene was an "A" student in grade school. She entered the convent after the eighth grade, stayed one year,

Fig. 2. Gene and Fran, c. 1946

and then returned home and worked as a domestic instead of completing high school. Later, she took secretarial courses and worked for an insurance company. Gene is remembered for having the best wardrobe of the sisters (her paycheck afforded her this), taking pictures of the family, and playing the piano. The older sisters are protective of her memory, and, without her own voice, I had to surrender to many of their edits regarding Gene's life.

Frances Ann (Fran) knew Gene the best because she was closest to her in age and they lived together for several years before Fran married a Czech American from Cleveland. Her husband earned an accounting degree (on the GI Bill) and they moved into a middle-class neighborhood where they raised three children. Fran dresses in expensive clothes that are easy to remember: a classically tailored beige short set, off-white pleated skirt and soft cashmere sweater, a jacket of rich burgundy and rust. She gets her hair done once a week and always has a well-cared-for public face—tasteful makeup, fashionable glasses, attractive jewelry. She does not drive and never needed to work (although she was an antique dealer for a while). She has had a comfortable and privileged life centered around her family and the church.

The only son, Joseph Stanislaus (Joe), was born after Fran. His sudden death at the age of fifty-eight (he died from lung cancer only six months after diagnosis) was one of the Grasinski Girls' greatest sorrows. His sisters feel "a special kind of love for him." He was talented musically and artistically, and, like his mother, he was a wanderer. He lived in Colorado before returning home to southwestern Michigan. He married and had four children and eventually designed and built a house near the Polish farming community of his childhood. He was a country-and-western singer early in his life and later became a commercial artist; when his company downsized and he was laid off, he reinvented his career, first as a prison guard and then as an auctioneer. Joe had an empathetic personality, a brilliant, flashing smile, and a hearty six-foot-one laugh. His sisters wanted a whole chapter devoted to their brother in this book. I compromised and gave them this paragraph.

Joe was closest in age to Patricia Marie, who took the name Nadine when she entered the convent. Nadine was a Felician nun for twenty-two years, during which time she earned a master's degree in home economics. After she left the convent, she kept the name Nadine, and acquired a French surname when she married a former priest. At the age of forty-five she conceived and delivered their only child. They built a winery and bed-and-breakfast near

Fig. 3. Nadine in front of her home, 1980

the upper peninsula of Michigan and today live as a modern-day baron and baroness. She challenges this description by noting that they "both work all day" running the business—and they do. She prepares gourmet breakfasts for the guests, and sews items she markets under the label Nadja. One sister describes Nadine as a "Russian countess." I see her as Polish. She has high cheekbones, a gracious manner, and almond eyes. Her clothes are detailed with ruffles and gold lamé, and, at the age of sixty-seven, when she walks into a room, people still turn their heads.

Angela Helen (Angel), the second youngest daughter, also started her adulthood as a Felician novitiate, but she left the convent after a year. She married the boy next door, a Dutch-Polish American, and together they had six children. Angel is located solidly in the working class. Her husband, a tool-and-die maker, worked forty years in the auto industry before he retired at the age of fifty-eight with a comfortable pension. Angel worked on and off as a secretary so that they could save up a down payment for a house, convert the basement into a family room, and buy a new car. She and her husband like to gamble in Las Vegas and take three-week group tours of Europe. For over

Fig. 4. Angel in front of her home, 1967

Fig. 5. Mary, Angel, and Gene at their home, 1952

forty years they have lived in the same house in a well-maintained, white working-class neighborhood of ranch homes built in the late 1950s.

Mary Marcelia (Mari), the youngest daughter, straddles the decades of the happy housewife of the 1950s and the return-to-college feminist of the 1970s. Like many white working-class women in her generation, she married a few years out of high school. She put her Irish-American husband through college and professional school and raised their four children. By her mid-thirties she was divorced and back in school. She earned a degree in fashion merchandizing, but never had an opportunity to develop this career. She worked instead as a nursing assistant. In midlife, she changed her name from Mary to Mari, moved to San Francisco, married a Filipino, and moved again to Manhattan where she lived for more than fifteen years with her husband before retiring to Phoenix.

These are the Grasinski Girls. Some will object, I assume, or at least wonder about the use of the term "girl" to describe the lives of women. Let me say first that the sisters themselves do not object to the term. I use "girl" because it captures their laughing personas, their gaiety and lightness, and, in many ways, the frivolity that comes from a combination of privilege (race and relative class privilege) and disadvantage (the "silly" gender). I also like to use the term because doing so subverts the power of the dominant group by co-opting a term that subordinates women. But this is not why the Grasinski Girls like the term. As "strictly a female female," they all simply "enjoy being a girl."[30]

‖ PART I ‖

Migrations and Generations

The Grasinski Girls' Family Tree

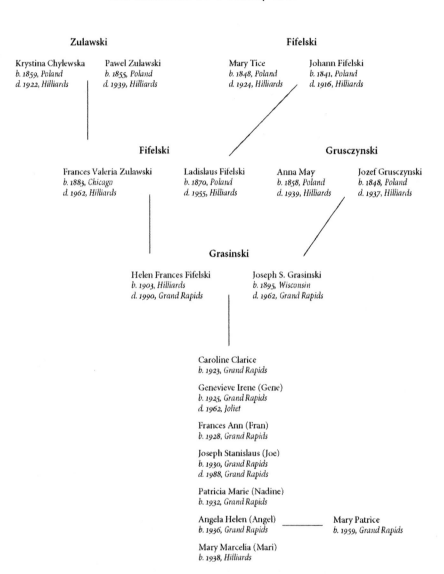

Zulawski

Fifelski

Krystina Chylewska
b. 1859, Poland
d. 1922, Hilliards

Pawel Zulawski
b. 1855, Poland
d. 1939, Hilliards

Mary Tice
b. 1848, Poland
d. 1924, Hilliards

Johann Fifelski
b. 1841, Poland
d. 1916, Hilliards

Fifelski

Gruszczynski

Frances Valeria Zulawski
b. 1883, Chicago
d. 1962, Hilliards

Ladislaus Fifelski
b. 1870, Poland
d. 1955, Hilliards

Anna May
b. 1858, Poland
d. 1939, Hilliards

Jozef Grusczynski
b. 1848, Poland
d. 1937, Hilliards

Grasinski

Helen Frances Fifelski
b. 1903, Hilliards
d. 1990, Grand Rapids

Joseph S. Grasinski
b. 1895, Wisconsin
d. 1962, Grand Rapids

Caroline Clarice
b. 1923, Grand Rapids

Genevieve Irene (Gene)
b. 1925, Grand Rapids
d. 1962, Joliet

Frances Ann (Fran)
b. 1928, Grand Rapids

Joseph Stanislaus (Joe)
b. 1930, Grand Rapids
d. 1988, Grand Rapids

Patricia Marie (Nadine)
b. 1932, Grand Rapids

Angela Helen (Angel)
b. 1936, Grand Rapids
————— Mary Patrice
b. 1959, Grand Rapids

Mary Marcelia (Mari)
b. 1938, Hilliards

Fig. 6. The Grasinski Girls' family tree

St. Stan's Cemetery

I WENT HOME to visit the family graves at St. Stanislaus Cemetery in Hilliards, Michigan. It was the time of the year when, more than a century earlier, the Grasinski Girls' grandfather first stepped off the train, the time of year when the hush of dense summer green muffles the afternoon crickets and the smell of clover expands in the heat of the day. St. Stan's connects me to the country—not the old country, but the farm fields of Hilliards.

In the cemetery, I record the names of the patriarchs and matriarchs of Hilliards: Fifelski, Jan, 1841-1916, and Maryanna, 1848-1924; Zulawski, Pawel, 1855-1939, and Krystyna, 1859-1922; Gruszczynski, Joseph, 1848-1937, and Anna, 1858-1939; Fifelski, Ladislau J., 1870-1955, and Frances V., 1883-1962. I locate my bloodlines etched in stone—Fifelski, Zulawski, Gruszczynski—and find my beginning in the cemetery, my connection to immigrant farmers and thick-waisted women who married young and had lots of children.

On a blustery March day in 1884, when he was fourteen years old, Ladislaus Fifelski, the grandfather of the Grasinski Girls, departed from the port of Danzig (now Gdańsk) with his parents Johann (Jan) and Maryanna.[1] They immigrated to Chicago to join his uncle, who had sent the family transoceanic tickets (costing fourteen dollars for adults and seven dollars for children). His uncle, who worked for the railroad, helped his parents get jobs: his father worked on the turnstiles and his mother cleaned Pullman cars.[2]

The Fifelskis came from the Prussian-controlled sector of Poland.[3] Poles from this sector began arriving in the 1850s, and the wave continued (roughly 450,000 in total) until the 1890s.[4] They built the first Polish communities in America, often located near German settlements, as was the case with the Polish communities that later became home to the Grasinski Girls—Hilliards

Fig. 7. Gravestone in St. Stanislaus Cemetery, Hilliards, Michigan. *Photo by Andrew Erdmans*

and Grand Rapids, Michigan.[5] As a Prussian Pole, Ladislaus had a border culture composed of German and Polish strains, and generations later there is some confusion as to whether or not he was (or we are) Polish, given his "German" roots. His father's German name (Johann) was Polonized (Jan) on his gravestone. Ladislaus spoke German and Polish, and was literate in German at the time of his arrival. He learned English at night school in Chicago, where he also learned to read and write Polish.[6]

Eight years after they arrived, the Fifelski family left Chicago. They traveled by train in the heat of July to the fields of southwestern Michigan and became farmers.[7] They settled in Hilliards, an unincorporated village in Hopkins township, situated halfway between Grand Rapids and Kalamazoo, the two largest cities in southwestern Michigan. I once asked Valentine Fifelski why his grandfather's family moved from Chicago to Michigan. He said it was because they had upset stomachs: "In Poland all they were living on were potatoes. And see, when they came here they were eating all this meat and it upset their stomach, so they decided to move to the country.[8] They had been living in Chicago when they got a letter from a friend from the old country, and this man wrote them and tells them there is a farm for sale here." This man was Michał Burchardt, a Kaszub (a member of a regional ethnic group in Poland) who had emigrated in 1868 from the Tuchola region north of Poznań.[9] Burchardt spoke Polish, German, and English. His language skills as well as his knowledge of the area allowed him to be a cultural intermediary and real estate broker for the Polish immigrants. Walter, Ladislaus's youngest son, said the Fifelskis came to Hilliards "mainly on account of this old Mike Burchardt. Understand, my dad learned how to speak some English, but his parents never did, and even my grandpa Zulawski never spoke English. [Burchardt] was the guy to fall back on, to look out for these immigrants." The Fifelskis, he continued, "knew him from the old country." They also "knew the Icieks and they knew the Klostkas," other immigrant farmers in Hilliards who came from Poland. So Ladislaus became a farmer in Michigan because of his networks in Poland.

Ladislaus was an immigrant, but the Grasinski Girls' grandmother, Frances Valeria Zulawski, was a native-born ethnic American.[10] Born in Chicago in 1883, she was the oldest daughter of immigrants Pawel Zulawski and Krystyna Chylewska, who also came from the Prussian partition.[11] Pawel is remembered as a landowner rather than a peasant, even though he emigrated because his family lost their land.[12] More than one hundred fifty years and five generations later, Pawel's grandson Walter makes sure his great-niece knows that: "My mother's folks were landowners, they were not peasants." Frances was also aware that her father came from land and that her husband did not. Walter said, "See, my mother [Frances] always thought she was a little higher class. My grandfather Fifelski, they were peasants, they were farm laborers [and] over there, a peasant was a peasant." Because social networks brought them to Hilliards, their status migrated with them.

Frances's father, Pawel, came to the United States in 1872 at the age of sixteen and worked in the steel mills in Pittsburgh. There he married another Polish immigrant. They had four children before his wife and one of their daughters died of typhoid fever. Another daughter died of sunstroke, and Pawel was left with two sons. Pawel then moved to Chicago and married Krystyna Chylewska, who bore him nine more children. Krystyna was an immigrant whose mother, Noah-like, sent her children to America in twos to escape the poverty brought on by their father's early death. Being the youngest, Krystyna and her brother came last, in 1881. They settled in Chicago with their older siblings, and she worked as a nursemaid. When the family make reference to Krystyna they remark on her religious devotion: "She was a religious nut," her grandson says; "[S]he was a very pious woman," her granddaughters write; and they all mention the altar in her house.

In Chicago, Pawel and Krystyna lived above a saloon in a two-story brownstone they owned on the corner of Paulina Street and 48th Avenue in St. Joseph Parish, a Polish community in the heart of the Back of the Yards district.[13] Pawel worked first as a tailor, and then his wife's brother-in-law got him a job on the Chicago police force. He worked the night shift, drank in the morning, worked his way up to the rank of detective, and drank a lot more. He grew so fat that his wife had to tie his shoes. Under the prodding of Krystyna, they left the city and bought a farmstead in Hilliards. If Johann Fifelski left because the meat was upsetting his stomach, Pawel Zulawski left because the liquor was.

Similar to the Fifelskis and Zulawskis, secondary migration also brought Józef and Anna Grusczynski, the other grandparents of the Grasinski Girls, to Hilliards.[14] Born in 1848, Józef, like Johann Fifelski, was a former Prussian soldier. He came to the United States with his wife and six brothers in the late 1870s. They emigrated to New Jersey, where the first of their eight children was born, then to Mt. Carmel, Pennsylvania, where three more children were born, then to Glenwood, Wisconsin, where the last three children were born, including Joseph Stanislaus Grusczynski, the father of the Grasinski Girls, in 1895. They finally settled in Hilliards in the early 1900s, about a mile and a half down the road from the Fifelski farm.

Anna Grusczynski has been referred to by her granddaughters as a *pani*, that is, a "real lady." She had worked as a cook on a large estate in Poland, meaning she was a house servant, where "she picked up a lot of nice things," including her mannerisms. Like Pawel, she escaped the status of peasant; as Walter says, she was "a couple steps above." According to the Grasinski Girls, Anna Grusczynski got along well with Frances Zulawski Fifelski, most likely because they shared the manners of the manor.

These three immigrant families in Hilliards—the Fifelskis, Zulawskis, and Grusczynskis—share features with other Polish immigrant farmers in Michigan. First, they came from the Prussian partition of Poland. Second, Hilliards was not their first place of settlement in the United States but represented a secondary migration.[15] Few immigrants arrived in America with the two to four thousand dollars needed to buy farms, so they worked in the steel mills in Pennsylvania or the railroads in Chicago to accumulate the necessary capital.[16] One other similarity is that they all arrived with families, intending to stay permanently. Toward that end, these immigrants set about establishing more permanent roots by creating an ethnic farming community in Hilliards.

Status within the Polish farming community derived in part from Poland. When Ladislaus's family migrated to America, their peasant identity clung to them like the smell of cow manure on a barn coat. A peasant was a peasant. But Frances's family had been landowners, and this status carried some prestige within the Polish farming community.[17] Routines, dispositions, and status get carried over oceans, over generations, and most certainly over the course of one's own life. Because they emigrated through networks, their social class emigrated with them and was used to distinguish ranks within Polonia, the general term for the community of Poles living abroad.

Outside the ethnic community, however, Polishness was a more salient status marker. As a structural locator, the ethnic identity ranked the group vis-à-vis other groups, which in Michigan at the beginning of the twentieth century included "Yankees" (native-born Americans of northwestern European descent). Poles ranked below Yankees, and they experienced prejudice and discrimination as a result of their ethnic identity. For example, at the dedication of St. Stanislaus Church in Hilliards on October 12, 1892, the local sheriff arrested two trustees of the church on charges of violating revenue laws for selling beer at a church fair (the Toledo Brewing Company had donated fifteen barrels of beer to be sold to help finance the new building). They were tried and convicted. The local newspaper, the *Saturday Globe,* reported that one of the trustees and his "compatriot with the jawdislocated cognomen" were given a deferred sentence.[18] His compatriot's name was Joseph Waynski. The real jaw-dislocating cognomen, however, was that of Józef Gruszczynski, who Americanized his first name to Joseph and whose son Americanized the surname to Grasinski to avoid just such derogatory statements.

Frederick Barth argues that ethnicity is important because it stratifies and structures intergroup relations, and that what is most salient is "the ethnic boundary that defines the group, not the cultural stuff that it encloses."[19] This is evident in chapter 1, where I show that when the children of these Polish immigrants moved into the city after World War I, ethnicity (coupled with religion) sorted the groups into neighborhoods and occupations. Polish Catholics were ranked below the Dutch Calvinists who were aligned with the Protestant Yankee leaders. At that time, and in that place, ethnic identity was embedded in relations of power and domination.

In chapter 2, I show that ethnic identity was less salient in the generation of the Grasinski Girls, most of whom acquired non-Polish surnames in marriage and moved into middle- and working-class non-Polish suburban neighborhoods. For them, whiteness, rather than Polishness, was the border between groups and the basis for ranking and sorting. And yet, Polishness continued into the third and fourth generation as a culture, a set of routines and values shared with family members. The Polishness of the Grasinski Girls is not articulated in class, politics, and social status, but instead is found in the dimples of a smile that reminds them of Aunt Antonia. What is important about this shared history is not the "cultural stuff" the ethnicity (as family) encloses, but the act of enclosing, of bring together, of connecting. In the private sphere, ethnicity helps the Grasinski Girls do the gendered kinship work that keeps the family together; it locates them in a concrete place and connects them to the textured faces of people they love; and it keeps present the memory of the matriarchs and patriarchs of Hilliards.[20]

1 ⟨⟩ The Mothers of the Grasinski Girls

We make our history ourselves, but, in the first place, under
very definite assumptions and conditions.

Friedrich Engels, letter to Joseph Bloch

Frances of Hilliards

In her wedding picture, Frances Zulawski Fifelski, the grandmother of the
Grasinski Girls, looks young and apprehensive. She was a short, slight woman,
only ninety pounds and less than five feet tall. The yards of cloth that make
up her wedding gown add a plumpness that foreshadows her matronly thickness. Her small frame is dominated by a giant corsage that covers half her
chest and a limp bouquet in her right hand (the pictures were taken on the
third day of their wedding). Both Frances and her husband Ladislaus Fifelski
look past the camera lens. No smiles—that was the style back then. Her left
arm rests tentatively on his shoulder. She was fifteen when they married in
1898. He was almost twice her age. Her father had arranged the marriage, and
she agreed to it. No stories of passion are passed down through the generations. Frances and Ladislaus were introduced, they married, and they had
their picture taken. Within a year a child was born, and Ladislaus kissed her
for the first time, or so the story is told. In the wedding picture, he sits stiffly
in a high-back chair. His brow is unlined, his face clean-shaven, the black suit
just a little too short in the sleeves, his collar starch-white.

Ladislaus's family arrived in Hilliards about the time the church trustees
were getting arrested for selling beer at the church fair. Frances didn't get
there for another six years, and when she came it was to marry Ladislaus. The
oldest child of Krystyna and Pawel, Frances was sickly and weak from having

contracted diphtheria as a child. After finishing eight years of schooling in Chicago, at the age of thirteen she entered the Felician convent in Chicago. Like her granddaughter Angel, she lasted about a year in the convent. (I am struck by how fortuitous my existence is as a descendant from this line—my great-grandmother and my mother both made attempts to lead celibate lives.) Her children write that the convent was "harsh"; the Mother Superior "felt that self-denial and poverty" were a necessary part of the training, and "Frances did not think much of this life."[1] Leaving behind this emotionally hostile atmosphere of self-abnegation, she returned to Chicago, lived with her aunts, and worked as a seamstress until her marriage was arranged. Nadine, her granddaughter, in an autobiography written while she herself was a novice in the Felician Order, wonders "how strange it was to be taken from the convent, where she spent a year, and marry a man she never saw before in her life." And in this situation, she praises her grandmother for being someone "determined to make her marriage successful."

The choices for a girl like Frances at that time were constrained by her class position. Once she left the convent, she had no education or resources to pursue an independent career. Frances's decision to leave the convent was almost by default a decision to get married in order to establish her own household. Despite the fact that her father arranged the marriage, the marriage actually afforded her some independence, even if it did mean establishing a dependent relationship with her husband.[2] In that new relationship of dependency, however, the matrifocal nature of Polish-American families gave her more power to determine her life in its frills if not its essentials—to decide how to arrange the furniture, what to grow in the garden, which curtains to buy. She became the matriarch of a household while living in a patriarchal family and society. In Frances's case, she also gained an edge in the marriage because of her nativity as an American and because her bloodline connected her to landowners in Poland.[3] Despite the fact that it was arranged, the arrangement afforded her some power vis-à-vis her husband and her family.

Frances and Ladislaus were married on May 30, 1898, in St. Stanislaus Church in Hilliards.[4] In addition to the church, Hilliards had six other buildings: a general store (which is still in operation) that also held the post office (in operation there between 1869 and 1953), a bar, a community hall, a pickle factory, a creamery, and a cheese packaging factory. Poles settled in this region in a four-by-four-mile area that straddled the townships of Dorr and

Hopkins, located along 138th Avenue.[5] Most of the farms in the two townships were owned by Americans of northern European descent (mostly English and German with a few Irish, Scottish, and Dutch); however, a defined Polish corridor appeared at the end of the nineteenth century, and by 1913 it was densely populated (see map 1).

Only four Polish families are identified on the plat maps of 1873, but by 1895 there were forty-six Polish farmsteads occupying almost 3,500 total acres, and by 1935 Polish immigrants and their children owned more than 8,000 acres on 104 farmsteads.[6] Between 1895 and 1935 the number of farmsteads grew more quickly than the number of Polish surnames in the area, signifying that immigration had slowed down.[7] By the twentieth century, growth in the community came from within, through the retention of the second generation.

A few years after they were married, Ladislaus and Frances took over his father's 120-acre farm.[8] Polish farms in that region survived through a combination of subsistence farming, market-oriented farming (grains, milk, and cucumbers for pickling sold locally), and intermittent work in industries (the creameries, breweries, and canneries in the rural towns, and factories in Flint, Lansing, and Grand Rapids). Every farm had a large garden, the women's domain, that provided fruits and vegetables for the family. They stored potatoes and carrots, canned apples, rhubarb, pears, and strawberries, and slaughtered pigs, chickens, and cows. They also made lard, head cheese,[9] and sausage from the pork scrap.

They called themselves dairy farmers because cows provided their most regular source of income, but they had a diversified agricultural economy that was labor intensive.[10] Their main cash crop was wheat, but they also grew a variety of other grains, in particular timothy hay, clover, and oats both for feed and the market. The other source of income was the pickle patch, which netted the Fifelskis some two hundred dollars annually by the 1920s, to be spent on school clothes in the fall. Pickling was a practice that Poles brought to Michigan, and growing cucumbers for market continued until the 1940s.[11] The farms survived by using family labor, which worked well for a farmer like Ladislaus Fifelski, who had seven sons. Their holdings, however, were never large enough to divide among many sons, so one son inherited the farm and the others bought their own land or found work in factories.[12]

By midcentury, the main source of family income was no longer the farm but the factory. No sharp line, however, demarcates factory work from farm

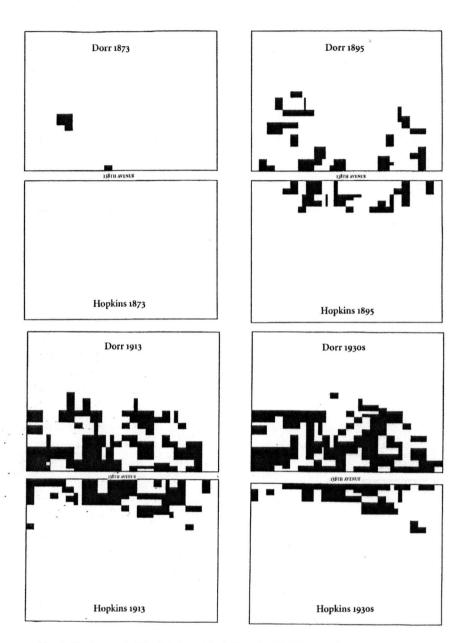

Map 1. Development of the Polish corridor in Hilliards, Michigan, 1873–1935

work. The farms were initially bought with wages earned in the industrial sector, and early farmers also supplemented their farm earnings with wage labor.[13] Ladislaus worked in a furniture factory in Chicago before he became a dairy farmer in Hilliards; when his sons were old enough to manage the farm, he once again found work loading freight in Grand Rapids. His seven sons also straddled the shop floor and the barnyard. Some worked full-time in factories and lived in the country, others moved from factory to farm to factory, and still others worked in factories only long enough to raise the money to buy their own farms.[14] Most of the farm boys in the second generation started working in nearby cities during World War I. Only one of Ladislaus's seven sons remained a farmer, and Ladislaus's own farmland was sold by his youngest son in 1947.[15]

||||

A year and a day from their marriage, Frances delivered her first child, a nine-pound boy, born to this slight seventeen-year-old girl who months before the delivery still naively believed that St. Joseph delivered babies. Ladislaus informed her that the baby would come out the same way it went in.[16] Over the next twenty-five years they kept going in and coming out. The second child was born the following May, the third the next year; she had all but one of their thirteen children two years apart.[17] She either was pregnant or nursing a newborn for twenty-six years. (Actually, she was too weak to nurse her first child, but she did nurse the next twelve.) All of them were big babies—the smallest was nine pounds, and her last child, delivered when she was forty, was twelve pounds.

Frances had a reputation for being a "tough bird." She cultivated a large garden, sewed and cooked for her large family, and cared for and cleaned a large

Fig. 8. Frances and Ladislaus, c. 1938

house. She worked—even if she received no wages, she worked, and this fact
is noted in the public and private memory banks. On the 1910 census—where
the occupational category for most women was left blank or listed as "keeping house"—Frances's occupation read "farm labor" and the census recorded
that she worked fifty-two weeks of the year. But she never did· "men's"
work, her son Walter defends. "She was short and kind of heavy. She was a
tough old gal, I'll tell you that. But she never worked on a farm. She never
worked the barn. Never! She was a hard worker, but she never worked out in
the field. Maybe like when they had to pick pickles or something like that,
but outside that, to go out and pull corn or work horses, no, never. And same
way with doing chores in the barn. I can never remember her ever going into
the barn." Women's work, though strenuous and significant, was separate
from the routines of men.

Frances was small, but there was nothing weak about the grandmother
of the Grasinski Girls.[18] Her strength was located in a set of traditional gender routines that included tending to flowers and family. Her namesake and
granddaughter Frances remembers "her peony gardens all the way from the
front of the house down to the road and, you know, as heavy as she was she
did all the work and everything herself. Always walking up the hill, pushing
the wheelbarrows, and planting her flowers, all her rose bushes and, well,
that was what she was kind of known for. Besides having thirteen children."
Pictures show her standing in a faded blue print dress, full apron, and white
sandals in front of her fiery red cannas. My aunt Caroline remembers that
her grandmother "instilled in me my love of flowers and planting. And she
used to say, 'We don't get in trouble. We don't talk about anyone. We talk
about trees and flowers.' [laughs]" Her granddaughters still have offshoots
of her peonies. And they all remember her laughing. Fran said, "Oh, my, she
laughed a lot and so did the aunts. That's where we get that from—Aunt
Sophie, everybody laughed at the drop of a hat, Aunt Clarice, Aunt Agnes—
oh, they laughed all the time. I mean, they laughed and kidded no matter
what age they were. That's where I think we get it from."

Thin ankles, thick waists, peonies, pickled cucumbers, laughter, strength,
piety, and an air of aristocracy because one time, long, long ago, someone
owned some land in Poland. This is what Frances passed on to her granddaughters, the Grasinski Girls.

Helen on the West Side

Helen, the mother of the Grasinski Girls, was born in 1903 in Hilliards. She was the fourth child of Ladislaus and Frances. She married the boy down the road, Joseph Grasinski (the son of Józef Grusczynski), at St. Stanislaus Church on August 22, 1922. Joseph had the air of a landowner, and when forced to work the fields he rode the tractor wearing a fedora. Helen shared his desire to move up and away from the farm. Given the restrictions placed upon her choices ("Frances and Ladislaus would not allow them to date other than Polish Catholic, and they had to know the family"), she thought that Joe was a pretty good catch.[19] Helen had more freedom than her mother (whose marriage had been arranged), but less than her daughters, who would be constrained only by religion.

When they married, Joe Grasinski was already living in Grand Rapids, a city about twenty miles north of Hilliards. In 1920, there were over 4,200 foreign-born Poles living in Grand Rapids and almost three times as many Dutch immigrants.[20] Poles and Polish Americans moved to the city because it held more promise than the farms, especially in terms of work.[21] They moved

into Polish neighborhoods situated near the local industries: the brickyards, the gypsum mines, and the furniture factories. Immigrants were more likely to work in these industries, especially in the lower-skilled positions that required heavy manual labor.[22] The second generation of men, however, including Joe Grasinski and his brothers-in-law, more often worked as skilled laborers, in particular as machinists and toolmakers in the nascent automobile industry. Throughout the early years of their marriage Joe worked at several factories. Between 1923 and 1936 he is listed in the

Fig. 9. Helen and Joe on their wedding day, 1922

city directories with the following positions: machinist, filer, die maker, auto worker (which he begins in 1929), and toolmaker (from 1933).[23]

By 1930, the census takers counted 4,690 foreign-born Poles in the city, and twice as many in the second generation, together representing about 8 percent of the total population in Grand Rapids.[24] The Polish community was dwarfed, however, by the Dutch community, which was twice as large.[25] Grand Rapids was the center of Dutch life in America and of the Dutch Reformed Church (also known as the Christian Reformed Church; its adherents are called Calvinists). Calvinists followed a strict moral code that prohibited drinking, dancing, gossiping, working on Sunday, and union and Masonic membership. Their presence cast a conservative pall over Grand Rapids. Prohibition came to Grand Rapids in November 1916, six months before the rest of the nation went dry. More than 160 saloons were closed in Grand Rapids (mostly on the Polish-populated west side of town). While the Polish Catholics voted against Prohibition, against regulations on theaters and other places of entertainment, and in favor of the eight-hour workday for city employees, the Dutch Calvinists voted just the opposite.[26]

Though not the largest ethnic group, the Poles' densely populated neighborhoods and Roman Catholic faith in a largely Protestant town made them a visible minority. The Dutch conservatism in Grand Rapids exaggerated the behavior of the "fun-loving" Poles, who enjoyed robust dancing and a strong drink. Sometimes their drunkenness spilled over into violence. One headline in the local newspaper in April 30, 1913, read, "Stab Six Men at Wedding, Polish Gangs Attack Guests Leaving St. Isador's [*sic*] Hall, One Fatally Stabbed."[27] While both groups were known for hard work, frugality, and home ownership, the Dutch comported themselves in a more austere manner. The Dutch kept holy the Sabbath by praying and sitting quietly. The Poles celebrated the day of rest by setting up stages in Richmond Park for polka bands and bringing out kegs of beer.[28] Grand Rapids historian Z. Z. Lydens writes, "Later the west side took Poland's sons and daughters to its bosom. The Poles were Slavs, Catholic, and given to fun even on the Sabbath day. The Hollanders were Teutonic, Protestant, with a more rigid religious behaviorism. The kinship therefore was thin. . . . The children had their taunts: 'When the angel rings the bell, Polacks, Polacks go to hell.' The taunt was automatically reversible and as effective one way as the other."[29]

It was the Poles' religious devotion that eventually saved them from the

Christian Reformers' tongues of fire. Reflecting on their ability to build magnificent parishes, a Grand Rapids historian writes, "The Poles might live in tiny frame houses, might labor at hard dirty jobs, might be slandered as drab and no-account, but through their faith they asserted glory and found radiance for themselves. For this, the core of their life and community, they would sacrifice."[30] And they did sacrifice, saving enough money from meager wages to build three magnificent churches near the areas where they worked. Prussian Poles founded St. Adalbert's Church in 1881 near the furniture plants on the northwest side, and the parish community became known as Wojciechowo (the St. Adalbert District).[31] St. Isidore the Plowman was organized in 1897 on the northeast side of Grand Rapids near the brickyards.[32] The densely populated neighborhood, referred to as Cegielnia (the Brickyard District), was composed of small, inexpensive single-family homes.[33] The third Polish parish, Sacred Heart, founded in 1904, was located in a neighborhood of Polish immigrants and second-generation Polish Americans which became known as Sercowo (the Heart District).[34] Reverend Ladislaus Krakowski, the organizer and first rector of Sacred Heart, was himself a second-generation Polish American who had been born in Hilliards.[35]

The immigrants living in Sercowo were more likely to have recently arrived from the Austrian and Russian partitions and often worked in the nearby gypsum mines.[36] This community, however, became home to many economically mobile second-generation Polish Americans.[37] The houses were larger and more expensive than those in Wojciechowo or Cegielnia. Many were built of brick and cement, had leaded-glass, beveled windows, large front porches, and bordered the green expanse of John Ball Park (newly developed by the architect Wencel Cukierski, superintendent of city parks from 1890 to 1908). One section near John Ball Park was even referred to as the Polish Grosse Point.[38]

The community grew rapidly at the beginning of the century. By 1913 there were three hundred families in the parish and twelve societies; in 1925 there were five hundred families, and most of the newcomers were second-generation Polish Americans. The number of baptisms swelled between 1915 and 1923, with an average 116 baptisms annually marking the initial growth of the parish, and then peaked again between 1947 and 1959, with an annual 125 baptisms consecrating the community's third generation of Polish Americans.[39]

|||

The grandiose twin-spired church of Sacred Heart Parish was dedicated on New Year's Day, 1924. Joe and Helen arrived in Grand Rapids six months before the first peal of its four large bells. According to the 1923 city directory, "J. Grasinske" rented a house at 1058 Pulawski Street, two blocks from Sacred Heart Church, and Helen's older brother, also named Joe, roomed with them.[40] Their first daughter, Caroline Clarice, was born on June 1, 1923 (forty weeks and two days from the date of their wedding). The following year they moved into Wojciechowo, four blocks from St. Adalbert's Church. Over two-thirds of the families on their block were Polish.[41] In 1926, they moved again, this time a half mile west to a neighborhood of Dutch, Germans, Lithuanians, and Poles (only three of fifty families had Polish names on the street). They remained in St. Adalbert's Parish and "Jozef Gracinski" is listed in the church directory.[42] At this time, Helen's brother Valentine boarded with them; meanwhile, Joe and Helen had two more daughters, Genevieve Irene (1925), Frances Ann (1928), and then a son, Joseph Stanislaus (1930).

On July 11, 1930, Helen F. and Joseph Stanley Grasinski took out a mortgage of $3,400 with The Industrial Company for a home in Sercowo.[43] They moved their three daughters and two-month-old son into a new three-bedroom stucco house at 215 Valley Avenue, less than a hundred yards from Sacred Heart Church, and only a few doors down from Helen's brother and his wife (who bought a lot next to her father) (see map 2).

The Grasinski house was elegant for that time and their people: it had a fireplace with a wooden mantel and ornate mirror above it, stained-glass windows, glass doorknobs on heavy wooden doors, and a solid brick porch. Caroline, the eldest daughter, describes the neighborhood:

> That was a godsend because in the Depression with no money, no nothing, and we were in a beautiful neighborhood, in the park and near the church, so it was just very nice. It was Polish, pure Polish. Father Karas was the one that baptized me and then there was Father Kaminski, and Father Kozak, he was a nice priest. And I still remember all the people that lived around there. I can go right down the line. Grupas lived there, and Girsz, Bobby Girsz was a lawyer, and Snow, he was a judge, and then Czechanski and Uncle Joe and Aunt Florence and her mother, father, and her brother, sister, and on the other side of the street were Paczkowskis and Borutas and

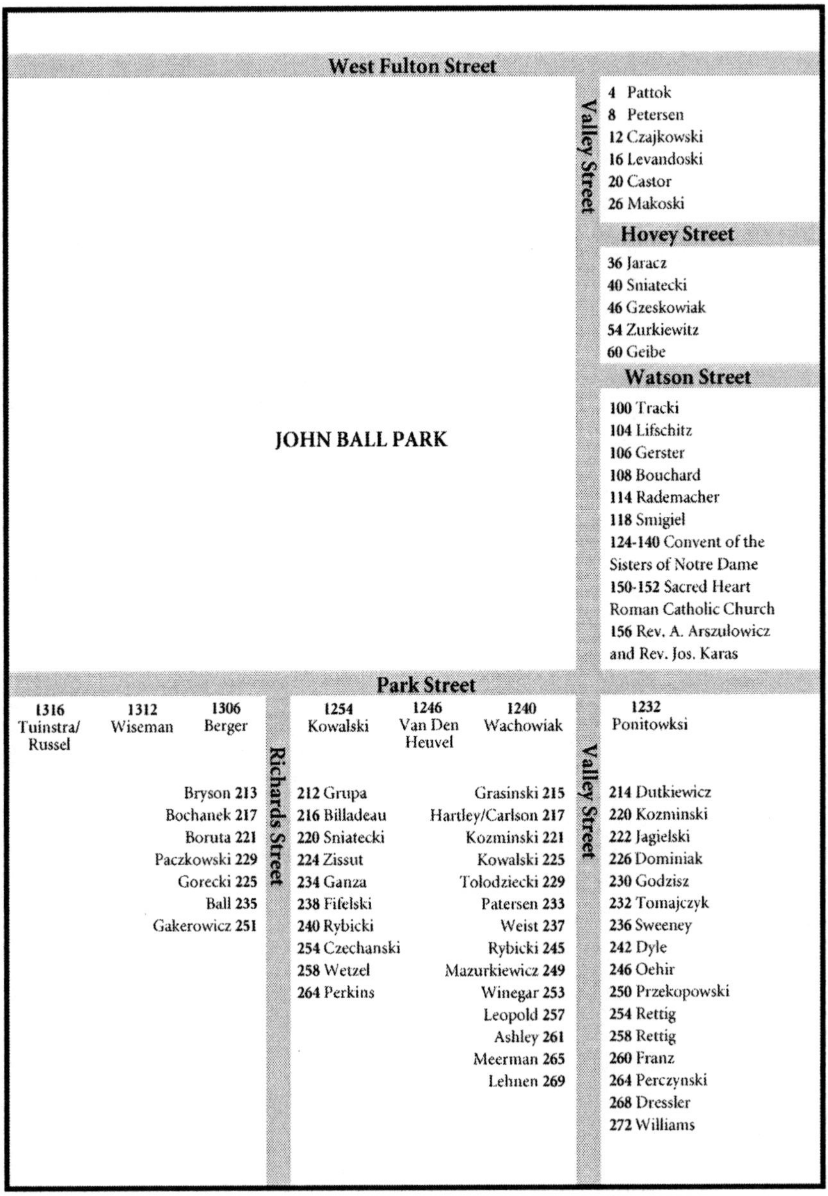

West Fulton Street

JOHN BALL PARK

Valley Street

4 Pattok
8 Petersen
12 Czajkowski
16 Levandoski
20 Castor
26 Makoski

Hovey Street

36 Jaracz
40 Sniatecki
46 Gzeskowiak
54 Zurkiewitz
60 Geibe

Watson Street

100 Tracki
104 Lifschitz
106 Gerster
108 Bouchard
114 Rademacher
118 Smigiel
124-140 Convent of the
Sisters of Notre Dame
150-152 Sacred Heart
Roman Catholic Church
156 Rev. A. Arszulowicz
and Rev. Jos. Karas

Park Street

| 1316 Tuinstra/Russel | 1312 Wiseman | 1306 Berger | | 1254 Kowalski | 1246 Van Den Heuvel | 1240 Wachowiak | | 1232 Ponitowksi |

Richards Street

Valley Street

Bryson 213
Bochanek 217
Boruta 221
Paczkowski 229
Gorecki 225
Ball 235
Gakerowicz 251

212 Grupa
216 Billadeau
220 Sniatecki
224 Zissut
234 Ganza
238 Fifelski
240 Rybicki
254 Czechanski
258 Wetzel
264 Perkins

Grasinski 215
Hartley/Carlson 217
Kozminski 221
Kowalski 225
Tolodziecki 229
Patersen 233
Weist 237
Rybicki 245
Mazurkiewicz 249
Winegar 253
Leopold 257
Ashley 261
Meerman 265
Lehnen 269

214 Dutkiewicz
220 Kozminski
222 Jagielski
226 Dominiak
230 Godzisz
232 Tomajczyk
236 Sweeney
242 Dyle
246 Oehir
250 Przekopowski
254 Rettig
258 Rettig
260 Franz
264 Perczynski
268 Dressler
272 Williams

Map 2. Valley Avenue in the Sercowo neighborhood of Grand Rapids, Michigan, 1932

Bochanek. Every day I went with this big bag of groceries. I ran to Lewandowski's grocery store and I remember a priest, we had an assistant pastor at that time, his name was Francis Kozak. And he always stood there with a nickel so I would buy him a cigar. [laughter] So I was always buying a cigar on top of them groceries. I was running all the time.

The ethnic homogeneity of the neighborhood produced a sense of comfort that comes from knowing one belongs, while the economic heterogeneity (the judge lived next door to the machinist, who lived next to the lawyer) stabilized the neighborhood, at least in the early years of the Depression.

The older Grasinski Girls remember the time with great fondness: the access to the swings in the park, strawberry pop, Mom in the house cleaning and singing "Genevieve, Sweet Genevieve," the young girls waiting on the porch for Dad to come home from Jarecki's factory, daily trips to the *grosernia* and *buczernia*, neighbors who were relatives and others whom they knew by their first names.[44] Most likely, Joe got his hair trimmed at *Polska Balwiernia* on Butterworth Street, bought coal from Stanley Gogulski, and read the *Grand Rapids Press*.[45] Helen had Lillian Rybicki set her hair in tight rollers with egg whites and shopped downtown at Woolworth's. The oldest Grasinski Girls, Caroline and Gene, were among the 880 students enrolled in Sacred Heart's elementary school.[46] In church they sang "Serdeczna Matko," and on Christmas they sang, among other carols, "Dzisiaj Betlejem."

They lived in a vibrant hybrid community that was becoming increasingly Americanized. Even when Polish Americans were listed in public documents with their Polish names, their neighbors called them by their American translations: Sniatecki was Snow, Paczkowski was Bell, and Rybicki became Fisher. While the Polish language was used in churches, schools, social clubs, and businesses, American-born Poles were more likely to speak English at home. The oldest Grasinski Girls rarely heard their parents speak Polish, and then it was only to each other and not to their children. Caroline, Gene, and Fran learned Polish in school and at mass: they learned to pray the *Ojcze Nasz* (Our Father) and the *różaniec* (rosary), and they sang "Twoja Cześć Chwała" and "Witaj Królowo Nieba." The oldest Grasinski Girls also made their confessions in Polish well into their teens.[47] It was mostly in the church that their language (and Polishness) was retained, through their participation in the religious pageantry of the holidays. They remember *Pasterka* (midnight mass) and the *kolędy* (carols), the sharing of the Christmas wafer (*opłatek*), the Sunday vespers during Lent chanting the Lamentations of Christ's Passion and Death (*Gorzkie Żale*), the blessing of food at Easter (*Święconka*), and the *Rezurekcja* (sunrise mass of the Resurrection).

The Polish church socialized them into ethnic routines at the same time that it reinforced American values and helped them to become accepted into the larger society. The pastor of Sacred Heart, Reverend Joseph Kaminski, a second-generation Polish American addressing his ethnic parishioners in 1923, stated, "True Americanism or patriotism manifests itself in industriousness, in religious and moral conduct, in the family circle, and in ownership of a home."[48] Framed this way, praying the *Ojcze Nasz* helped define them as "true Americans"; as such, the ethnic institution became a springboard for their assimilation into the larger society.[49]

|||

Helen never worked outside the home, but she did take in family members as boarders.[50] Women's work during that period was physical and time-consuming. Helen swept the carpets, rolled them up, and took them outside to beat them; she boiled the clothes on a wood-burning stove in the kitchen, scrubbed them on a washboard, wrung them out by hand or through a hand-operated machine, hung them out to dry, and then ironed them. She washed the curtains seasonally and cooked daily. She cleaned the wooden floors every Saturday, and the girls polished them by skating around with rags on their feet. She sewed her own and her children's clothing by hand, using meticulous, tiny French stitches. In addition, she took care of their growing family. While living on Valley Avenue, Helen and Joe had their fifth child, Patricia Marie, in 1932.

At that time, Joe worked at Jarecki's, a factory that made machine parts. He was soon laid off from that job and found a part-time position at Hayes Body Corporation. When Hayes Body Corporation began to feel the effects of the Depression, Joe was laid off again. Without a job, they could no longer make the mortgage payment, and on October 4, 1933 the house was turned over to the Metropolitan Life Insurance Company for the sum of twenty-five dollars. As a condition to the indenture, the family was allowed to live in the house for another ten months, paying rent at market rates.

Home ownership was important for Polish families, providing respectability and helping immigrants reconstruct themselves as Americans rather than foreigners. In the 1920s, 50 percent of the homes in Grand Rapids were owner-occupied, and the Poles and the Dutch had the highest rates of ownership of all ethnic groups.[51] In one study, one-half of the Polish furniture workers in Grand Rapids owned their own homes in 1910, many of them small and modest, yet burdened with mortgages at high interest rates.[52] Because of heavy mortgages, foreclosure proceedings started sooner than among those with lower debt-to-value ratios. The failure of the Polish American Bank also had a ripple effect through the Polish community.[53]

The loss of these homes was not just a material loss but a loss to dignity. Leaving the home on Valley Avenue is something the older sisters vividly remember. Caroline said, "I remember the day we had to leave that house. I still can hear it. Mom had Joe in the green stroller and Fran sitting down on the bottom and Gene on one side, me on the other, and I still can hear the wheels on that stroller going."

While Sercowo remained stable during the first part of the Depression (between 1930 and 1932, only five of forty-seven residents on Valley Avenue moved), 43 percent of the residents left between 1932 and 1935. Sacred Heart Parish also went through difficult times. The church, which was completed in 1924 at a cost of $250,000, was built on borrowed money. The parishioners banked on the continuation of immigration and general prosperity, but when the quota laws closed the door to immigration in the 1920s and the Depression hit, Father Kaminski had to "go door-to-door begging for funds to meet the mortgage." Unfortunately, at that time, the church could barely raise $30 in its Sunday collection.[54]

The Depression hit Grand Rapids hard: at its bleakest point, one in four Grand Rapids workers was unemployed.[55] The furniture factories, machine shops, and the embryonic automobile industry laid off men. Grand Rapids City Manager George Welsh, a progressive Republican, created public works projects for men, believing that "a man had a right to save his honor by working for his keep."[56] Most jobs were aimed at developing the city's infrastructure and required manual labor; men with families were given hiring preference. Joe Grasinski, who now had six children, was given a WPA job digging ditches and laying pipes. His daughter Fran recalls, "I can remember when we were going to St. James, when I was in the first or second grade, my father worked for the WPA. He worked digging some kind of tiles or water pipes, right in front of St. James school. I can remember I'd run out on my lunch hour and he'd be there, sweated up and everything. He'd be diggin' that hole, and I's so proud of him, so proud, that was my dad." He eventually found work in an automobile factory in Flint, where he commuted weekly. In 1936 he relocated to the newly opened Fisher Body Plant, a subsidiary of General Motors, just south of Grand Rapids. He started as a tool-and-die maker and worked his way up to foreman before he retired in 1958.

|||

After they lost their house on Valley Avenue, the Grasinskis moved from house to house on the West Side, "but we never lived in crummy, crummy areas," Fran says. "We lived on rent, but it was still always, you know, it was still nice areas." Helen was a "meticulous" housekeeper and, even though they were poor, they dressed with style. Fran said, "We always got a dress with a pocket, and then this hanky had to be hanging out of the pocket. And our hair, there was no money for ribbons, so we had to tie it with bias tape.[57] But she'd iron it out, and she'd put knots on the end."

In 1936, during this period of bi-yearly moving, Angela Helen, their sixth child, was born. Eventually, Helen and Joe gave up on city life and moved back to Hilliards. In 1939, they bought the eighty-acre Walnut Hill Farm, the farm adjacent to her parents.[58] Joe continued to work in the city, on the third shift. During the day he would help his father-in-law in the fields. They also

raised chickens and had a large garden but their income came primarily from his job in the factory. The thirty-mile round trip he made daily is something all of his daughters have mentioned—every night, in the snow and in the rain, they recall, he kissed the girls goodnight and drove into town to work. He is framed in their narratives as a good father, someone into whose lap they climbed, someone who cried for them when they left home, someone who loved to sing, and drink, and enjoy a good laugh.

Fig. 10. Helen and Joe, c. 1946

Helen did not want to move back to the country. Despite the openness of the farmland, the country represented an enclosed traditional society more conservative in dress, gender roles, and lifestyles than the urban community.[59] Helen and many of her sisters had an elegant manner of dressing that perhaps they inherited from their own mother, Frances, the descendant of landowners in Poland. Helen would wear wide-brimmed black hats decorated with opulent silk flowers and high-quality wool coats. Yet she was also frugal; she bought her clothes on sale, put her own roses and ribbons on her hats, wore the same coat and hat for years, and made her own soles. Her daughters remember her clothes. Caroline fondly recalls, "She had this soft wool coat and it had white fur going around the collar and going all the way down. She made a two-piece from white crepe that had big, big flowers appliquéd on it. And then she had a hat, pink crocheted silk on top of the brim, and then the underside was all pale pink crepe and then on top were flowers, a whole bouquet all made out of ribbons." Helen's style was noticeable when she showed up for Sunday mass or the Saturday night chicken dinners at St. Stan's. Joe also came to church nattily dressed, with his six daughters in high heels and silk stockings preceding him down the aisle of the small country church. The old village did not always embrace them warmly. Caroline recalls:

> Coming from there [the city], it wasn't very easy comin' out here. We would go to church, there was no pews. They used to pay twenty-five cents for a pew and then you got your pew. And I remember comin' into church, nobody was sittin' but one person in that pew, and I would come into church, and kneel down, and they wouldn't move and let me in. [laughs] Then, finally, they found one pew for us, and that was the first pew, way up in front. And all seven of us would pile in there. Then they started tellin' us we were showing off and ooh, dear! It wasn't very easy. I mean, well, when you come with six young girls like that, and everybody all dressed up, it wasn't a very easy thing.

But they went, every Sunday they went. Joe sang in the choir (and later Fran and Nadine sang with him). They went to Sunday mass, to the Stations of the Cross, to midnight mass on Christmas Eve, and six o'clock Resurrection mass on Easter Sunday, when, as Nadine sighs and smiles, "this whole pew was filled with these Easter bonnets, Mom and Dad and everything."

Caroline, the oldest, was fifteen when they moved back to Hilliards;

Fig. 11. The Grasinski Girls: Mary, Angel, Fran, Gene, Caroline, 1951

Gene was thirteen, Fran ten, Joe eight, Patty (Nadine) six, Angel three, and Mary was born in Hilliards that same year. The Grasinski kids grew up out in the country. Caroline and her dad listened to the opera on Saturday afternoons; Genie and Fran had Halloween and Valentine Day parties; Joe and Patty fought over radio stations while doing chores in the barn; and Angel dressed up as the queen and made Mary her handmaiden. On Sunday afternoons it was Jasiu on the radio, who "played all polkas. And we'd turn that radio up and the whole house was smelling and Mother would be cooking dinner." She would be cooking chop suey, they remember.

Caroline, the oldest, stayed in Hilliards. She and her husband bought the family home when Joe and Helen moved back to the city in 1954. Fran and Gene left the farm before their parents. They worked and shared an apartment in Grand Rapids until Fran married. Joe went into the army and Patty became Nadine when she entered the Felician convent. Angel finished high school out in the country and Mary finished it in town. The house in Hilliards remains the family home, and, along with the church and cemetery at St. Stan's, a site for doing ethnicity.

Frances Ann

My Aunt Fran, the third Grasinski Girl, is steeped in memories and things of the past. A weekend antique dealer, she has a large house with bedrooms now empty of children and full of valuable dolls and Depression glass. She has boxes of black-and-white pictures and can produce detailed, sensuous images of her childhood: for example, discovering empty brown candy papers in her mother's apron pocket and holding them to her nose to inhale the lingering scent of chocolate. Fran is an engaging storyteller and I sought her out at family gatherings to listen to her. She talks about people and things that came before me but still seem to matter: my great-grandmother who had thirteen children, my aunt Gene who died of a cerebral hemorrhage, my grandfather who smoked cigars, the house they lost in the Depression.

I went to Fran's house on a Sunday afternoon and we talked for several hours in her prim, soft-colored, floral-patterned living room while her husband Albert whistled in the den. He never came into the front room, but we were never alone. Later, when I transcribed the tape, I could hear his whistling.

When we finished the first side of the ninety-minute tape she was only at age six, and she said, "That's as far as I go." I coaxed her through another forty-five minutes by asking her some questions about her parents, the other houses they lived in, her ethnicity. She responded to the questions and they became springboards for more storytelling. At the end of the second side of the tape, her story was up to the age of sixteen. She was flirting with sailors, hanging out with her sister Gene, taking singing lessons in Kalamazoo (she inherited her mother's beautiful voice). And then she stopped and wouldn't tell me any more. I tried several times to interview her again, and finally, two years later, after I sent her a small piece I had written based on the first interview, she agreed to another session, in part because I had not written enough about her being a mother. When I arrived, she had an outline I had sent in front of her and she wanted to know why there were only question marks after her name in the section on motherhood. I said it was because she had not yet told me anything about mothering. She was surprised. "We talked so long and I didn't say anything about them?" I told her No, she didn't say anything about getting married or the children or her antique collecting. "Those antiques are nothing," she said, but she did want to tell me about her children and her years of work with the Boy Scouts and Campfire Girls. She also talked about her sister Gene, her involvement with the church, and the gratitude that she feels toward her mother for instilling in her a strong faith and love for Jesus.

|||

After she finished high school, Fran worked briefly at Fannie Farmer's candy store in downtown Grand Rapids, and when she was twenty she married Albert Hrouda, a Czech from Cleveland who graduated from Case Western Reserve University. She met Al only six times (though some visits lasted for five days) before he proposed to her. She got to know him as a pen pal while he was in the army. They were married at St. Stan's in Hilliards and then moved to Cleveland for a few years, where she remembers riding the trolley to "the other side of town" on Wednesday nights to dance the Slovenian polka. After a few years they returned to Grand Rapids and she has been in the city ever since.

Her husband became a successful certified public accountant, and she raised their three children. Now they have four grandchildren whom she enjoys greatly. She doesn't drive. From her middle-class suburban house she can walk to a small shopping center, and her husband takes her to the other places she needs to go. When she was in her forties, she started buying and selling antiques, dishes and dolls mostly. She is

Fig. 12. Fran and Albert Hrouda on their fiftieth wedding anniversary, 1998

a devout Catholic and has always been active in the church, but even more so nowadays. Currently she organizes prayer groups and works for the pro-life movement. Every Christmas she sends me a Christmas card with a pro-life card tucked inside or a "pray the rosary" sticker on the envelope.

This is her story of the Grasinski Girls' early years.

The Lights of the City

I was born in Grand Rapids on Tuesday, at home, we were all born at home. All the way up to Mary. We lived on Powers Avenue until I was about eight months old, and then they moved to Valley Avenue. They just rented that house on Powers, but they owned that one on Valley, and they lost it during the Depression. They needed 345 dollars and they didn't have it. I guess they were too proud to ask anybody in the family, you know, for that, so we lost that house. That was in '32 or '33 and I was born in '28.

When we moved away I was four and a half, but it seems like I remember the most of my life there. The day we were moving I can still remember, we came down the driveway and we had all our toys and everything in this red wagon. [starts to cry] I can't talk about it. And in this wagon, piled up in this red wagon, [muffled tears] and we were pulling it to the house, to our new house, which was, oh gosh, I don't know how many blocks away, long ways away. But we had to take it there. They had a small van, I guess to move the big furniture, but I can still remember coming out of the driveway, Caroline had the handle and Genie and I were holding all the stuff so it wouldn't fall off the wagon. Here I'm only four years old, Genie's seven, and Caroline is ten.

We took that wagon with those toys and we pushed it all the way to our new house. [laughter] And I'm trying to think, that was on First Street. It was probably about six blocks, maybe, that we had to go, maybe more than that. I don't know if you want to listen to all of what I'm saying. [Me: Yeah, yeah, go ahead.] Then we went from First to Fifth. Then we moved to Third. We tried to figure out, Caroline and I, why we moved, why we moved as much as we did. It was on rent, those three times were on rent, and then they bought, out in the country. I was ten when we moved out in the country. But like she [her mother, Helen] says, Valley Avenue was her home. That's the house that she really loved and it was really nice inside and everything. It was a stucco house and it had the three bedrooms, and it was nice. Anything we lived on rent didn't compare with that.

I can remember from the time I was probably three to four and a half. That's a lot. I can't figure out how I can remember all of that, I mean, I can still *feel* 'em! [laughter] I can still feel all of that. I think I took everything in. There was a little porch where we used to shake the *pierzyna* [down quilt] out every Saturday morning, and then there was the fence in the backyard with all the hollyhocks. She used to hang up the clothes and those dresses and stuff. Genie and Caroline, they would go to school at Sacred Heart, which was just across the street, and they had these chinchilla coats, with those hats, and boy, I just couldn't wait, 'cause when it was too small for Genie, then I got that chinchilla coat with that big chinchilla tammy, oh goodness!

Dad was working. I think he worked part of the time and then he got laid off, that was why we couldn't keep the house. I think he was working at Jarecki's, a factory. It was some machine parts or something like that. I used to wait for him, he would come home from work, and we had this porch, this brick porch, and there's always the little cutout window on the porch, I don't know what that was for, but anyways, we had it and I used to lay on the porch on my stomach and watch through that hole. As soon as I could see him coming way down the block, you know, then I'd ask my mom and she'd say, "You can go now, if you can see him you can go now." And he had this cap on, he looked just exactly like they show them people from the Depression. [laughter] With the cap, yep, and them kinda shaggy clothes and everything. Well, we were poor.

When I was six years old, I had all the baseball cards 'cause I was the one [my dad] used to take to Valley Field to baseball games on Sunday afternoon. And I can remember at that time when Joey and I were little, Mom used to dress us, we had sailor suits, him and I had look-alike sailor suits, and she used to dress us all up in them sailor suits and then we'd go walkin' down the street. He was very proud of us. He'd meet people on the street and he'd say these are my two children. But they say he always used to pat me on the shoulder when he'd tell people and he'd say, "This one shoulda been the boy, though." [laughter] See, Joe was very delicate. He was pale, and he wasn't a healthy boy to begin with, but he grew up to be big and strong. I

Fig. 13. Fran, 1951

guess I was healthy. Depression or no Depression. And so, when he would go places and this is what he would say, he'd tell the guys who we were, you know, and then he'd pat me on the shoulder and say, "But this one shoulda been the boy." And I did do a lot of things with him. I was the one that went fishing with him. I don't know if Joe ever went fishing with him. I went fishing with him. And I used to have all the Babe Ruth baseball cards and I knew all the baseball players at that time.

It was at that time that [my mother] sold her engagement ring, because we needed money for food. Then we moved, when we got a little bit older, when he still didn't have a job, and then he finally went to Flint, and he'd come home just for weekends, and oh, I can remember times we went to bed hungry. You know. She'd say, "Well, there's oatmeal if you want oatmeal," but, you know, there's nothing in the cupboards. I can remember many days where we just got eggs and potatoes, and those big egg pancakes—they're still my favorite. That used to be our main meal. So, we were just poor.

But that's when we always had a Christmas tree but we didn't always have presents. I remember the one year when we didn't get any presents, but Joe got one present because he was the boy. [laughter] Well, you know, it didn't make any difference to us, you know, it didn't bother us. He got this fire engine and I remember we were all down on the floor playing with it. We got fruits and nuts and stuff like that and maybe we got a pair of stockings, something like that, but that was, uh [pause] that was a real poor Christmas.

After the Depression my dad didn't want to be caught with that happening again. He figured that at least out in the country he could grow food, vegetables, and he could have a cow, and that's what we did. We had a cow, one cow! [laughter] And, uh, chickens, lotta chickens. He just didn't wanna be caught with six children with a Depression again. But see, I can remember that's how Daddy was, that was the reason, because what are we gonna do if this happens again? At least if this happens again we can put in our potatoes and we don't have to *buy* everything.

Oh, Mom didn't want to move out there. But then, oh, we had to move and I can remember she didn't wanta move. But she did. And here she's moving [to Hilliards], you know, right among all her friends and relatives. This is where she lived before, the same church and everything. But she complained about it. It's probably the only thing I remember her really complaining about. And she just didn't like it. She didn't want to move back out in the country. She loved the city. She's like me, I gotta see lights. I gotta see lights and people, I gotta see them moving around. And maybe I got that from her.

2 ⠇ Ethnicity in the Belly of the Family

> It's not something I think about, but it's with me every day of
> my life.
>
> > Mari

AT ONE POINT in the middle of this project, one of my aunts pulled me aside and confided, "You know, there's not much that's Polish about us except the name Grasinski, and that isn't really Polish, it's Russian." Other family members pointed out that our bloodlines are predominantly German. Johann Fifelski, rumored to have been born out of wedlock, would have been a Von Wagonner had his father the lord married his mother the peasant. Instead, the single mother's surname got passed down, and with it, Polishness. Or so the story is told. Johann's great-granddaughter and granddaughter-in-law wrote a detailed Fifelski history that never mentions this bloodline slippage. But my aunts and my own sisters have all heard this. The story that we come from aristocracy through illegitimacy is a rewarding fantasy of origin that helps us to accept our class position while at the same time reminding us that class and status do matter. In this case, status was linked to ethnicity because the lord was German and the peasant Polish.

Not only are we German, but we're supposedly Russian as well. Mari believes she is mostly Russian; Nadine acknowledges Russian bloodlines (she sells her crafts under the label "Vineyard Couture, made by Nadja," using a Russian spelling of her name); and Caroline, the most "practicing" Polish American of the sisters, laments, "I'm not even sure they were Polish. That Gruszczynski, he could have been Russian, 'cause you see that name a lot on the Russian side, and could even have been Russian Jewish or something a little bit in there, I mean. And then my dad is German, too, because his mother was pure German, you know, Grandma Anna was pure German. And then on the Fifelski side, they say there was a lot of German and then Polish [laugh]." The older sisters support their claims to Russian ancestry (and perhaps even that they were Russian Jews) by noting that the priest wrote their father's name with a "y" ("Grushinsky") on his baptismal certificate (evidence of his Jewishness is found in a Catholic ceremony?), that their father spoke some Yiddish words (they remember the word *shiksa*), that their brother "looked Russian," and that their mother Helen told them that their grandma and grandpa Grusczynski had Russian blood (yet, in the same breath, they tell me that their grandma Anna Tice Grusczynski was "pure German").

The confusion in part relates to the political morass of history: because Poland was annexed in the 1790s by its more powerful neighbors Prussia, Russia, and Austria, the emigrants who left before Poland regained its independence in 1918 were not Polish nationals. The Grasinski sisters vaguely understand this. This ambiguity of borders allows them more freedom to construct their myth of origin, though they would never think of themselves as actively constructing their ethnicity. They confess to blood-mixing and lineage confusion because they understand ethnicity as a descent identity— something that is passed down the generations, that is "given" to them.[1] Polishness is in the blood; they feel its primordial pulse in their toes tapping to the accordion and their fingertips moving over the shiny amber beads of the rosary. Mari finds her Polishness "in my face, my legs, and my mannerisms." Nadine says the Grasinski Girls may be more Russian and German, but they "still got that Polish blood."[2]

Their reputedly thin Polish bloodline is more than offset by their thick Polish heritage. They were raised by ethnic Poles. All records indicate the Fifelskis, Chylewskas, Zulawskis, and Grusczynskis were Polish Roman Catholics. They came from the Prussian partition of Poland and spoke Polish; their gravestones were written in Polish; they moved to a Polish rural community in the United States, were part of a Polish Roman Catholic parish, and taught their children that they were Polish.

Leaving aside bloodlines, Fran makes a more sociological argument for why "we are not Polish!" The Grasinski Girls don't "do" Polish things, she says: they don't follow many Polish traditions, cook or eat much Polish food, speak Polish, belong to Polish organizations, or visit Poland. Compared to her friends who are actively Polish, she and her sisters fall short.

Do you keep Polish traditions? I ask Nadine. "Not that much. I guess

Polish traditions to me would be having the *opłatki,* getting blessed food for Holy Saturday." Do you do those things? "No, not really. Sometimes." But she "loves Polish food," especially "the sauerkraut and *gołąbki* and some of the Polish things." Yet even though she edits the first draft, insisting I include that she "enjoys cooking this way," she seldom does—in fact, only on Christmas, and then not every year. Nadine finally concedes, "Aaah, not that many Polish customs."

And yet, she said, "I love being Polish, I love Polishness." All the Grasinski Girls expressed a similar affection for being Polish. While they may not "be" or "do" Polish in terms of bloodlines and behavior, Polishness still gives them something. So, what does it give them? What does ethnicity mean to third- and fourth-generation women of European ancestry?[3]

⫼

ME: Once you got married, you had the Erdmans name, so no one really knows that you're Polish.

ANGEL: No, but I tell everyone I'm Polish, because I don't want them to think I'm a Hollander. So, I say, "Now, my name is really Grasinski, that means I'm Polish. I'm not Dutch."

While working in the Grand Rapids library collecting data for this book, I wrote out a check for photocopying one day, and the librarian who had been helping me smiled and said, "Oh, I didn't know you were an Eerdmans." In Grand Rapids, home of Eerdmans Publishing Company, the name identifies me. It places me both in an elite circle of prominent names and in the Dutch ethnic community—and class and ethnicity overlap. I smiled at the comment, ego-pleased to be identified, but self-conscious of the fact that my class and ethnic heritage were both mislabeled. While distant bloodlines connect me to the publishing company (my great-grandfather was the cousin of William B. Eerdmans), my lived experiences do not. I tell him, "Yeah, I'm an Erdmans, but I come from the Polish side of the family that no one mentions." He didn't laugh.

In the early twentieth century, the Yankee Protestants and Dutch Calvinists were the industrial, political, and moral leaders of Grand Rapids. Poles and other new immigrants (e.g., Lithuanians and Italians) occupied the lower class rungs.[4] The Poles were paid less than their Dutch co-workers, they were politically underrepresented, and they were morally criticized for their more unrestrained leisure activities.[5]

This all changed, however, by midcentury. With immigration sharply curtailed, the community became mostly second- and third-generation Americans of Polish descent. That descent was often hidden, as in the case of the first Polish-American mayor, Stanley (Dyszkiewicz) Davis, elected in 1953. Class mobility accompanied cultural assimilation and the practices and homes of the professional middle class outgrew the Polish West Side. Moreover, with the strong post–World War II economy and the presence of the automobile industry and its labor union, the United Automobile Workers, many Polish Americans occupied secure working-class positions. While the Dutch remained the cultural, religious, and intellectual leaders (Calvin College and Hope College, both Calvinist institutions, are the most prominent local schools), Polish Americans were moving on up.

The only discrimination the Grasinski Girls identified occurred more than forty years ago and was linked to their religious identity. In Grand Rapids, this identity is bundled with ethnic identity, so that we speak of Polish Catholics and Dutch Calvinists. Fran recalls that, during the Depression years, "We had a hard time finding [a place to] rent because, uh, because we were Catholic. I mean, there were a lot of people against the Catholics at that time." Angel had the most explicit examples of discrimination. One of the reasons she was conscious of them was because she moved through Grand Rapids under the cover of her husband's Dutch surname. She could then see people treat her differently when they found out she wasn't Christian Reform or Dutch, and, as she said earlier, she made it clear she was not.

> We were discriminated against twice. The first place was when we got married. We wanted to rent a home from a lady, and it said, "Christian couple wanted." And we are Christian, we're Catholic. And everything was fine and dandy, she was going to rent it to us, and then Dad asked her where the nearest Catholic Church was. And just like that, she looked at us and said, "You're not Christian, you're Catholic. I would never rent to you." I said, "Okay." I guess I didn't want to live in a place where somebody didn't want me.

A second, similar instance occurred when they tried to buy a home in a predominantly Dutch suburb.

Forty years ago, ethnic identity was still a basis for ranking in Grand Rapids, but it was linked to religious identity. Even so, the discrimination they experienced was mild and infrequent; those were the only examples that any of the five sisters reported. By the time they married and bought houses in the suburbs, the Grasinski Girls were structurally and culturally assimilated, as were most third- and fourth-generation European Americans. This assimilation, along with the increased presence of blacks and Latinos in the city, made race the more salient basis for delineation of neighborhoods, friendships, and jobs.

While Poles were subject to prejudice, discrimination, and racist beliefs of inferiority in the early part of the twentieth century, by midcentury they had been racialized into the dominant white category.[6] As early as the 1960s, census reports show that on measures of median school years completed and family income, Polish Americans were doing as well as other ethnic groups of European ancestry and better than nonwhite groups. Polish Americans were still more likely to be found in working-class positions, however, and their aggregate income levels were influenced more by unionized high-wage blue-collar positions than by a significant movement into the white-collar middle class. While there has always been a Polish-American middle class, the occupational mobility of Polish Americans was stunted until the 1970s, when the sons and daughters of the blue-collar aristocracy began graduating from college.[7] By the 1980s, however, Polish Americans were as similar to other European descendants on indicators of income, occupation, and education as they were distinguishable from the descendants of African slaves and Latin American immigrants.[8]

Despite these indicators of parity, some scholars continue to argue that Polish Americans are a discriminated group, underrepresented in corporate, political, academic, and ecclesiastical hierarchies.[9] And, in fact, there is evidence that Polish Americans are still negatively stereotyped as dumb, racist, and uncultured.[10] Antidefamation groups continue to fight the stereotypes perpetuated in joke books, television sitcoms, advertisements, and documentaries.[11] While there is some evidence that Polish Americans experience discrimination, this was not the case for the Grasinski Girls.

The Grasinski Girls did hear Polish jokes, which they brushed aside with self-confidence. Angel said, "Once in a while, somebody'd say a Polish joke, but you can make it Polish or Dutch; I don't get offended by that. Wherever I've worked, I've always managed to convince them that I was much smarter than they were." I laughed when she said this. "No! I'm not kidding you!" she responded. I found this somewhat incredible. Polish-American antidefamation organizations actively fight the Polish joke, scholars write about the problems of the Polish joke, and this Polish-American woman hears Polish jokes and it does not bother her because she believes she is smarter than the joke tellers. She sees no need to repeat Stanley Kowalski's defensive moan, "I am not a Polack . . . I am a hundred percent American!" Angel's American status is not threatened by her Polish ancestry because, despite the lingering jokes, her family and most Polish Americans have become secure in their identity as Americans. Their acceptance as Americans gives them the confidence to more openly embrace their Polish heritage. Since the 1970s, the stigma of Polishness has given way to a "Kiss-me-I'm-Polish" attitude. Some of the factors accounting for this overt ethnic pride include the government-supported policy of multiculturalism, the identity movements of the 1960s, as well as the election of a Polish pope in 1978 and the international attention on the Solidarity movement in Poland in the 1980s.[12]

The valuation of their ethnic heritage comes in part from their reference group, their co-ethnics. Except for Mari, each of the Grasinski Girls, while she was a "Grasinski," lived in Polish-American communities where their ethnicity was valued. As Angel explains, "Growing up in this community of Polish Catholic people, you have gotten all your self-esteem, so by the time you're grown up, I mean, if somebody wants to say something about Polish, you don't care, because your self-esteem, it's already high. Like I said, when we went to high school, we were always looked up to because we were the Polish girls, you know, the pretty girls and smart and respectful. So that sort of validated it." When they left the safe haven of the Polish neighborhoods they also left the mark of their stigma, their Polish names, behind. The two sisters who kept their Polish identifiers, Caroline Matecki and Nadine Grasinski, also remained within Polish communities—Caroline in Hilliards and Nadine with the Polish Felician Order of nuns. The others, as they moved into non-Polish neighborhoods, did so with non-Polish married names, which gave them the choice of whether and when to reveal their ethnic identity. For European Americans, the surname is a patent ethnic marker which becomes the lightning rod for prejudice and discrimination. Without their Polish maiden names (and by marrying men without Polish surnames), they decreased their chances of experiencing discrimination.[13]

For the Grasinski Girls, ethnicity is not a structural identity; that is, it does not determine social ranking, it does not determine resources and opportunities. For them, race is the structural identity. While their whiteness was seldom articulated in their narratives (they never talked about being white, but they did identify others as being black or Hispanic), they also did not use their ethnic identity to hide their race. That is, they did not claim to be Americans of Polish descent as a substitution for being "white." Scholars such as Mary Waters have argued that European ethnicity persists into the latter generations because it helps whites to hide the privileges of their whiteness and gain access to multicultural resources.[14] But I did not see this to be the case. The Grasinski Girls never pretended that their ethnicity was a structural identity. They never even hinted that being Polish was similar to being a racial minority. They do not claim the status of victims—that is, that Polish Americans are an oppressed people and therefore deserving of affirmative-action preferences.

While vestiges of historical discrimination may produce disproportionate underrepresentation in government, education, and religious institutions, while negative labels may still accompany Polish names, and while working-class Polish Americans do not have the economic power and status of the professional middle class, Polish Americans are nonetheless white.[15] And, in a racist society, that matters. In order to understand ethnicity in the third and fourth generations, we need to separate it from whiteness.

For the Grasinski Girls, whiteness is an identity, while ethnicity is a culture. Identities locate us in the social structure, determining who is above and below us. It is in the presence of the other (e.g., the Dutch, or African Americans) that we see our relative position. In contrast, culture is a set of routines and values and as such it requires in-group members to teach these values and participate in the routines.[16] Identities are salient because they order resources, opportunities, and networks, as well as determine privilege, define power relations, and differentiate positions of subordination and domination. But culture is meaningful because it patterns the routines of our lives, and it is those routines that challenge or reproduce the social structures. It is in culture that we find agency. So, what does Polish-American culture look like in later generations at the end of the twentieth century?

|||

Today, the parish priest at St. Stanislaus in Hilliards is Father Vinh Le, an immigrant from Vietnam. They buy Polish rye bread in old Sercowo from the

American Bakery, owned by Asian Indians. Polish is no longer spoken on the streets of the West Side, the dance halls are vacant, and today it is not the Poles who are being arrested for public drunkenness. The Polish Catholic Cemetery was renamed Holy Cross Cemetery in 1947, and the last issue of the Polish-language newspaper was printed in 1957. A few meat markets selling *kiełbasa* and herring remain open, enough so that we can still refer to the West Side as the place to buy Polish food. But Highway 131, built in the 1950s, slashed through Wojciechowo and Cegielnia. The houses left standing under the belly of the highway are unkempt and board-ragged. Suburbanization pulled many Polish Americans away from the city; urban renewal pushed out others. Declining property prices and wasted interiors lowered rents and brought in the poorer populations, which, as in other U.S. cities, have darker skin than the descendants of Europeans.[17] Banks contributed to the destruction by redlining the highway-ravaged, racially torn neighborhoods.[18]

This transformation of the Polish neighborhood is recapitulated in Polish-American individuals. The Polish community no longer stands as a community apart from the city, and Polish-American culture no longer uniquely defines the self. By the later generations, these Americans claim some Polish (or German and Russian) ancestry, but they are not Poles, or even Polish Americans. Commenting on the draft of the manuscript, Fran was annoyed that I kept referring to them as Polish Americans: "I am an American first before I am Polish." I asked her if she preferred the term "American of Polish descent" and she nodded in agreement.[19] Caroline agreed.

Polishness for later-generation Americans of Polish descent is a consent identity—it is a choice. Like purchasing *kiełbasa* on the West Side, they can buy into their Polish heritage if they want. John Bukowczyk writes of the third generation, "Homogenized—or, for the upwardly mobile, assimilated —they were Polish-Americans only when they wanted to be."[20] And this homogenization was also partly a choice. The same assimilation processes affecting other white ethnic groups—intermarriage, suburbanization, mass consumer culture, and religious ties—took them away from co-ethnics and led them to forget and discontinue many of the cultural routines of Polishness.[21] While some of the attrition was forced, assimilation also represented a conscious desire, and ability, to join the dominant group.[22] They changed their surnames to avoid discrimination, but also so that their neighbors could more easily pronounce them.[23] Thus, Gruszczynski became Grasinski became Grayson (the name Joe Jr. used when performing as a country singer). And the Grasinski Girls married into Hrouda, Erdmans, and Hillary surnames.

Assimilation is linked to social mobility. Moving up the social ladder usually means moving away from the ethnic community.[24] Yet, members of the middle class do not necessarily lose their ethnicity when they move to the suburbs, because they can keep ties to the community through participation in ethnic organizations, and keep an affinity to the culture through the reproduction of ethnic rituals.[25] But the Grasinski Girls without the Grasinski name did not belong to ethnic organizations, did not share their everyday routines with co-ethnics, and did not consciously practice many Polish rituals. So, what does it mean when Mari says that her Polishness is "not something I think about, but it's something that's with me every single day of my life"?

|||

A few years ago I visited Pittsburgh. I was living in North Carolina at the time, and I was looking forward to going "north" to an "ethnic" city with a history of Polish and Italian immigration. I could find only one Polish restaurant listed in the telephone directory and I convinced my non-Polish-American colleagues to go there for dinner. From the highway, we could see a large Polish eagle painted on the brick wall of the building, with an inscription written in Polish. When we arrived at six-thirty, a white-haired Polish-American matron gave us a menu that included *pierogi, gołąbki,* and *kiełbasa.* They served Budweiser. By eight, the mood of the place began to change. The waitresses were counting their tips and getting ready to cash out and go home, while young twenty-something kids in spiked blue hair and pierced body parts started arriving and a rave band set up on stage. A Polish restaurant by day was one of the best venues for new music at night. They had newspaper clippings framed on the wall to attest to both sources of fame—winner of the prize for best *pierogi* in town eight years in a row, and a glowing write-up on the music scene by a local critic. Polishness in a postmodern America.

We assume, perhaps too quickly, that Polishness derives from Poland. While it is certainly true that many routines within the ethnic culture originate in the home country and are carried over to the United States with the immigrant group, they always get transformed within the sociohistorical, class, and race culture of the new country. For example, the polka, traditionally working-class music, has changed over time as it was adapted to changes in class structures, musical tastes, and residential patterns. Today, polka bands are performing in non-Polish venues and blending the strains together with the sounds of big band, rock, and country music.[26] Ethnicity is constructed and reconstructed over time so that what takes hold is a Polish-American culture, which at most bears only a shadow of a semblance to something from Poland.[27] In fact, the polka, while certainly part of Polish-American culture, did not originate in Poland, where it is seen as something American. In 1987, I was in Poland, eating alone at a restaurant that had a dance floor and a band. A persistent middle-aged man, speaking Polish, asked me several times to dance. I refused by saying I did not know how. Waltz? No. Tango? No. American? Yes. Where? Chicago. He smiled and walked away. I figured I had convinced him that Americans did not know how to dance. The next song the band played was "Beer Barrel Polka," and he was standing next to me insisting I knew this dance because "I came from America."

The stuff of Polish-American culture is often named: foods (*kiełbasa, gołąbki, pierogi, pączki,* and *chruściki*), dances (polka, mazurka, *oberek, krakowiak,* and *kujawiak*), religious rituals (Advent, *roraty, Wigilia, opłatek, Pasterka,* the Christmas blessing of the house, the blessing of the Easter baskets, May processions for Mary and June processions for Corpus Christi), and religious icons (Our Lady of Częstochowa, the wreath of thorns around the Sacred Heart of Jesus).[28] In addition, Polish-American culture is reputed to include lavish flower gardens, stable marriages, robust men and women, modest small-frame homes, and strong workers who are thrifty and resourceful. Polish-American values include family solidarity, well-disciplined children, humble acceptance of social class, hard work, well-cared-for lawns, and clean homes.[29]

But what does the Polishness of the Grasinski Girls look like? If I make a checklist and find that they eat three of the four basic Polish foods or celebrate five of nine religious rituals, does that make them Polish? Caroline makes all of the Polish dishes mentioned. And they have flower gardens, work hard, adore the Virgin Mary, and pray to the Sacred Heart of Jesus. Does that make them Polish American?

Polishness may be a derivative of Poland, but the Grasinski Girls have no connection to Poland, neither political, nor social, nor intellectual. They carry no memories of Poland, have no understanding of Polish history, revere no Polish heroes. They know neither Sienkiewicz nor Kościuszko (though the older sisters tell me they recognize this name), nor Mickiewicz, Piłsudski, or Jaruzelski. However, the older sisters do know of the pianist Ignacy Paderewski, and they all know Karol Wojtyła as Pope John Paul.

Despite their minimal intellectual, affective, and political ties to Poland, they nonetheless posit Poland as the source of real Polishness, and in doing so they minimize their American-grown Polishness. For them, Poland creates genuine Polishness, the right way to be Polish, and they question their own ethnicity in this language of "realness"—we are not "that Polish," my friends are "more Polish" than me. In talking about the West Side of Grand Rapids, Caroline said that, during the 1930s, the people who lived a few streets over from them "came right from the old country, you know, like the *busia*s with the scarves and stuff like that, but the people on that side, they were like, they were the real, you know, like the Polish people, Polish-Polish people." If that from Poland is real, then is that from America fake? One Christmas, Angel made *chruściki* [a pastry] for the first time and said, "They are not like the ones from Little Warsaw [a Polish restaurant on the West Side of Grand Rapids, now closed], but mine are the real *chruściki* like they make in Poland."

It is when they ground Polishness in Poland that they feel "there is not much that is Polish" in them. Their own Polishness is diminished when they define its constructedness as some sort of bastardization, while that which originates from Poland is blue blood. Caroline asserts, "I like my Polish ancestry, I mean I wish they would have kept Grusczynski instead of Grasinski 'cause that has no meaning, that Grasinski, that's something they just made, you know, just made up. And the Grusczynski, that's a good strong name. I feel really bad 'cause Grasinski, it doesn't belong to anybody. You know, and this is what you are, and that is a pretty good name, 'cause I've seen in books, that one book, the Russian one, his name was Grusczynski, the captain of that boat."

Grasinski is a Polish-American name. She is Polish-American. But to her, the name is weakened by the fact that it was "made up." Angel agrees, and wishes they would have kept "the real name." And yet, Grasinski is a real name.

|||

Looking back toward Poland does not necessarily help us find the meaning of ethnic culture in the later generations. After a century of American assimilation, Polishness is a shadow, a childhood faded, a language read but not understood. The Grasinski Girls can phonetically read Polish, sing Polish Christmas carols, and pronounce Polish names, but they have no understanding of what the words mean, beyond the rudiments, like *Jezu* means Jesus.[30] As a result, their Polishness is hidden behind a cluster of pronounceable but incomprehensible consonants that beg for a vowel. They wish they knew Polish, but no one taught them, neither their parents nor the Felician nuns at St. Stanislaus.[31] Nadine recalls that

> [a]t home it was the Polish church and school you attended, followed by a Polish convent. I taught at St. Stanislaus and St. Florian's in Hamtramck and Detroit, big, huge, huge, wonderful churches, and I remember sitting there and listening to these Polish sermons and not knowing a word that they're saying. . . . I went to the convent, and everything was in Polish. When we went there all the signs were in Polish, and they would tell us, "Go do dishes" and we didn't understand. [laughs] So they changed the signs in a hurry. But in 1950 everything was Polish, the signs, everything.

And Angel tells me, "We never knew what we were reading. [laughs] We just had Polish readers; I never knew what they were. But that stopped in about the third or fourth grade. I just remember something about *reba*, r-e-b-a is fish[32] or something. [laughs] It's the only word I remember out of the whole Polish book." Neither Joe nor Helen spoke to their daughters in Polish; they used Polish only when they didn't want the children to understand them. "She would talk to her sisters on the phone when she didn't want us to hear." Polish was the secret language, the cryptic code of their ancestors, the haunting melody of the Polish song their aunts and uncles sang as they lowered the coffin of their grandmother into the ground—though they don't understand the words, they understand the feelings of sadness and connection evoked by the melody.

Their ethnicity, like their language, is present but not spoken, hidden not absent, private not public. It is housed in the words that they can sing but do understand, it is in the daily prayers to the Sacred Heart of Jesus and the Blessed Virgin Mary, it is in the icons hanging on their wall that tell the symbolic history of Poland that they do not know, the dark-faced Madonna of Częstochowa with the two slash marks on her cheek, the grieving Mother of Jesus, and the twisted thorns around the Sacred Heart.[33] When their mother Helen was dying there were two icons in the room—Our Lady of Częstochowa and the Sacred Heart of Jesus. These are familiar icons. I ask them if they know why Our Lady has cuts on her cheek. What they know is that this is their mother's icon; they have seen it on the wall in every one of her houses and apartments. I explain the story of the Swedes invading and overrunning Poland in the seventeenth century, and how the tide of the war changed and the Swedes were repulsed at Częstochowa. A miracle occurred when a Swedish soldier slashed the cheek of the Madonna and real blood flowed. I tell them the story one afternoon while we are sitting around the bed of my dying grandmother. They don't care that much. Their mother is dying. They turn to her, their mother, and to the icons on the wall, the familiar Madonna and the bleeding Sacred Heart, comforting familiar pictures from Hilliards that have nothing to do with Swedes and swords.

They are not genuine Poles, they lament, because they don't speak Polish or belong to Polish organizations. But they are ephemeral Poles. Polishness is tucked away in their prayer cards and icons, in their laughter, cheekbones, skinny ankles, and wide hips, in what gets passed down and what gets reworked. It is in them but overlooked, like so many private and small religious shrines and crosses in fields and backyards in rural central Wisconsin that remain unknown to us because we don't see them as part of our Polish heritage, part of the way that Poles shaped the landscape of America.[34]

Some of their Polishness is hidden in the class-biased nature of defined ethnic artifacts. For example, Polish peasant fare, like potatoes and boiled beef, is not considered Polish. As Caroline puts it:

My mom cooked good but she cooked very simple stuff, just like we do today, your meat and your potatoes and stuff like that and not any of the good Polish dishes you hear people talking about all the time. I know that she used to do pig's feet—clean 'em off, and then cook 'em and put 'em in a pot, and then you'd have them Sunday morning for breakfast. They'd turn that pot over upside down and the pig's feet were all in that gelatin setting. [laughter] They didn't eat stuff like you read in Polish cookbooks, like the real stuff, like they did in Poland. They didn't eat that kind of stuff. But I know they made brains [chuckles], must have been pig brains or cow brains or something, my dad would bring them and they would fry them up with egg or something like that.

Gelatin pig's feet were Polish fare for the peasants, as were potatoes. Ladislaus is memorialized in the family history as a man who loved potatoes, heaping plates of steamed potatoes. But pig's feet and potatoes do not get counted as Polish food because they are not in the cookbooks. High-class culture gets constituted as authentic culture, while peasant culture gets discarded from the collective memory like the birth of an illegitimate child.[35]

Ethnicity is also hidden in women's work, the kinship work necessary to maintain relations between households.[36] These inter-household relations include intergenerational relations, so kinship work involves "passing it down": keeping the family photo album, telling the stories, deciding who gets Helen's 1920s button-up shoes (Nadine) and her 1970s mod hot pink sunglasses (me).[37] This kinship work provides women with a cultural power as they select what is kept, what is forgotten, and what is transformed.[38] But it is also work that is less obvious to those residing only in the public sphere, less known to people who don't do this type of work. Being an administrative secretary of a Polish organization will secure one a place in the public archives as someone involved in ethnic work, but sitting around a kitchen table telling stories of life in Sercowo gets defined, if defined at all, as kinship maintenance (women's work) rather than ethnic work.

What did they pass down? Some may argue that they didn't keep much. Angel says she knows she's Polish because she laughs all the time. "Who else do you know that laughs, maybe the Italians, but we are always laughing. That's how you know we are Polish." And they kept a few religious pictures and phrases like *Jezu kochany* (often uttered in frustration, it translates as "Jesus my love"). But we need to look harder. Ethnicity remains, in phonetics without semantics and religious icons that have been converted into family history.[39] And it is here, in the family, that we see their Polishness. Thomas Gladsky, referring to the short stories of Monika Krawczyk, states that the only things Polish about her characters are their names, but then he looks again and finds that, in her stories, "Polish ethnicity is in the prosperity and continuity of the family."[40] Discussing a children's book written by Anne Pellowski, Bernard Koloski writes, "The family is living an undeclared Polishness. The people do not work at being Polish; they do not much think about themselves in a Polish context. . . . Yet the opening pages of the first volume make clear that this is a distinct community of people bound together by an intense closeness of family, a fervent attachment to the Catholic church, and an unaffected acceptance of a body of folkways that identify them as Polish Americans."[41] In the same way, the Polishness of the Grasinski Girls is present in their familial relations and religious attachment. Their ethnicity is done in the family, through the family, and for the family.

Polish culture in their private sphere embraces a set of values and routines that help them perform their gender routines and reaffirm their gender ideals.[42] Polish women are valued for being hardy. Fran remembers her grandma Frances as the little woman pushing a large wheelbarrow. Caroline admires her mother Helen as someone who hung a set of curtains when she was nine months pregnant, standing alone on top of a table. They also respect emotional hardiness, women who can manage the household when the husband is not present. Polish women also value cleanliness and Polish homes are remembered as orderly and neat, and Polish women as good housekeepers.[43] Talking about her mother, Fran said, "On Saturday she'd wash all the floors and the linoleum and everything, and they'd all get covered with newspaper so they wouldn't get dirty right away. It'd come off Sunday morning then. But maybe that was a Polish [laughter], something from the Polish neighborhoods."

In addition, Polishness supports the role of women as beautifiers. Through flowers and song and the rosary, Polish women engage the soul and humanize the world. Through rituals, lightness, tears, and laughter they transform the drudgery of the night into the lightness of the day. These gendered ethnic routines are acts of resistance against capitalism's instrumental rationality. Thaddeus Radzilowski writes of Polish-American women: "Whatever light, beauty, love, and humanity appeared in the ugly landscapes of industrial America was in large measure their work."[44] And, as a subversion of the dominant order, Polishness celebrates their role as the matriarch of the family. Polishness in women is strength, intelligence, beauty, and responsibility. These traits become manifest in their care of the home, their children, and their husbands. Reproducing family reproduces ethnicity.

The private, gendered meanings of ethnicity are often missed by scholars who interview people like the Grasinski Girls whose ethnicity is suggestive and understated.[45] Their "undeclared Polishness" is also invisible to scholars who look for ethnicity only in the public space of formal institutions (e.g., newspapers, organizational documents, phone books, government records, plat maps).[46] This documentation of public Polishness overlooks the ethnic work of kinship maintenance done in the private sphere. What is important is not the "cultural stuff" of ethnicity but the shared history of the family, and it is not ethnicity that creates a shared history but the shared history that creates ethnicity.

|||

Ethnicity for later-generation white working-class women is intermingled with religious routines. When I asked Angel what she did at home that was Polish, she said, "Probably the traditions." What traditions? "Well"—she pauses—"Easter and, uh, going to church."

I scrunch my forehead, breathe through my nose in frustration, and shoot back, "Well, the Dutch Christian Reformers also go to church and celebrate Easter!"

"It's different," she said.

"Okay, how?"

"Well, all the Lenten services, going to church a lot. I mean, we would never think of not going to the Stations of the Cross, and going to mass, and going to confession once a month, I mean, if you needed it or not. And all, like, May devotions and Corpus Christi, and, you know, during those days there was like lots of processions, and all that was so much part of your life. Christmas and Easter, probably those were like special times."

She also described the peripheral aspects of religion, such as the joy of eating chocolate on Easter morning after six weeks of Lenten fasting. Her Polishness is part of her life unconsciously today, when she resurrects the willpower to not eat chocolate with the pleasant memory of how sumptuous chocolate tastes on Easter morning.

When I asked Fran how she knew she was Polish, she also pointed to the routines of the church—"all them processions and everything like that"—and the celebrations of the two main holidays, Christmas and Easter, at home.[47] "We had our Polish food, your ham and your sausages, and you get your coffee cakes from the Valley City Bakery, and then they'd take that down to the church, and your sausages, all your sausage, take that down to church and they'd bless it for us for Easter. And then I know that we would all dress up and everybody'd get up in the morning and run and kiss Dad and Mom, one right after the other we'd go give them their Easter morning kiss. And we had our Easter candy and stuff." At another point she exclaimed, her eyes smiling, "And Polish songs! I mean, I sang in the choir. They had only one choir and I sang in the choir when I was ten and I was singing Polish songs. I was singing down here and my dad was up there, singing up above, we were in the same choir!" When asked to talk about her Polishness, Nadine also mentioned Christmas, when "the *kolędy* are played, and 'Bóg się Rodzi' always brings back my daddy singing in the choir." Ethnicity is performed both at church and at home, both in the public processions and the morning kisses.

|||

Even though I grew up in Grand Rapids with a Dutch name, I never defined myself as Dutch.[48] I was raised by Polish Americans, and called myself Polish. On my working-class suburban street only one other family was Polish; the others were Dutch Calvinists, German Catholics, Scot Methodists, Baptists, and Heinz 57 atheists.[49] They all celebrated Christmas on December 25th, while our family began Christmas at sunset on the 24th. We sat down for a fish dinner of shrimp cocktail, creamed herring, fried oysters, and fish sticks; we then sang American carols (including "Rudolph the Red-Nosed Reindeer"), Santa dropped off presents at the back door, we unwrapped them, played with them, cleaned up the paper wrappings, and then went to midnight mass. After mass we came home to a big meal of *kielbasa* and ham drenched in horserad-ish on rye bread bought the day before on the West Side.

My young friends were puzzled by the fact that we opened presents on Christmas Eve and told me I did Christmas wrong. Confused, I confronted my mom as she stood at the sink doing dishes: "Mom, why do we do it like this?" She answered very matter-of-factly, "Because we come from Hill-iards." Okay. Made sense. My relatives who came from Hilliards did the same thing. Twenty years later, in a language class in Poland, the teacher asked us to describe our Christmas celebrations. She was bemused by my description. She had not defined me as Polish American (because of my last name and the fact that I didn't speak that "funny" Polish that Polish-American students often spoke), so my description puzzled her. She said that it was similar to how they celebrate Christmas Eve in Poland. "Well," I informed her matter-of-factly, "that's how they do it in Hilliards."

Our Polishness comes from Hilliards. It comes from the fact that we do things the way they did in Hilliards and because we look like the people from Hilliards. Our ethnicity locates us in southwestern Michigan—it defines who we are not (the Dutch) and gives us connections to the local communities of Sacred Heart Parish on the West Side and St. Stan's Parish in Hilliards. A few years ago my mother sent me a card with a picture of the St. Stan's altar decorated for Christmas; she wrote inside, "This is where it all began." Ethnicity does not connect us to an abstract nation, but to a concrete place, a geographic space within America.

Co-ethnics share space as well as a history, and the later generations keep returning to the locality, to the rural and urban landscapes, to do ethnicity. They return for the funerals, sitting on metal chairs in a grade school auditorium, drinking weak coffee out of Styrofoam cups. An aged aunt brings the photo albums and they talk about this old uncle or that dead grandfather, and all the others who died before and those yet to die. Polishness in Anthony Bukoski's rural Wisconsin town is a barren landscape of closed churches, vacant buildings, faded signs, and diseased minds: "Overgrown fields now grew where the church stood. . . . It's come down to remembering people in a graveyard."[50] In writing this book, the five sisters all wanted me to include their brother, "because he's a Grasinski, too," as well as their sister who died. Polishness is something that was here but has not fully left, it hangs around like a dusty red film on the bushes alongside the unpaved country roads. Polishness is cracked pictures and mangled names, younger generations who have moved away, and routines that are no longer practiced but not completely forgotten. Talking about church rituals, Angel says, "You really miss it now, and everybody says the same thing, 'Why does everything have to be eliminated?' The May processions, it was just so much to it. And I think it just gave you a background or roots."

Their Polishness is a life they shared with others in a particular time and place. Fran's story centers on her childhood when her family lived on the Polish West Side, which provides a comfortable place to visit through storytelling on a fading Sunday afternoon. At the end of one such afternoon she said, "Every time you leave I am caught back in that place for days." The locale of Polishness. In that locale, she sees her mother in her large hats, plays in the park across from Sacred Heart Church, wakes on Sunday morning with her father sitting in a chair smoking a cigar and her mother in the kitchen

Fig. 14. Nadine, Joe, and Gene, 1949

frying sausage. As an older woman remembering her childhood, Polishness brings her past into the present and connects her to generations of family.

Their ethnic history is a family history. Historians Roy Rosenzweig and David Thelen, in their book *The Presence of the Past,* show how family histories give meaning to present-day selves. When I ask, What's Polish about you? Caroline responds, "My love of flowers, my love of music, my love of color, my love of family." And she connects some of these values to her Polish grandmother's fiery red cannas, and her admonition to talk about plants and not people. The Grasinski Girls use the history of the family to define their life spaces and choices.

Their values located in an ethnic childhood are also used at times to evaluate contemporary society.[51] When Polishness taps into the rhythms of childhood, for them a pleasant childhood, it becomes linked to an all-is-right-with-the-world feeling. Fran, describing a Polish Christmas celebration, said, "We just cried and we laughed and sang and they danced. They danced all these songs like Mom used to do, the *oberek* and everything, it was just, it was so wholesome. I didn't even want to put the television on when I came back. You know, it was just so good. Oh, it was just real Polish!"

Ethnicity stretches into yesterday to provide routines for today's traditions, routines that connect us to the bloodlines swirling through concrete local places. Traditions bring the past into the present and the self into the family. We affirm our connections by acting out our traditions, which in our family means eating mounds of horseradish, wearing large hats, and pickling cukes.[52] Ethnicity also joins us at the hip. Caroline comments, "I can see, in Emily, I can see some of the Grasinski in her, and I can also see in Eddie, I can see that Grasinski smile. Grasinskis, they all got that smile real big. They all got good smiles. And Annette's girl, Carrie, she's the one that we call 'Grandma Helen the Second.' [chuckle] She looks like a Fifelski. She looks like one of Aunt Adele's—I don't know if you remember Antonia, do you remember Antonia? Oh, I keep thinkin' you know these people, but you don't." They want me to know. They want me and their children and their children's children to know, to remember. Gendered, private ethnicity in the later generation is about connections and relations. Having family and knowing family are important to these women.

Polishness connects the generations of the family and the generations of the self (the old self to the young self). Ethnicity is a mediating process. Helen named her babies after dead Polish relatives and contemporary American songs. The sixth generation is connected to the first generation when the grandchild cries out to *Busia* for a hug. The fifth generation is connected to the second generation when the grandfather with the highball breath whirls his granddaughter around the wedding floor in the one-two-two polka. Great-aunt Adele played in a polka band, Angel played the accordion, and as a young girl I watched two women dancing together, holding onto each others' arms, laughing and twirling.

|||

For the Grasinski Girls, Polishness is a wisp of a thread floating from the ribbon of one generation to the next. It is in the nuances of the social world that we detect the traces of ethnicity hidden in the third and fourth colors of the weave. Caroline:

> I remember when I was little, Grandma Gruszczynski, you know, they never told us their names [laughter]. It was Wayland Grandma and country Grandma [laughter]. No names, I didn't have any names. Anyhow, this Wayland Grandma, she'd come out by us and help Mom make *pierogi*. She's the one that taught Momma how to do a lot of her cooking. She'd make *pierogi*, [pause] and I can remember walking behind her in the yard, I'd just see a faint shadow, and she used to pick all the dandelion greens, you know, the little greens, she'd pick those up, bring them in the house and she'd cook 'em like that. And, she taught my mom how to make *czarnina* [duck blood soup]. But my mom didn't like baking. We make more *babkas* [cakes] and stuff than they did at that time.

In the later generations, ethnicity is something that has no name because it was not named, it is the shadow of a grandmother the child follows behind, it is what was taught (*czarnina*), what was refused (baking), what was reclaimed (*babka*-making). Ethnicity is not a cover for whiteness, it is not a culinary recipe, an organizational membership, or a vocabulary list. Ethnicity is an ethos, a soul, a connection, not to a community in some foreign land but to local spaces and generations, the generations of their selves and the generations of their families. And that's why women do it well. Ethnicity reaffirms their connections.

Polishness goes back to Hilliards and the West Side, but not to Poland. They feel a connection to Frances's zinnias and hollyhocks and their mother singing *kolędy*. Their Polishness is not a public identity, and they don't claim Polishness as some sort of ethnic revival. They don't wear "Kiss me, I'm Polish" buttons or join antidefamation groups. Polishness is an unspoken language that holds existential meaning, that signifies "this is me," this is who I say I am, a vestige of this family, the remains of this day. Like the incense at midnight mass, it wafts through the air and reminds us of whence we came; it's the familiarity of routines, the soak of tradition, the way they do it in Hilliards. This is who I am. A Grasinski.

Ethnic culture is in a constant state of construction. Ethnic rituals are altered as each generation, like a pianist who is a little tone deaf, reconfigures its cultural sonata; something new is intermingled with the old. Grandma's recipe with her daughter's new ingredients gets sent as an email; the seeds of a country grandma's peonies are replanted in the suburban backyards of her daughters, and repotted on the urban apartment balcony of her granddaughter; the tatted-lace doily gets matted, framed, and hung on the wall. Like soil and recipes, ethnicity gets reworked so that even in the latter generations we find threads, seeds, yeast, an old photo, the dimple in the chin, that laugh, the love of music that binds them to the generation before. But ethnicity is not about what gets passed down; rather it is about the process of passing down.[53]

‖ PART II ‖

Choices Given, Choices Made

Nuns and Moms

THIS SECOND PART of the book describes the choices the Grasinski Girls were given and the gender identities they constructed. I present three life stories: Nadine, who was a Felician nun for twenty-two years before she married and had a child; Angel, a working-class mother of six who has been married for forty-five years; and Mari, the youngest Grasinski, who went to college after her divorce in the 1970s. While I will talk about the choices these women made, I wonder whether they really had "choices." Is joining the convent a "choice" when it is defined as a "calling"? The same question applies to motherhood, often described by these women as more like a destiny. Can destiny be a choice? Was singlehood a sufficiently attractive alternative to marriage that they could choose one or the other? Given their Catholic upbringing, was divorce a real option, or was it something that just happened? Did they choose not to go to college?

Their choices and gender identities were constrained by class position, shaped by religious expectations, supported by ethnic culture, and privileged by racial standing, but their lives were not determined. Nadine and Angel chose to answer Jesus' call, Angel chose to stop having children, Mari chose to pursue an extramarital affair. The structures within which they acted, however, predisposed them to making certain choices. To hear Jesus calling, they must have first been aware of what His voice sounds like, so that they did not mistake it for Allah's.

Life choices represent the intersection of history and biography. The Grasinski Girls came of age in the 1940s and 1950s. In the post–World War II era, an expanding economy gave married working-class white women more freedom to stay home, especially if their husbands had union jobs that paid well and provided benefits. In addition, the cultural superego redirected women back into the home as wives and mothers. As Betty Friedan phrased it, "the spirited New Woman" of the 1920s was "replaced by the Happy Housewife" in the 1950s.[1] The age of first marriage plunged to its low point for the century (around twenty for women) in the 1950s and fertility rates rose between 1947 and 1963. The proportion of middle-class women attending college declined, and women's liberation took two steps back with a return to more puritanical views on sex and more narrowly defined gender roles.[2] Many young women dreamed of getting married in white organza, and feverishly asked their secretarial coworkers, "Are you pregnant yet?" Mari said, "The thinking at twenty was, if you weren't planning your marriage, you know, life had passed you by, honey. So you better get on the ball. I'm saying that was the social climate."

The social climate helps to sort individuals into meaningful life grooves. And it is within these grooves, or fields of opportunities, that individuals act. The groove is not just a conduit for resources (e.g., money, education, networks) but also contains a stream of attitudes and values that shape our perceptions of the objective conditions that give rise to our grooves and choices. French sociologist Pierre Bourdieu referred to this as the *habitus,* a durable set of dispositions formed by our early life experiences that (while altered by later life experiences) survives into adulthood as a matrix of perception that shapes how we think, feel, and act.[3] The habitus represents structure (an objective set of opportunities) made real in the individual as a subjective perception of those opportunities, and, as such, the habitus mediates structure and agency, it is the dynamic intersection between the choices we are given and the choices we make.

The "conditions of existence," that is, our social location within a particular sociohistorical context, creates our "definitions of the impossible, the possible, and the probable," and we make choices within this perceptual worldview.[4] For the son of a middle-class professional family in the 1950s, a college education was possible and probable. At the same time, for the Grasinski Girls, the convent and motherhood were possible and probable, while having careers as priests or professors was not. The notion of habitus stresses that it is not only our objective conditions, but our perceptions of these conditions that construct the realm of the possible and the probable. And it is our background that shapes perceptions and our ability to imagine. Nothing is possible unless it can first be imagined. Caroline understood this. "I really wish that somebody, when I was in school, would've told me more about how important education was, how good studying is, 'cause I really was that type of a person. *But you have to find something out first before you can do something about it* [emphasis mine]. And that's the thing, I wished somebody would've told me how important it was." The Grasinski Girls could imagine going into the convent because they knew women who did. They could imagine being married, because most women were. But they did not imagine going to college because it was not a part of their conditions of existence. While they did choose to become moms and nuns, it was a structured choice shaped by dispositions.

The term "choice" as used here does not imply conscious intention. To the contrary, we are often not cognizant of the habitus, and are therefore unaware of how our options are shaped and constrained by our perception of the already limiting objective conditions. The habitus eclipses the possible so that choices often feel like destiny or "just the way we do it."

Whether we intend it or not, our ways of acting very often reproduce the social structure.[5] For example, the choice of a middle-class professional couple to send their child to college is not perceived as an act intended to reproduce class structure. And yet, it does.[6] The choice to pursue the mother career in the home rather than an occupational career outside the home is not intended to reproduce gender inequality, and yet it does.

Even though dispositions are often experienced as a personal feeling or a personality trait, they are not individual attributes but group traits. People are more or less predisposed to certain life grooves because of their social location. The Grasinski Girl generation was inclined to become mothers. Caroline said, "I never thought about anything else. I just wanted to be a good mother and make my home safe and secure." Regarding marriage, Mari shows how dispositions are like strong currents. "Everybody was getting married at twenty. I was wearing white clothes and carrying a purse and a hat, so that told you you were a grown woman, because you were dressing like Jackie Kennedy. She was thirty-four, but you were twenty, but you were still dressing like her. I mean, it wasn't like anybody forced you. Nobody said, 'Okay, this is the fifties, you're twenty.' I mean, no, nobody said that."

Dispositions are strongly suggestive cultural maps that guide our decisions. They tell us, at each stage of life, what we are supposed to do. Dispositions are not permanent, though they are durable within the self; they are not deter-mined, but they do represent, as Bourdieu notes, "a past which survives in the present and tends to perpetuate itself into the future by making itself present in the practices structured according to its principles."[7] This is how we, as ac-tive social agents, participate in the reproduction of structures of inequality. We don't choose inequality, but we are disposed to make choices that repro-duce the social structure, and, as such, reaffirm our positions of subordination (and domination).

Being single did not necessarily represent a rejection of the "nun or mom" choice in the Grasinski Girl generation. Gene Grasinski was neither a mom nor a nun (she did enter the convent after eighth grade but stayed less than a year). She worked in an office, bought beautiful clothes, played the piano, and took nice vacations. She dated a lot of men. She never completed high school, but she did go to secretarial school when she was in her twenties. By her midthirties she was still single. While she would have preferred to be married, she never found the right man—someone to whom she was roman-tically attracted, someone who was not married or divorced, someone with

whom she could start a family. While she did not choose singlehood, she did choose to not marry men who were not suitable to her. But she would have preferred marriage.

In the first draft of the book I had written about Gene as a sad woman. The older Grasinski Girls thought that I had mischaracterized her and pro-vided numerous memories to show that she was fun-loving, generous, and had a zest for life. Fran, the sister closest to Gene, wrote me a short essay about her. When Fran was fifteen, she lived with Gene in Grand Rapids.

Fig. 15. Gene and Fran (holding Caroline's daugh-ter Annette), 1947

We lived in an apartment, which was one room. We had so much fun together. We would spend most of our money on clothes, then we had to split a sandwich or bowl of soup the last two days of the week. We roller-skated at the Coliseum every week. We took trips together. We double-dated a lot. We always laughed about who had the cutest guy. It was such fun. We used to shop our heads off. She had such good taste in clothes.

Later on she took courses in secretarial and office work. This got her a better job. But things changed. She had her friends, and she dated, but it never seemed to be the right one. After I got married and moved to Cleveland for three years, and our younger sisters got married, I think this was probably a sad time in her life. I am not saying she was a sad person. She had her happy days and her not so happy days.

Gene was a lively, animated woman. Any disposition toward sadness was produced by her structural conditions. In this case it was because she was in her early thirties and she was not married. As Mari said, "the thinking was, if you were not married, life had passed you by—that was the social climate." Gene was single, but not called to a life in the convent. She was Roman Catholic, which made it hard to imagine marrying a divorced man. She was working class, so she did not have the education or encouragement to pursue a professional career. For Gene, as for all of us, the probable and the possible were shaped by her social location within a particular historical context.

Our choices are structured within a system of interlocking privileges and disadvantages that are influenced by race, class, and gender locations, as well as religion, ethnicity, nationality, and sexual orientation (and this list is not exhaustive).[8] Initially I tried to separate the following chapters into work (class), motherhood (gender), ethnicity, and religion. Later, I found that when examining the life worlds of these women, gender is classed and heterosexual, class is raced, religion is gendered, and all the other various permutations. When Angel talks about raising six children in a neighborhood where the mothers stayed home while their husbands worked in factories, it is obvious that gender, as motherhood, is classed. When Nadine earned a master's degree, quite a feat for a working-class girl forty years ago, it was as a Felician nun working in Polish-American parishes in Detroit. When Mari engages in oppositional behavior because she is frustrated in her marriage, she has an affair with a black man. The many streams running through us are present when we dip into the waters for a cup of narrative. What follows is a long, tall drink of water.

Nadine née Patricia

NADINE LOVES MUSIC. A picture of Julio Iglesias hangs on the wall of family photos leading up to her home on the second floor of their bed-and-breakfast cum winery, Chateau Chantal. The chateau was built in the middle of their vineyards, on a ridge that forms the spine of the Mission Bay Peninsula in northern Michigan. When I interviewed her in early March, the land was just beginning to awaken from its long hibernation. Nadine had spent the shortened winter afternoons watching the snow tumble endlessly from the sky, listening to Placido Domingo singing "Kumbaya" in his sexy, sonorous tenor. That March day she replayed the solitude of those afternoons (her only daughter in Chicago, her husband downstairs taking care of business), volume loud, booming tremulously loud, the loudness you have when there is no one else around. Placido's voice sounded holy and humble—"Kumbaya, my Lord, Kumbaya"—wringing every tone from every syllable, he sang slowly, resonantly, reverently. We sat in La-Z-Boy recliners positioned in front of the bank of windows and watched the sun suspended behind a heavy clump of clouds arching over the bay. "Someone's praying my Lord, Kumbaya."

Early the next morning, Nadine walked my mom and me down to the eastern shore of the peninsula to sing up the sun. She took us to the spot on the beach where she comes "to pray and scream and sing and cry," and passed out sheet music. Three women in holey sweaters and colorful scarves stood on the sand singing "Lord, When You Came to the Seashore." We sang all three verses, first in English and then in Spanish ("Pescador de Hombres").

To narrate her life story, Nadine chose a quiet room where we would not be disturbed. She is a good storyteller. She has a wonderful sense of humor and her laughter is infectious. "I laugh a lot," she said. "When I was in the convent my penance was for laughing and singing in the wrong places." We were alone when she told me her life story. Sometimes simultaneously laughing and crying, she constructed her chronological narrative around pivotal events in her life: growing up on the farm, entering the convent, teaching, leaving the convent, getting married, having her child, going to Europe, opening Chateau Chantal. She is flamboyant yet honest with her feelings. Mary Nadine was born Patricia Marie in the house on Valley Avenue in 1932. After she left the convent, she kept her name, Nadine, because at that point she "had been Nadine for more years than Patty."

I Gave My Youth to Jesus Christ and My Old Age to Bob

I was in the seventh grade at St. Stanislaus, and the nuns, the Felician Sisters, would talk to us about the lives of the saints. St. Teresa was my favorite. I wanted to be just like her—and she was a Carmelite. I even tried sleeping on the hard floor. And [that was] when I really felt like I had this calling to be a nun. Deep inside I wanted to be a Carmelite nun because I wanted just to pray all the time. And my mom said, "If you want to go to the convent, go, but you're not going to be a Carmelite nun." [laughs] And I was glad she said that, after a while. "If you want, go to the Felicians." I listened to her. And I'm glad I did.

It was a very real—being called, it was a very real thing to me, like, at certain times there would be a lot of music and things, and I just wanted to be myself and think about the Lord. And He touched me from time to time. And then at other times I thought, "Well, do I want to go or don't I want to go?" I remember agonizing, and I remember writing down all the things: I loved to dress up, I loved to dance, I loved to look pretty and go out (Jerry was his name), and all this, and the shopping. And there was only this one thing on the other side, the love of Jesus. He was there, saying, "Come!" And that was it. And so, up to the time when I actually went, I had doubts, I was never sure whether I should go or not. And when I did leave it was like I walked into the convent, and I can hear that door close today, and it was like that door closed on all these doubts. From the time I walked in, it was like, "This is for me, this is what I wanted to do."

Well, my mother was very happy. But my dad, aah, it was like, when I was going, I can cry to this day because I can still see him sitting in the chair, and I walked into the room three times trying to say good-bye to him. I could not say good-bye. [crying] He was crying. Mom didn't cry. Mom didn't cry as much as Daddy. Dad cried, you know, when

Gene was in the convent, and we were sitting down at the table and she's not there and he started crying. Not my mom, but my dad. And I remember, just before I left, he said, "Patty," he said, "I'll buy you anything you want, just don't go." He didn't want any of us to go.

I remember Joe [her brother] taking me to the train station, and I got on the train and there was Sister Patience, and she made me say the rosary the whole time, and I thought, "Oh, God, what am I getting into?" And then when I got to Livonia, Sister Teresa was there, and she was young and vibrant and happy, and I thought, "Oh, boy, this is more like it." [laughs]

And what was really strange was that all these seven years of thinking I want to be a nun, did it ever occur to me what I was going to be doing as a nun? [laughs] Did I really want to be a teacher? That's what I was doing. I knew I was going to teach, but it was, like, so far back in my head. The important thing was that He wants me to come. He wants me here. That was *the* thing. Bo-oy, shock of my life, two years later I'm standing in front of fifty kids, not knowing what to do, and I said, "Ooh"—you know, realization struck. I had one year of college and one year of religious training and then in those days you went out. I really learned on the job.

The first year was like another year in college. I had fifty second-graders at St. Michael's. And then I moved to the third grade, and then seventh grade. I was finishing the rest of my college education while I was teaching, so I would go to school in the summer and in the afternoons. And then I got my master's of science from Madonna [College] and I went on to get a master's degree in food and nutrition and clothing and

textiles from Wayne State. So, once I had all that education, I was able to teach in high school.

I've been many places. Every two years they would send you somewhere else. I taught in Bay City six years, and I taught most of the other time in Detroit, at St. Stanislaus, and at St. Florian's in Hamtramck. I was teaching home ec. I don't know what they call it now, but it was home economics. So that's what I did for the next twenty years.

Fig. 16. Sister Nadine in her room at the convent, 1970

So that's how it was. You teach all day, you get up and pray, and then you teach, and so it wasn't really a lot of time for anything else. It was mostly preparation for teaching, and studying and going to college. But you always made friends with someone, or with two or three, and you would chum around with those. I never felt out of place. People liked me wherever I went, I liked them, and I seemed to get along. I never had really any problems. There were a few superiors that were, you know [laughs], they took a lot out of you. They scolded you for things that you didn't think were important. Some were nice and some were very strict. On average, they were strict, but they didn't make you want to run away or anything.

The thing that struck me was that when I was home my mother would always lift us up on a pedestal, she would always be saying, "Patty, you're beautiful, you can do whatever you set your heart and mind to do." And then when I went to the convent it was the opposite. They were always preaching to us, "You're nothing! You're misery and sin!" And instead of telling us we were all beautiful they were putting us down, but that was the way they taught them in Poland, that's the way they taught them now, to learn to be nothing and then you can be everything to all people. It wasn't good, but it didn't really affect me because once you went out to teach you knew that you weren't only misery and sin. [laughs] All the little kids are saying, "Ooh, you're so wonderful!" And all the affirmations when you make friends with the nuns, and with the kids, and so you felt loved and worshiped to a certain degree. Not worshiped, but they looked up to you.

When I went to the convent I really missed Joe [her brother]. He was one of the things I was giving up when I gave up everything. And we did a lot of things together. We both loved country music and we used to listen to it in the barn when we were doing our chores. I grew up with him. And he's a year and a half older, and I just really liked him. And then I went in the convent and it was, like, ooh, I just missed him so much. I was praying rosary after rosary so that he would find success. And, anyway, he was getting married this one Saturday, and back then, we could not go to weddings.[1] We could go to funerals, but we couldn't go to weddings. I was so sad that I couldn't be there. Oh, gosh. It was really hard. It was really difficult not being there. And then I remember when his first child was born, named Patricia, he sent me this picture of her. She looked like an Eskimo, I can still see that picture he sent to me. [laughs]

Anytime he wanted to give me some help or anything, he would write. [crying] He was always there, encouraging me and sending me wonderful letters. All the time he was, like, encouraging me. All the time. And my mother wrote such beautiful letters.

One day I had this idea to get rid of everything. This was not new to me. I wanted to give myself totally to Jesus and detach myself from all material things. So I took all these beautiful letters out to the burning pit behind St. Stanislaus Church and I threw them in this fire. I took all these beautiful words and threw them in the fire and watched them burn. Isn't that crazy! And that was so stupid. I was thinking, "I'm gonna give up everything to the Lord."

One of the best summers [1968], we were sent to Orchard Lake. I cooked breakfast for the priests and I served them. So, that was my job. And the other nun there, she was a chauffeur. We would work all morning, and then we would be free from one to four, and so we would head out to the water. At that time we still had the long habits, and so, of course, we would have the long habits on, and we'd be sitting there on the beach in these long woolen habits. And then one day this Christian Brother was driving by on a bicycle and he said, "Hello, I'm a Christian Brother." And so we said, "Hi, we're Christian sisters." [laughs] And he said, "Don't you think you need a bathing suit? I can bring you a couple from the cook." And we said, "Sure. Bring us some bathing suits." And so, we used to put the bathing suits on underneath the habit, and then once we'd get there we'd hang the habits on the branch of the tree and then we'd sit in the sun, and talk, you know—I was knitting at the time. And so we'd do that, a couple days a week we'd put the bathing suits on and then the habit. And then there was this one time we did that and we went looking for our habits, and we couldn't find them. We're thinking, "How are we going to walk in the seminary in our bathing suits?" We said, "God, please help us find our habits." [laughs] Actually, nobody took them, we just forgot where they were and then we found them. [laughs] But that was a nice experience. All the priests were nice, and they all kissed my hands.

After twenty years, I requested a different kind of a job because I was getting tired of teaching. The Reverend Mother put me as the food supervisor at St. Mary's Hospital. At the end of summer, I reported to the hospital and the sister that was in charge, Sister Columbine, gave me three reasons why she didn't want me there: I didn't have enough education, my skirt was too short, and I couldn't get along. She had someone else in mind for the position, so she didn't want me there. I started walking back to the Mother House and some nuns passing by in a car offered me a ride and said, "Only you, Nadine, could get fired at seven-thirty in the morning." And I said, "Well, what do you do!" And I think the rest of my life is changed because of the one who said, "No, we don't want you here."

And I went to the Reverend Mother, and she allowed me to find another job. I joined this one experimental group of Felician Sisters. The experimental group wore no habits, there was no Mother Superior, but you had your vows. We were living in a regular house across from the church. And I ended up teaching again, it was an inner city school, and it was a very bad experience for me. But all the teachers were just wonderful, we were friends. It was also different because we had this little community life. We would pray together in the morning and then everybody would go to their job and we'd come back and have dinner. Well, in that community was Bob, he was the pastor of St. Margaret Mary's, and there were a couple of brothers, Jesuit brothers, and there were a couple of married couples. And it was just a different situation. We all lived around there and we would meet for prayers. So that was new, it was exciting.

And then, Sister Columbine became the Reverend Mother and she no longer allowed the experimental changes. So, at the end of the year she called us in and said, either you come back, put the habit on, go where we want you to go, do what we want you to do, or leave. That was it. Okay. There was no way we could go back and put the habit on. After the year, once you were out, once you were away from that and you saw that you could be just as happy serving the Lord, and there was a little bit more freedom, you know, we all asked for exclaustration, which was to get dispensed from the vows [by Rome].

Once we got the dispensation, then I left [in 1972]. I moved to Madison Heights, and I went to teach one more year at Bishop Foley, a high school.

|||

When I left the convent my mom was quite sad for about two weeks. And then she said, "Patty, do you want me to send you some curlers?" I said, "Send me some eyebrows, Mother!" [laughs] I moved out by myself. I found this apartment, I got a car. My brother helped me buy the car. It was so much fun! And the thing I remember was, for the first time in my life, I did not have to consider another person. No one! No one! When I was home there was always family; when I was in the convent you always had to be considerate of others. And now I didn't have to answer to anyone. I was totally free. I remember it was such a good feeling [laughs] that nobody was around, that I could do whatever I wanted to do.

And so, Bob was also thinking of leaving [the priesthood], and, of course, there wasn't anyone there that wasn't hanging around him. [laughs] A good-looking guy, and I always say that I won out because I knew how to cook. [laughs] And so, then he [left the priesthood], and we started dating, and then the following year he took me to the Steakhouse in Windsor, and as we were driving up there he's showing me pictures of a house that he bought on the Detroit Golf Club. And so, that night we were at dinner sitting in front of a fireplace, and he holds up this glass of wine, and in French I get this

Fig. 17. Nadine on her wedding day with
her bridesmaid Angel, 1975

proposal.[2] I was pretty sure what he meant,
but I said, "Say it in English! Say it in English!"
[laughs] I wanted to dance on top of the table.
That song was popular, "I'm the Happiest Girl
in the Whole USA," I went around singing that.
[laughing]

I would have been content to stay my
whole life in the convent, I really would,
because I really liked it there. I had all these
intentions to spend my whole life in there and
then here this man's proposing to me and I'm
getting married. [laughs] I don't know,
sometimes I still find it hard to understand
what went on. But I figured that since initially I
had nothing to do with it, you know, like the ball started rolling and just rolled and rolled,
and like, she said no, and this one said yes, and things just kind of fell in place.

And when I got married my brother Joe wrote me this letter and he says he feels
that he no longer has to take care of me [crying] because Bob would take care of me, but
[crying] I just remember that. "I feel like I don't have to take care of you anymore." Oh,
gosh. [crying]

I stayed in my apartment until we got married, another, about six months. I was teaching
at a reading program when we got married. And then he said, "If you don't want to work
you don't have to," and it sounded pretty good after teaching all these years, and so
then I didn't work. We got married, went on this honeymoon to Acapulco, came back, and
tried to get pregnant. Well, we tried to get pregnant before we came back, and it was just
not working. We were both in our forties, and we were just not relaxed enough. And the
doctor said, "Maybe if you went on a cruise it would help you relax and you could get
pregnant." And so we did and it rained seven days and seven nights and I still didn't get
pregnant. [laughs] And we said, "Hell!"

And so I think to myself, "Oh, God, I don't want to become a selfish person." I had
this beautiful home and everything and I knew Mari was struggling with her kids, and it
doesn't look like we're going to have a baby of our own. Maybe I could just invite them to

come in and stay with us until she gets herself together and goes to school. And I think back, and oh, my God, you always do something and you never really know what you're getting into. And then, it was hard. We took three of them. Jean Marie didn't work out, so she went back after a couple of months. But Charles, Charlie was in the third grade, and Beth was in the seventh, and they were with us for two years. All of a sudden you are the parents of these two children, and you think back, and it was a joy but then it was sad, too, because then they would go back and we would be missing them.

And then in the course of the two years I got pregnant. And I thought, did I have to do something as good as this for You to send me this baby? First when I got pregnant, I thought, "Oh, my God," and then all the prayers started, all the rosaries, to support a healthy baby. But we didn't really have any problems. I thought it was going to be a boy, but it was a girl, the doctor holds up the baby and says, "Oh, a beautiful girl." And I says, "What? It's not a boy?" And he says, "Hell, no, you have to have five girls before you get one boy like me!" I told him, "Don't worry about it, I'll take the girl." [laughs, wiping eyes] Oh, you know there is a lot of emotion in my life. And a lot of wonderful things, really good things happened in my life.

And so, there she was. And then for the next years I couldn't do anything, all I did was take care of her. She was my life. It was wonderful. I loved living on Hamilton [in Detroit], you know, I had this little baby, and I would walk down the street with this long cape and her in her stroller. [laughs] It was fun. We had theater tickets, and all my friends that I had known in the convent lived right around there.

And then [Bob] decided that he wanted to get out of the city and to accomplish one more thing before he was too old. And the thing he wanted to accomplish was to have this winery. That was his dream, to have fields, and to work in the fields. And I said, "Yeah, yeah, work in the fields." And so then, we moved, from this beautiful home on Hamilton to Dunn Drive [in Traverse City, Michigan], right on the water, it was absolutely beautiful, you could see the sunset everyday and walk on the beach. In 1983, the

Fig. 18. Nadine and Marie Chantal, c. 1982

three of us spent nine months in Europe, we toured and then we settled down, and he learned a lot about the architecture, and harvesting, and wine-making.

All that I did was take care of Marie Chantal—curl her hair and sew these dresses, and take pictures, take her to ballet and to piano lessons. And I was working hard at it. [laughs] And I loved it. And then, well, she got a little bit older, and not even that much older, and so she didn't want the curls and she didn't want the dresses. She went to school and started being more independent. She still was the main attraction, but I had more free time.

Then Marie grew up and I didn't have that much to do. We also were buying the farm [for the vineyard, started in 1983], and all our money was flying out, tractors, and shakers, and all this stuff, you know, to do the harvesting. So, actually, I went to work because [Marie Chantal] was [in school]. I wanted to do something, I wanted to help out, and I got this job working in the assisted living place. Three days a week I would cook all the meals for the twenty people there. I can only cook one way, and that is the best as I know how, and it has to be good. I made all these cream puffs and sauces. They loved it. And so, that's what I did for a year. [During this period, they built the winery, Chateau Chantal, which is also a bed-and-breakfast.]

And then I got busy with decorating [the bed-and-breakfast]. I worked with two different designers and that was the most fun, all the colors, and I just loved buying all this stuff. Every day they're bringing things in and unrolling them, and I thought, "Oh, my gosh," and "Ooh," and then all of a sudden it stopped and I thought I was gonna die! [laughs] I had to go out and buy something, anything! [laughs] But I really enjoy doing that, you know, picking out the stuff. I'm very good at colors.

The first summer Chateau Chantal was opened, it was, I swear, like being back in the convent [laughs] because I was doing the laundry, and there was this church there and they were playing all these holy songs. I'm walking up the steps with this laundry, and I thought I was back in the Mother House! It

Fig. 19. Nadine, Bob, and Marie Chantal at the opening of their winery, Chateau Chantal, 1990

had that same feeling! You know, 'cause it was a big building and there were a lot of people around that weren't your family. "This feels strange! I've been here before!" [laughs] We got Rosa now and she does the rooms, and the ironing and the laundry. She does all that. I work like from six in the morning to eleven. I get up and do the breakfast.

Ever since high school, when I took home economics, I've been in clothing and textiles and cooking. And I figured out that that's really my true vocation, because fifty years later I'm still doing it and I'm still enjoying it. I love to try a new recipe, I love fabric, and all the colors and textures, and being able to find the right fabric for this right pattern, and take it home and sit down and open up that fabric and cut it and then make something. I mean, you're creating something. That's fun! I do enjoy that very much. And then I put it downstairs in the armoire [in the lobby of the winery] and then pray that it sells. [laughs] And then I will make a little extra money and give it to Marie Chantal for things that she needs. And the success makes you happy.

So, that's it. We got a lot, we got the marriage and the baby, and, you know, I probably forgot a lot, but that's it. From that little girl growing up on that farm to have experienced all that is pretty good, I think. I don't regret a day of my life, not a day. I loved being in the convent, I don't regret that I gave Him all my youth, I say I gave my youth to Jesus Christ and I gave my old age to Bob. [laughs] That's the way it goes. Every phase of my life, wonderful things have been there, I have to admit it. I like what life has given me.

3 ‖ What's a Polish-American Girl to Do?
Working-Class Girls in the Convent

GENE, NADINE, AND ANGEL all joined the Congregation of the Sisters of St. Felix of Cantalice, of the III Order of St. Francis, commonly referred to as the Felician Order.[1] Nadine stayed for twenty-two years; Gene and Angel each left after a year. The Felicians are the first, most prominent, and largest Polish-American women's religious order.[2] The order was founded in 1855 in Poland by Sophia Truszkowska (Mother Mary Angela). Twenty years later, Resurrectionist priest Reverend Joseph Dąbrowski invited the Felicians to teach in the school he had recently established in Polonia, Wisconsin. He wrote that, without Catholic Polish-speaking teachers in the immigrant community, "all will be lost for God and country."[3] So, on a leafless November day in 1874, five Felician sisters arrived to help Polonia keep its commitment to the Roman Catholic Church and Poland.

The Felician Order grew quickly.[4] The number of candidates peaked at 335 in the decade between 1909 and 1919, but the order attracted less than half that number when Nadine and Angel presented themselves in the 1950s.[5] At that time, however, it was still a fairly prominent order, representing more than a third of the roughly ten thousand Polish-American nuns (see table 1). They had 313 houses in seven Felician provinces in the United States, and Livonia, Michigan, was the largest province, accounting for roughly one-fifth of the Felicians in the United States.[6] It was in the Livonia Province, which included Grand Rapids and Hilliards, that Nadine was a candidate, Angel a postulant, and their sister Gene an aspirant.[7]

Having come to America to teach, the Felicians kept this as their primary mission. Within a decade after their arrival, the Felicians were teaching in nine different states, and, by the turn of the century, they were teaching in

Table I. Polish-American sisterhoods in the United States, 1957–1958

Apostolate	Totals for all Polish-American sisterhoods (N=17) # sisters=10,162		Sisters of St. Felix (Felician Order)			
	# of institutions	# of persons served	Total in U.S. # houses=313 # sisters=3,632*		Livonia Province # houses=63 # sisters=33*	
			Inst.	Pers.	Inst.	Pers.
Teaching						
Elementary schools	690	250,255	271	99,913	56	22,769
Catechetical instruction centers	518	63,250	284	35,820	52	5,053
Kindergartens	170	8,760	117	5,751	15	849
Other: high schools, colleges, schools of nursing, special ed., publications	146	31,445	57	15,349	18	3,915
Care of the sick						
Hospitals	51	388,665	9	57,669	—	—
Other: clinics, nursing homes, rest homes	13	1,535	2	128	—	—
Care of altars and sacristies	558	—	283	—	57	—
Orphanages	18	2,082	7	284	2	142
Homes for the aged	19	1,694	2	292	—	—
Free lunches to the poor	—	—	—	27,559	—	3,134
Other: nurseries, boarding homes for girls, residences for women, summer camps, lay retreats, social work centers, liturgical vestment workshops, census-taking, domestic departments at seminaries	627	12,651	28	4,215	6	869

*Includes professed, postulants, and novices, but not aspirants.

Source: Doman (1959), columns 1–2, p. 603; columns 3–6, p. 470

Fig. 20. Final profession of vows for Sister Nadine (first on left), 1958

fifty-three schools in sixteen states.[8] By 1914, close to seven hundred Polish-American parishes existed, and most of them, like St. Stan's in Hilliards and Sacred Heart in Grand Rapids, had elementary schools.[9] Initially, the sisters taught only at the elementary level. This is a reflection of their inexperience as teachers as well as the fact that less than 10 percent of all American children (and this included Polish immigrants) completed high school in the first part of the twentieth century.[10] Child labor restrictions legislated in 1916 and 1918 increased school attendance, and as high schools became more popular the Felicians moved into the higher grades. Yet most Felicians continued to teach at the lower levels. By 1958, the order had 3,632 sisters working in 445 schools in 31 states, but over half of the schools were elementary schools, and another quarter were kindergartens (see table 1).

The Felician teachers were both religious and ethnic workers. The purpose of the Polish parochial schools was, first, to educate children, but second, to help immigrant children retain their Catholic devotion and their Polish identity, and toward this end they gave religious instruction and taught Polish language, history, and culture.[11] Reverend Dąbrowski brought

the Polish sisters to America to help "save Poland" in the immigrant communities, and Thaddeus Radzilowski claims that the "very existence of Polonia"
is in large part due to the "efforts of these women in religious orders."[12] As
Catholicism was mainstreamed, however, Polishness faded out of the rituals
of the Church, and as Polish Americans assimilated, Polish instruction left
the schools. Nonetheless, as late as the 1940s, the Grasinski Girls were being
taught to read Polish by Felician teachers in Hilliards. By the 1950s, however,
the Polish-American order was struggling to maintain its Polish mission. The
Felicians were still teachers, but less instruction was given in Polish and
about Poland. Yet, while Nadine and her Polish-American cohort of Felician
sisters were certainly not Polish, "neither were they all-American. The sisterhood evolved into a blend of the two cultures."[13] The convents "maintained
the Polish spirit," encouraging the American-born candidates to speak Polish, and Polish remained the official language until almost 1960.[14]

|||

"Swoosh, swoosh, swoosh! That's what I remember," said my cousin
Helene. "Real picturesque, you know, pious, kind of holy, you know, always, swoosh swoosh, swoosh." The Felicians in their modified version of
the Franciscan garb—flowing brown habit, a long, white cord, and large
wooden cross—evoked awe in my memory as well. This group of women,
living without men and working as teachers, represented liberation and
foreshadowed my own aspirations. Aunt Nadine was my Mary Richards,
"making it on her own," mixed with the charm of the singing nun.[15] The
convent gave her an advanced education and a professional career, both of
which I admired and emulated, first, when my sisters and I played make-
believe school in the classrooms of her parish school, and later when I became
a teacher myself and my jeans made their own swoosh swoosh swoosh.

Unlike the Felicians in Poland, who, especially in the nineteenth century,
often came from petty nobility or wealthy families, the Felicians in America
attracted the daughters and granddaughters of farmers and laborers.[16] Thaddeus Radzilowski contends that the primary reason the Felicians were so
popular in the United States was that the sisterhood provided status and mobility for working-class women. "The order appealed strongly to all of those
daughters of Polish American families, mainly working class, who wanted education, position, social status, power, travel, or who just had an adventurous

bent. . . . The Felician congregation provided the one major, socially acceptable and relatively inexpensive way of achieving a career."[17] The convent, he
added, also "offered an attractive alternative to marriage, domestic service, or
factory work."[18]

While that may all be true, Nadine clearly states that the convent did not
represent status and a job, but, instead, her love of Jesus. In fact, she was un-
prepared for the job. Teaching "was, like, so far back in my head. . . . He
wants me to come. He wants me here. That was *the* thing." She frames her desire (though not a decision: "I had nothing to do with it") as grounded in her
devotion to God. For Angel it was the same. When asked to talk about the
women she knew growing up who had careers, she named mostly nuns.[19] I
questioned her on this matter. "Look it! You don't know anyone who has a
professional career except those who are nuns. Maybe this is why you
joined?" "No! No!"

> ANGEL: I had in my mind I was going to be a nun and a teacher, and I thought
> I would be a good teacher because I liked teaching and so forth and so on.
>
> ME: So, it's not just that you were going to be a nun, but you were going to
> be a nun and a teacher?
>
> ANGEL: Right, right, but I think the nun part came first, the part of wanting
> to be a nun.

And, in fact, after Angel left the convent, she did not pursue a teaching career.

It would contradict the nun narrative for Angel or Nadine to claim that
they entered for any other reason than to dedicate their lives to God. And
yet we must allow that we do not always see how social structures (e.g., ethnicity, class, and gender) work behind our backs to influence not only the
paths that we take but also the paths not taken. Neither of them ever considered college or professional careers outside the convent walls.

Still, there is something unique about a profession that requires a "calling." As a young novitiate, Nadine wrote that her "greatest happiness can be
accounted for by the fact that God has chosen me, a very unworthy and poor
creature to work for Him in His vineyard."[20] And sometimes He did *not* select them to be nuns. As you will see in the story of Angel in the following
chapter, her leaving the convent was seen as "being rejected by God. . . . I
was willing to give my whole entire life, everything I have, and He didn't

want me." Even if she did want to be a teacher, that is, even if she was motivated by educational and occupational status, if God did not want her, then the convent was not an option.

For Mari, the "call" was necessary if she was to submit her life to the dictates of others. No matter what career possibilities the convent offered, something more than the promise of education was required for her to join this total institution.

> MARI: But I have to say, in my eighth grade I had a teacher, her name was Sister Teresa. She was just totally lovely. We were always used to the ugly old nuns and yet here she was, probably about twenty-seven or something and just as cute as a button, and we just latched onto her.

> ME: Did you ever think of becoming a nun?

> MARI: Oh, Sister Patience wanted me when I was in the eighth grade. She was, like, pushing, putting the pressure on. But it's strange, because I would go visit Nadine with my mom and dad. She was, like, very happy, and I wasn't attracted. I just kind of thought they were like saints and they were something that you just kind of looked at from afar. I didn't identify. I identified with her education. She got her master's and I thought that was cool, you know, all these women continuing their education. But when I found out there was a Mother Superior, that was it. I don't think so! [Laughs] And then, when she told me some of the stories, you know, where they would humiliate you, and I mean, of course, it was for God! [sarcastic] But, I mean, I would have been a basket case if they would have made me get down on my knees. So, even though I loved Sister Teresa, and we were friends and I admired her, I maneuvered my way around Sister Patience and made it through without getting hooked. For one thing, they were always, like, "It's a ca-alling," and nobody ever called me! [laughs] I didn't hear nothing, so I'm clear.

She did not defy destiny by ignoring a call. And, while she was attracted to the educational possibilities, without the call she would not choose the convent for her career.

Nadine did hear the call. Silently, in her heart, Jesus was calling to her. The experience of the calling, however, does not mean that the educational and occupational opportunities provided by the convent were not important. In fact, the decline in the number of women entering the convent today is not because fewer women are getting "the call," but that women have a greater range of choices. That said, we still need to understand this profession as different from other professions. Because of the totality of the institution, we need to understand the convent as more than simply an occupational career and a means of social mobility. For the Felicians, their religious vocation is as important as their occupational vocation. The Felician Order stresses both contemplative prayer and active service.[21] They are not just teachers, they are "brides of Christ."

I believe these women when they tell me they had or did not have a calling. But the calling does not erase the fact that the convent was one of the possible life routes for Polish-American working-class women. Their ethnic groove as much as their class groove predisposed them to the choice. In some ways it is their Polish Catholicism that responded to God's call in their entering the convent. In her history of the Felicians in Livonia, Sr. Ziolkowski argues that it was something about the Polish character that inspired women to join. "Women of Polish descent served in religious orders in numbers greater perhaps than any other ethnic group. To be a 'Polish' woman was to possess a profound spirituality and to practice that spirituality in lay organizations and in religious orders."[22] Without conscious intention, joining the convent reproduced gender and ethnic routines.

We often do not see larger social structures manufacturing choices for us, but, instead, experience ourselves operating somewhat freely in making life decisions. My friend Nancy Jo, who grew up as a Presbyterian in Texas, has always admired the rituals of the Catholic Church, and she herself has a deep and serious relationship with God. Nonetheless, as an eighteen-year-old, she did not define her desires and longing as a call from God to join a sisterhood. She felt the impulses differently than did Nadine, who writes of her first such experience, "It was in the upper classroom, the second row from the window and the fourth bench that the Sister casually said something that set my heart on fire. This burning was the actual beginning of my religious vocation . . . that was the inception of my romance with Jesus."[23] It is within the framework of Roman Catholicism—as interpreted within a Polish-American parish which values religious orders, within a gender dynamic that prescribed marriage (to God or a man) as a form of gender legitimation and life fulfillment, and within a class structure that did not encourage higher education—that Nadine responded to her religious passion by joining the convent. It is within this framework that she interpreted her desires and feelings as a calling. It is in the space of the Hilliards country-side, among the family praying the rosary, sitting in the pews of St. Stan's, that she was open to and then responded to a religious vocation.

|||

"The third year was one of importance because in that year I received my future Spouse into my heart for the first time. As I walked down the aisle I felt just like a little angel ascending the throne of heaven. With my beautiful white net and lace dress, my veil, and Jesus in my heart, I lived the day like a saint." This is Nadine's description of her First Holy Communion when she was eight years old.[24] Her relationship to the Lord is defined even then within the gendered roles assigned to women. Nuns are "brides" to Christ, and her first communion like a wedding march. The roles created for women in the convent paralleled their gender roles in secular society: brides, sisters, and mother "superior."[25] The title of Mother Superior for women who do not bear children extends the concept of motherhood to include women who give birth to the spiritual selves of their flock. In her biography of Sophia Truszkowska, the founder of the Felician Order, Maria Winowska writes, "Failure to comprehend this fundamental truth accounts for many miscarried vocations, because nothing revolts a woman so much as the stigma of sterility. She is made to be a mother and when she is called to *total gift* and to sacrifice of physical maternity, it is not to be *less* but *more* of a mother."[26] Celibacy does not preclude them from developing maternal feelings or traditional gender routines.

The Felicians undertook women's traditional social reproductive work by feeding the poor, teaching children, taking care of priests, and ministering to the aged and the sick.[27] The order was founded with a special dedication to young girls, orphans, and needy women, especially in the early years in Poland but also in America, where they formed sewing workshops and staffed orphanages, nurseries, and kindergartens.[28] They also cooked and cleaned for seminarians and priests (as Nadine did that summer at Orchard Lake), maintaining the domestic routines at seminaries and in this way providing wifely duties for the priests. Even though nuns did not participate in the conventional gender routines of marriage, childbearing, and housekeeping within a family context, they performed traditional gender roles by caring, nurturing, cooking, teaching, raising, protecting, and comforting.

Perhaps the best example of continuity between the convent life and the married life is Nadine's description of her life inside and outside of the convent. Asked to compare the two phases, she said, "Actually, there's not that much difference. [laughs] Because my life as a nun was a giving life and every life is a giving life. Most life is a giving life. I'm always giving—I'm giving to Marie Chantal, I'm giving to Bob. I actually feel like I am the same person that I was, that I became in the convent." Gendered expectations become manifest as durable dispositions easily carried from one setting to another.[29] Expected to nurture, these women were caretakers in the home, the church, the community, and the workplace.

The feminists' master narrative on Roman Catholicism acknowledges that the Church is an extremely patriarchal institution. Both the organizational structure, which does not allow women to hold positions of power, and its underlying ideology, that women should submit to men (fathers, husbands, priests), have misogynistic tones.[30] Carol Lee Flinders, however, has written eloquently on how the Church can be liberating for women despite the patriarchy and misogyny. Flinders argues that medieval nuns—Teresa of Avila, Clare of Assisi, and Catherine of Siena—may have been the first feminists. Enclosed behind the walls of the convent, "they found a scope for their energies and a freedom of expression women enjoyed nowhere else in the 'civilized' world."[31] They lived longer, developed their skills, and found a voice stronger and louder than their secular sisters. They had connections to themselves, to each other, and to the sacred, and they liberated their selves through these connections.

As "brides of Christ," Flinders writes, "they were freed from the authority of fathers, brothers, husbands, and sons."[32] In this cloistered environment, medieval women developed and created hospitals, the arts, and scholarship. To say that these women crafted a space of their own does not mean that the institution was liberated. Rather, it is an example of how counter ideologies and institutions were created within, but in opposition to, the dominant ideologies and institutions. Through their accommodation, they did not confront or try to change the patriarchy, but they did create a safe space for themselves to develop within it. Entering the convent was, consciously or unconsciously, an act of resistance that set up the opportunity for a more radical self-expression, such as pursuing professional careers. As a result, the convent helped women develop their selves with dignity even within a system of structured inequality. Entering the convent was not an act of resigned acceptance but a means of accommodating the constraints of the system to escape some of its oppressiveness. Flinders writes, "Women religious were able to transcend patriarchy, I saw, because they knew themselves to be the subjects of their own biographies after all—individuals who could make meaningful choices and live by them, braving if necessary the stigma attached to the women who made their own decisions—and also because convent life allowed them to form their own female cultures and communities."[33] Catholic women mystics, she argues, "were not pale and silent brides of Christ at all; they were passionate and vivid, eloquent, resourceful, funny—and impressively stubborn."[34] Given these qualities, these religious women were admirable gender models and not simply pawns of patriarchal priests and lords.[35]

The choices available to medieval mystics were different from the choices available to Nadine, and those available to me. As women's spaces for freedom expanded, the need for the convent's liberating shelter subsided. In the early-to-mid-twentieth century, the convent still provided some opportunities that were not as available to working-class women outside the convent. As noted earlier, Radzilowski argues that the rapid growth of the Felician Order was in part caused by the occupational rewards the convent offered. Whether or not this is what attracted the women to the convent, it is nonetheless one of the results of the religious life. John Bukowczyk provides evidence that, in one particular context, nuns were more academically active than their lay sisters. The sister-scholars played a central role in the formative years of the Polish American Historical Association (PAHA), founded in 1944, especially within its main organ, a biannual academic journal, *Polish American Studies* (*PAS*). In 1947, 71 percent of the women in PAHA were nuns.[36] In the 1950s, women, mostly nuns, held a third to almost two-thirds of the officer and council positions; articles written by women made up 41 percent of the contents of *PAS*, and over two-thirds of the fifty-seven pieces written by women were written by nuns. By the 1970s, when secular scholars replaced the religious control of PAHA and *PAS*, the number of nuns participating declined, and, along with, it the overall number of women who were active in the organization as members, leaders, and authors.[37]

The decision to be a nun is influenced by the choices available at the time. As women's choices and freedoms expand, by gaining reproductive control, equality of opportunity, and protection in public spaces, the convent may be less necessary for women (but still necessary for spiritual folk). Fewer women are entering the convent today, and even Nadine understands that her vow was a reflection of the times. I asked her, "If you were growing up today, would you still go in the convent?" She answered, "Probably not. Probably not. When I was growing up there were nuns around. They would encourage you, and you would see some of them, what they were doing. It was a totally different time, 1945 and '50, than what we have now. I probably wouldn't."

Angela Helen

I HAVE KNOWN ANGEL only as a middle-aged woman; before that I could not distinguish the woman from my mom. She had six children close together (at one point, five children, ages six, four, three, two, and newborn), and for decades she was monolithically "Mom." She was (and is) the kind of mom that your friends called "Mom," named their children after, and converted to Catholicism for. More than half of her first, almost hundred-page interview transcript was related to children; only her younger sister Mari spent as much time talking about her children. Perhaps this is a result of the fact that I am one of those children and so I unconsciously asked for, and she unconsciously gave me, information about my siblings and myself. But, in contrast with Caroline and Fran, who have detailed memories of the first twelve years of their lives, Angel's story begins when she is in high school, explores her one year as a nun, and then launches into marriage and children and stays there: her best and worst moments were defined by her children's antics; her turning points in life were related to her children's life cycles; the things she most regrets had to do with children; and what brings her closer to God are her children.

We began the first of many taping sessions with me asking about the convent experience. We children grew up knowing Mom had been in the convent. (It was always a way to one-up anyone in a conversation about strict parents—"Yeah, but my mom was a nun"—when, actually, she was more lenient than most parents.) I knew bits of the story about why she left—something gory about nightmares—but I wanted to hear it all again. The "scandal of the convent" was the most sordid thing I knew about her. And it wasn't even sordid. I was fascinated because, in every other way, Angel presents herself as a problem-free woman.

Fig. 21. Angel, Jim, and Mary (author) in front of their home at Mary's First Holy Communion, 1967

Angel was eager to have me interview her, and of all the Grasinski Girls, I got the most from her. It started in 1998, when I went home at Christmas. I took a tape recorder and we found time to sit and talk. Dad was in the house, but she would not allow him in the room while we were taping. She chose the evening hours when he was downstairs watching television. One time he wandered up and leaned his tall body into the archway of the living room, and she stopped talking and told him to leave. "I don't feel comfortable," she said. It was a simple statement—not mean, nor aggressive, but very assertive. I was impressed. "Please leave." And he did.

Angel, born Angeline Helen Grasinski on February 8, 1936, was baptized as Angela Helen at St. James Church in Grand Rapids. The family moved out to Hilliards when she was a baby. She was a skinny kid with large dark circles under her eyes. We have one black-and-white photo of her standing poetically, D. H. Lawrence-like, in a field of daisies, innocently posed with a piece of hay in her mouth. She looked emaciated. At sixteen, she had contracted rheumatic fever and spent the summer in bed. That summer she also decided to be a nun, but she says the two events were not related. After attending St. Stan's grade school in Hilliards, she went to the public high school, where she and her Polish-American girlfriends were known as the "four 'skis"—bright, pretty, social girls who became the "in-group." From her high school pictures it doesn't look much like she was in training for the sisterhood, but as soon as she graduated she entered the Felician convent in Livonia.

The Best Time in My Life, and the Worst Time

I started thinking about becoming a nun when I was about sixteen. I don't know, there wasn't any exact time or date or place, but it was just something that came about, some longing, something that I wanted to pursue. And I just did. My sister was already a nun at that point, but she had never encouraged me or my younger sister to enter the convent. No one really was, like, drawing me to there. It was just something I felt that I wanted to do.

I decided I would become a nun rather than getting married, because nuns don't get married. I mean, I always thought, when I was growing up, that I just wanted to meet a boy, and get married and have children, have a family. But then this other feeling or this other dream just sort of took precedence over that. I didn't care to get married anymore. That didn't have nothing to do with wanting to be a nun, though. You didn't make a choice of "Well, I don't want to get married, and so I'm going to be a nun." It's just, well, that doesn't even enter the picture. It's just, you just want to be a nun, and that's it.

I started going with Jim when I was seventeen, and he wanted to pursue this further. And I said, "No, no, I'm going to be a nun. I'm sorry, I'm going to be a nun." And so I went steady, but I was going to be a nun, and so I never did anything. [laughing] But then, when Jim went overseas in February and I was going to the convent in June, I thought, "Well, what the heck!" So, in that period of time I met some really nice guys. One wanted to get married to me, just fell in love with me. "No, no, I'm going to be a nun!" [laughs] And another guy I had met through a pen pal, he was in the service and he wrote me these beautiful, intelligent letters. And he came home on furlough, this was like a week before I was going to the convent. So, we went to a picnic, and went to a show, and I just told him, "No, I'm going to the convent." I mean, he was an Italian Catholic, he understood.

My mother supported me because she, well, probably the fact that she never had, maybe, like a real happy marriage. And so, having her daughters being nuns, she knew we would never have to go through trouble with husbands or having babies and all this stuff. So, she was all for it. Not that, you know, like some people are so proud because their children are nuns or priests. I mean, she was happy because she probably thought that we would be relieved of all the hardships that she went through. But I could see other people who were happily married, and I knew that there was choice, I didn't have to be running away. I just never thought of that. It didn't influence me that much. And probably by the time I was growing up, my mother had gone through the worst parts of her marriage, so I didn't really see this part.

After I graduated I went to the convent. I went right on Father's Day, June 18. I went to the convent dressed in my pretty dress, and my make-up, and no one thought I was going to stay. [She met the five other girls in her group, and they all had attended the Academy, the high school run by the Felicians.] And none of them had ever even dated a boy, so I had to sneak in my scrapbooks [laughs] and tell them about all my boyfriends. [laughing] And they just had to hear everything. I used to think, you know, they'd never had a boy kiss them or put their arm around them. That was, like, really sad. [laughs]

The first couple days I said, "What am I doing here? I made the wrong decision." I cried all night long, and I just was, like, "I don't know what I'm doing here. I really don't want to be here." [laughs] "I want my dresses back, and my boyfriends." But then it was, maybe the third day, it was just like something overcame me, and I thought, "No, this is what I really want." And for all them six months till January, I was just the happiest person—probably, you know, probably ever in my whole life this was my happiest period.

I didn't really miss anybody. I missed this Ron, because that was the one I was dating before I left. I didn't miss my mother and Jim, because I had been away for a whole year before, living with my sister Caroline. And I missed hearing music, because I played music all the time, and not being ever able to hear a radio or music, I missed that. But, other than that, it was such a joyful time. I mean, I loved going to the college, and I loved getting good marks. And I liked being with all these other women, you know, and we just got closer every day. Some you liked, some you didn't like, some you became very close to.

In the summer we took [courses in] children's literature and something else. The process was, you went to college, and basically you started out as an elementary school teacher. And then from there you pursued and got master's degrees in different fields. I thought I would be a good teacher because I liked teaching. In the fall, we went to regular college with all the regular girls, Madonna College. So we took biology, English literature, and world history, and theology, and French. I could not write, and I still can't. I'd sit there for hours, and I'd have a paragraph wrote. [laughs] But in French I got As, and in biology—I loved anything where I could memorize and didn't have to write. World history, I liked world history!

Then, this was after Christmas, we had a nun in our order who was older. Her name was Sister Jane, and she had been in World War II. And she was a dentist, so they welcomed her with open arms, because she set up her whole practice, and nobody ever paid to go there. And she had a nervous breakdown. They kept her there for two days, and she was laaaughing and screaming, and, you know, it was just the most scariest thing for an eighteen-year-old who had never seen mental illness or anything like that before. And finally somebody came and they wrapped her in a sheet and dragged her out. I mean, it was just, it was terrible. And then, about three days later, my girlfriend Maryann left. She says, "I just feel like I'm going crazy. I cannot stay." I asked her, "Oh, how can you leave Jesus? You know, you're breaking His heart." And at that point I'm okay. This has happened, but that's no big deal, you know, I can deal with this.

And then, one day, one morning at prayers, I started to pray, and I couldn't pray. Now I realize, all it was, was, like, a panic attack. But not knowing it then, I just, uh [pause] my hands started sweating, and then, it had to be more than that. My nerves must have just been on edge. Well, they put me to bed, saying, "Oh, you have a virus." And then, it was like this perfectly still quiet. And the more you think, the worse, the crazier you get. They sent me to the doctor. How do you explain to him you think you're going crazy? You can't do this.

Oh, and I couldn't drive. The girls that could drive used to drive the nuns to the hospital and so forth. And they asked who could drive. This was in my good time. "Oh, I can drive." I loved to drive, and I would drive periodically. And then, one time after I had this panic attack, I was driving on Grand River Road, five lanes going each way, and I had this old nun [in the car], and I had one of these attacks. I mean, it's just [sigh], you know, you just, uh, your hands sweat and you're just, like, dizzy. And [the old nun] said, "She don't know what she's doing!" [spoken in a harsh tone] I was going, "You better believe I don't." [laughs] And the other girl that was sitting with us said, "You're okay, you're okay." But, so, then that was another thing, every time I'd drive, I was afraid this was going to happen.

I mean, this all works in your mind, but it's so common now. I mean, they have these workshops to get rid of it, but you didn't know this till thirty years later, that this is what you were having. And so I had a problem with that. And I had a problem of never being able to be in a place where I couldn't see an exit door. I could never go to a concert or anything. I had to sit right by the exit door, because I would get these same feelings. Most of that's gone now. The only thing I probably can't do now is speak in front of a large group of people, and every once in a while, I get these feelings again and my palms start sweating. I think, "It's just gonna go away. It's just a feeling. It's nothing. I'm not going to pass out. I'm not going to die or anything." And so, they go away. But I didn't know enough about it then to say, "I can't speak. I'm really upset." Every time I had to get up to say something those feelings would all come back to me, this panic attack.

This had happened in January, and I just prayed and prayed. I was still going to classes and every time I would have to get up and speak, I would just be petrified. And I couldn't explain it to the teachers. I just thought, "I'm gonna lose my mind." That's exactly how I felt! And I kept thinking, "This is the devil testing me. I really love it here." But in my mind, I was going, "Aw, you can't stand it here, you're going to go crazy. I don't want to leave, I don't want to leave. No, I'm going to go crazy if I stay."

And the Mother Superior, we had a Mother Mistress Lucille, and a Vice Mistress, Mother Amelia. I went to Mother Mistress and told her exactly how I felt. "Oh no, it's just the devil. You are to be a nun. You're just like Nadine. Both of you are beautiful nuns. You just are, you're smart." And blah, blah, blah, all this stuff. Okay, so I go back, pray some more. [laughs] "This is the devil tempting me." It was just really hard—probably the best time in my life and the worst time.

I couldn't do nothing to distract myself. If I was home I could go shopping or play some music or something, but there it was just this dead silence. After I was in bed there for a week, and I couldn't even walk, I was trembling, I had to get up, and I was scared, and it was just horrible. And there was nobody to talk to except Maryann, who had already left. So, then I wrote her a letter, and I thought, "Okay, I think I'm going to have to go home." [laughs]

Well, no, this was what really happened. You know, I prayed and prayed for some sign that either I stay or I don't stay. I mean, somebody's got to help. "I come here to please You, God! Why [pause] why aren't You helping me? Why are You making me go through this?" So, I was doing some ironing and big tears are rolling down my cheeks, and this Mother Amelia, she said, "What's the matter?" And I told her the whole story and she said, "You just pray to Jesus that you just . . ." Let's see, how did she word it? She says, "Whatever He gives you," and something about the highest place in heaven. "You follow that life. It doesn't matter if you're here or there, or whatever, but just pray that you will follow whatever Jesus wants you to do." And, I called my mother the next day. "Come and get me." [laughs] This is all I needed, for somebody to say that. I could not stand it anymore. I mean, I was losing weight, I wasn't eating. I should have probably went to the psychiatrist or somebody to help me. It didn't help me none that somebody told me I got a virus, which I know a virus does not make you mentally ill.

So, but before that, I wrote to Maryann. We had a mutual friend, who was a college girl, and I snuck out a letter [through her], 'cause all of our letters got read. We never sealed them; everything incoming, outgoing, got read. So, I snuck a letter out to Maryann. "I think I'm leaving, you know, what's it like out there once you get home?" She wrote me back, "Oh, it's beautiful! You know, you could get some help. Nobody ever says anything like, 'Why did you leave the convent?'" So, I thought that was, like, reaffirming, so then I called my mother, and just like that, I said, "I'm going." But that was really hard. [starts crying]

It was just hard that morning that I left. The postulants all gathered around me and were singing, "May the Good Lord Bless and Keep You." [crying] And it was just so touching. [crying, pause] I mean, it was just so beautiful. Everyone was crying and singing. And I thought, I'm leaving all these girls that I really feel so close to. And when you're doing something, you have this bond, you know, we were all just wanting to be brides of Christ. I mean, this was our whole goal in life. They were just these good people, everybody trying to be good and overcome evil. [laughs] But they all gathered around me, started singing. That's when I realized I must be really nice. And they were giving me little presents, and saying they'll never forget me, and it was really hard. But then, when I got married, I went back there on my honeymoon. [laughing]

The nuns, especially some of the older nuns that were teachers, they were bitter and crabby. Way back then I used to think, "My mother has a lot more love in her heart and her soul than any of these nuns." I mean, she was a lot holier, a lot more spiritual. And she was a lot more kinder. And I think, maybe, you know, I would have become bitter or something; I don't know. I think, "I, I tried. I really tried." That's all you can do. And then you think, "Well, I could have stayed longer." But I couldn't have; it was at the point of really having a breakdown. And like she said, "God doesn't ever ask that of you." But you think, "Oh, that's the devil's tempting you." Oh, okay, I realize the devil can tempt you, but this was a bit long, like from January till June?

I had decided to stick it out, to complete my first year of college, so I would have one year. Otherwise, I probably would have left earlier. When I came out of the convent it was, it was [pause] hard for me to have to think, "Now that I'm not going to be a nun, I have this whole different life ahead of me, of getting married and having a family." It was just strange, feeling that way, when for the last three years all I had in my mind was I was going to be a nun and a teacher. I thought I would be a good teacher because I liked teaching and so forth. And now I come back, and this is, like, all taken away.

I think I learned lessons that first six months that I probably carry with me my whole life. Oh, just about faith and trust, you know, that things actually do work out. But, I mean, at the time, you think that you're all alone, and no one cares about you. It took me a long time to get over these feelings of being rejected by God. I was willing to give my whole, entire life, everything I have, and He didn't want me. I mean, it's really a sad, sad feeling.

4 ⫿ Mothers on Boone Street

ANGEL WORKED ALL THROUGH high school in what we now call the service sector—first at Buzz's Bar and Grill for forty cents an hour when she was sixteen, then at a dime store for sixty cents an hour, and finally at a bowling alley her senior year, where there was "talk" because the twenty-eight-year-old divorced owner gave her a ride home every evening. "But he was always a perfect gentleman, never even said innuendoes or nothing that I ever had to be afraid of him or anything." In Grand Rapids she worked at a dress shop owned by a Russian immigrant who wanted to train Angel to become a clothes buyer. Angel politely declined the offer; she was going to be a nun.

For the Grasinski Girls, the life grooves were motherhood, sisterhood, and singlehood. In the first track, they worked in an office or the retail sector for a few years between high school and marriage, and then up until their first child was born.[1] After this, motherhood defined their routines in the private sphere as well as the public sphere (for example, children influenced where and when they would reenter the labor market, what roles they played, what organizations they joined). Motherhood was the career—that is, a field in which to complete a life ambition, involving a continuous rather than temporary activity, invested with moral intent so as to provide meaningful purpose. Careers have the potential to fulfill the aspirations of the self.[2] Both motherhood and the convent provided careers. The third track, singlehood, required paid labor which was not a career, but a job they had to accept if they did not have a husband. A job provided neither a moral mission nor meaningful purpose; instead, it was a holding pattern, a survival strategy. Gene Grasinski found herself on this track, and Angel did not envy her. "I always thought she was a very lonely person. And she was. And I never wanted to be that way. I never thought that was cool, like, she was living in town by herself. I remember thinking, 'This is sad.'" The values, ex-

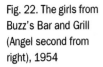

Fig. 22. The girls from Buzz's Bar and Grill (Angel second from right), 1954

pectations, cultural capital, and education of working-class girls did not prepare them to be unmarried career women.

While both Fran and Mari confess to wanting to become airline stewardesses, their young-girl fantasies were just that: fantasies, not career dreams. As Fran puts it:

> I really thought I was gonna be an airline stewardess. [laughter] When I was a young girl, that's what I used to think. I was like about ten or eleven years old, and I used to sit on the step of the front porch, and I used to look at all those clouds up there, and oh, I'd just be in one of those planes that go, you know, up above the clouds. Yeah! But then as I started getting, like, sixteen or seventeen, then I guess I wanted to get married and have a family. I guess that's what I wanted to do. I didn't ever want to go to school, you know. I didn't. At one time I thought about going to the convent, but that's probably because Gene went.

For her, an occupational career requiring advanced training and a long-term commitment was not a perceivable possibility—though it was a dream, an easy-to-dismiss, head-in-the-clouds dream.

From our social location in the world, we are predisposed to follow some tracks and overlook others. These dispositions, as Bourdieu notes, are formed by the structural conditions that generate doable "aspirations and practices," while, at the same time, "the most improbable practices are excluded, either totally without examination, as *unthinkable,* or at the cost of the *double negation* which inclines agents to make a virtue of necessity, that is, to refuse what is anyway refused and to love the inevitable."[3] In other words, we learn to not want what we cannot have. Learning to love the inevitable goes a long way toward helping these women find happiness. They do not choose life courses that are incompatible with their life options; that which is possible is only that which they can imagine as probable. Frustration and discontent grow from dwelling too long on the improbable.

I pushed Angel into telling me what sort of work she might have chosen had she not decided to become a nun. She hedged, paused, and then said that she could type ninety-three words a minute and "had the notability of being the fastest typist in Hopkins High School. And so, I enjoyed doing that, so probably, possibly, I probably would have thought I would like to work in an office where I could do that." But she wasn't imagining an occupational career. She pursued the convent and then motherhood in a way she did not pursue an office career. When Angel left the convent, she did what she "probably, possibly" thought she would do—she worked in an office, developing her craft as a secretary, along with countless other working-class women since the 1920s.[4] She got a "nice" job at Auto-Owners Insurance. "It was a very nice place. There was four of us girls, and the office manager was pregnant with her sixth child. And so, she was going to quit or at least to have the child. Back then, they didn't give you maternity leaves, you just had to quit. So, then I became office manager after six months. I was over all these other girls, but it was

Fig. 23. Angel and Jim on their wedding day, 1956

fine, because I didn't have to discipline anyone, and I just got a little bit more money."

In August 1956, just over a year after leaving the convent, Angel married James (Jim) Erdmans, the boy down the dirt road in Hilliards whom she had dated in high school. After the wedding, she continued to work for Auto-Owners Insurance until she had her first child thirteen months later. Her story continues.

In those days, once you got married it was like a trick to see who would get pregnant the fastest. I mean, that was the only thing on your mind. It's like, "Can you get pregnant on your honeymoon?" [we both laugh] No, I'm not kidding you! And it was this dumb thing to do. I mean, I had this nice job, and I could have gotten to know him better. We could have done something together, but no-o, this was number one on your mind. There were four girls: Evelyn Rosma, another girl that worked with me, and then two girls next door worked at Occidental [Insurance]. We all got married that summer. And it's just like, "Are you pregnant yet? Are you pregnant yet? Are you pregnant yet?" every month.

Well, three of us did, and the one girl never did, so she ended up adopting. But three of us did, I mean, and this was number one. That was the only priority. And then, you know, once you started having babies, there was nothing else. But this is what you wanted. It wasn't like, "Oh my god, I'm pregnant!" It was like, I'm "finally" pregnant, after, like, three months. But when I think back, I think if I had to do it over again, I was only twenty years old, I could have worked for two years. We could have taken a trip or two and really got to have fun together, I mean, just us, me and him, you know, 'cause I was so deathly sick when I was pregnant.

I got pregnant that December; it was four months. And I worked till about two weeks before Jimmy was born. I quit in the summertime, and they paid me six weeks severance pay, which was really nice. But then they kept calling me back, "Can you come?" This was vacation period. "Can you come?" I mean, and I wasn't doing nothing; I felt really good then. And so, I came back and helped whoever needed help.

Jimmy was born in September, and in January my mother said to me, we were living in the one-bedroom apartment, and she says, "If you want to work for a year," she says, "I will take care of Jimmy for nothing, and you can get your house." And so I says, "Well, okay." And I just hated it. I hated getting up, taking this four-and-a-half-month-old baby out in the dead of winter. I found a job at Dun & Bradstreet. And jobs were really scarce, and the pay was not as much as I was getting at Auto-Owners. And so, I went to work there from February until I got pregnant in November, and I quit then. I just hated it because I would have to get up at maybe five forty-five AM to get ready and to get the baby ready because Dad had to be at work. We would leave Jimmy at my mother's on 32nd Street, and then I would have to take a bus downtown and then take a transfer to where I worked. I hated packing that baby up every morning, I hated that with a passion. And then I would go to my mother's, I just hated leaving him. He was only four and a half months old, and he was this beautiful child, and I missed out on so much of his growing up, because by the time I got out of work at five, I had him maybe, like, two hours and he was ready for bed. I had the weekends, but I hated working.

I loved being a mother, just every little smile and everything—I just loved it, and I was just so proud of him, I was showing him off to everybody and dressing him so cute. And I had to take him to Christmas Eve midnight mass, that was, like, really important to me. On Easter Sunday, we had to be all dressed up, and I had to take him to church. When you have a few more children, you don't do that, but with the first one, it was important.

[ME: But why did you go to back to work? I mean, if you didn't want to go back to work, why did you?]

Because I thought this was my chance to get a house. Otherwise, we couldn't afford the down payment; we could more or less make the payment, but you needed a down payment. But I just hated it. I mean, I just hated it. I missed so much. And when I had you [the second child], then I didn't work anymore after that, except for periodically. Once they called me back at Auto-Owners, and I worked for two weeks. I was pregnant with David that summer. I went to work two weeks only, but, oh, it was so much fun to get out and get dressed up. [laughs] But that was just, you know, for a summer to fill in.

Angel initially enjoyed working, both before her marriage and during the first year of her marriage. She enjoyed getting dressed up and being in an office with other women. She was good at her job: she was a smart, fast typist, and she "got along wherever I worked." She had the correct demeanor, necessary skills, and preferable skin color for office work.[5] Angel defines her satisfaction by job conditions rather than by the nature of the work: she was more satisfied at Auto-Owners because of her wages and the severance pay. In contrast, the same work performed at Dun & Bradstreet was not as satisfying because it paid less and transportation was more complicated.

In hindsight, Angel wishes she had delayed the onset of children, but she also clearly understands the strong social expectations that pushed her, and other women of her generation, into early marriages and motherhood. Angel also sees the relation between working and baby-making. Sociologists Myra Marx Ferree and Beth Hess observed the "link between a woman's employment expectations and her fertility behavior, although the direction of cause and effect probably runs both ways. That is, women are able to enter the labor force because they have few children, and a commitment to work reduces both the desire and the need to have many children."[6] In Angel's case, the cause and effect ran one way: her fertility and mothering expectations influenced her employment behavior. Once she had a child, work became burdensome. The burden was not the work itself but the fact that work interfered with her ability to mother. Her routines were not easy; she had to get up early, go out in cold weather, leave her child with her mother, and be away from him for long periods of time. Her problems were related to both gender dispositions and class location. Gender expectations pushed her into early childbearing, which would have been easier to manage if she did not have to work. The reason she worked was because they needed the second income for a down payment on a house, and, as a result of limited resources, she had to take the bus to work and fit herself into her husband's schedule. Simply having a second car would have given her an extra three hours with her child at home in the morning.

Once Angel and Jim moved into their house and had a second child in 1959, she did not go back to work until 1970. She spent those early years raising her children on Boone Street, in a white working-class neighborhood. Boone Street was a new street when Angel, Jim, and Jimmy Jr. moved in. There were twenty-six houses on their block and another eleven around "the bend" on Boone Court, almost all built between 1955 and 1960. Because they were new homes, it was easier for homeowners to get federally backed loans through the Veterans Administration or the Federal Housing Administration.[7] The families in the neighborhood aged together: they moved in as young married couples, had babies, commiserated over chain-link fences while raising teenagers, and then retired and took Caribbean cruises together and learned to play blackjack on the Indian reservations near Michigan's Upper Peninsula. The neighborhood was built on cleared farm land (an asparagus field that continued to put forth stalks in undeveloped areas behind the houses) and required the new homeowners to landscape their expansive lots. As a result, the trees in the neighborhood—red burgundy maples, eerie white birch, tall twin-trunk oaks, and weeping willows—are the age of their oldest children. The permanent residency of their neighbors, a function of a stable economy and their location in the labor market, reinforced the stability of the neighborhood. Almost a half a century later, a quarter of the homes are still occupied by the original owners, and four others are owned by children of the original owners.

At that time (and, for the most part, still today), Boone Street was racially and economically homogenous—white and working class. No blacks or Asians lived in the neighborhood and only one mixed Hispanic-Anglo family. The neighbors were at least third- or fourth-generation Americans, and while most would identify themselves as "American" their surnames marked them as having Dutch, German, Scottish, English, Polish, and Lithuanian ancestry.

The homeowners did not have college educations (but many sent their children to college) and most of the men worked in the manufacturing sector as skilled and unskilled laborers. Angel's husband, Jim, was a tool-and-die maker at General Motors from the time he was eighteen until he retired at the age of fifty-nine. Asked to describe "where" the men worked, Angel listed the local factories: Steelcase, American Coveralls, "some factory that closed down," Lear's, Reynolds Metal. (In the middle class, people ask each other "What do you do?" In the working class, people ask each other, "Where do you work?") When I asked her if they "worked in skilled or unskilled positions," she said, "not skilled" for many of them, and yet, for one, she said: "He wasn't skilled, but he worked his way up to be the head of the whole maintenance. So, in a way, he worked his way up very well." Reading a draft of the manuscript, Angel wrote in the margin, "You need to talk about Dad who worked his way up to lead man."

As young adults, the men found work in the robust 1950s industrial economy; by the time the economy fell into a recession in the 1970s and the manufacturing sector began its decline, most of their positions were secured through seniority, unions, and Grand Rapids' more diversified manufacturing base.[8] Had they lived only one hundred twenty miles east, in Flint, a town more heavily dependent on the auto industry, or if they had been twenty years younger, it would have been a different story. As it was, most of them retired from their factory positions after forty years and returned home with their toolboxes, gold watches, and comfortable pensions.

Boone Street's narrative is different from that of the more common working-class suburbs. Joseph Howell's classic study, *Hard Living on Clay Street*, describes the "working-class" neighborhood he studied as having deteriorating buildings occupied by the working poor. Lillian Rubin's books, *Worlds of Pain* and *Families on the Fault Line*, describe the economic desperation of working-class families. From the title of her first book, it is clear that she plans to document the culture of the working class as a negative experience. In *Families on the Fault Line* she refers to working-class neighborhoods as being neglected and describes them as "junky." Visiting one of those neighborhoods, she is affronted by the "stench" and steps around a "child's tricycle lying forlornly on its side, its handlebar pitted in rust, a rear wheel askew." She comments on a house with "sagging parts" with countertops "cracked and mottled gray." She writes, "The buildings that line its path would look dingy and decrepit on any day. But on this drizzly, gray November afternoon, they're particularly depressing."[9]

These narratives of the working class presented by Rubin and Howell (see also Judith Stacey's *Brave New Families*) do not describe the working-class neighborhood on Boone Street (nor the numerous other streets in the suburbs surrounding Grand Rapids). In stable economies, where workers are protected by unions and respected by state policies, it is possible to be a member of the working class and not suffer miserably. Unfortunately, in the history of the United States, these periods are rare and the privileges of a living wage and sufficient benefits have not been extended to all workers, all races and ethnic groups, or both genders.

The residents of Boone Street were not depressed and their homes were not neglected. It was just the opposite. The houses were freshly painted eggshell white or corn yellow, the shutters a contrasting black. Red-potted geraniums adorned small front porches laced with wrought-iron railings, pale orange roses flowered alongside the driveways, and purple hyacinths were planted sparingly among the trimmed shrubs. The hedges were clipped, the lawns edged, and the sidewalks swept. There was no garbage or litter in the neighborhood; everyone responsibly (almost obsessively) cared for their yards. The tricycles were not left out to rust but instead were parked in orderly garages, along the wall with the lawnmowers, rakes, and, nowadays, leaf blowers and snow blowers.

The people who lived on the street mirrored their weedless lawns. They had stable families with few visible "dysfunctions." On Boone Street, only three families were divorced, and these families did not stay in the neighborhood. Two other couples separated but then reunited. Most families attended church on Sunday mornings. Angel knew of no abortions, only one instance of spouse abuse, no drinking or drug problems among the adults (the children are a different story), and only one extramarital affair and one potential case of incest (a stepfather passed lewd notes to his sixteen-year-old stepdaughter). This last was one of the two couples who divorced, which Angel refers to as the "dysfunctional" family. Dysfunctional behavior such as alcoholism or child abuse was found more frequently in studies of working-class families by Lillian Rubin and Lyn Mikel Brown, but was atypical on Boone Street.[10]

For many scholars, the working class is conflated with the working poor and the nonworking poor, and poverty (with its pain and suffering) rather than economic stability (which affords privileges and makes it easier to laugh) becomes the defining feature of the working class.[11] The families on Boone Street had tight budgets, but they were not poor. Angel did not feel financial insecurity because her husband always brought home a paycheck, even though when the children were young they were "living from paycheck to paycheck. We never, ever could save, you know, a penny. No matter. We just couldn't." "Did you feel insecure?" I ask.

> No. Because we lived in suburbia where no one was any better off than you. You had this nice, clean house, and you always have clothes, and you always have food. And my whole life I was thankful for these things, and that I had healthy babies, and that I have a husband that goes to work every day. I didn't wish for anything. Maybe a bigger house, just so there would be some space, because it seemed like there was never any space to go anywhere or be by yourself. I would go in the bathroom and it ended up like a conference room after a while. It was my only quiet time, when I was in the bathtub. But I never felt like that [insecure], and my friends didn't either. I haven't one friend that was, like, just unhappy.

She understands that her security was related to a steady paycheck from her husband's unionized position, as well as the "excellent insurance. They didn't have eye insurance or teeth insurance. That came later on. But, I mean, we didn't really have those kind of worries. And the cars, well, if they needed fixing, we would fix them." But they did not have a lot of luxuries. "We never had money like to go out or to go on vacation. Everything you bought was on sale. Like clothes. But that, I don't know, it just didn't bother me, and it still doesn't bother me." There was little feeling of deprivation, because they were no worse off than many of their friends.

The mothers and fathers of Boone Street were not depressed, did not apparently feel oppressed, and were not obviously dysfunctional. They were law-abiding citizens, disciplining parents, and responsible neighbors. Many had, at most, high school educations; they worked as skilled and unskilled laborers in the local factories, and retired with good pensions. As in a Garrison Keillor sketch set in Lake Wobegon, the women were strong, the men worked hard, and the kids all played sports. Or, as Neil Young sings, "the women all were beautiful and the men stood straight and strong. They offered life in sacrifice so that others could go on."[12]

|||

Then we moved to Boone Street, into our brand new home. We moved in July of '58. [Jimmy] was not quite a year old. So we had the nursery all fixed up for him. With just one child in this house it seemed empty, because there was this one little baby and you had three bedrooms, and it was just really nice. I worked at Dun & Bradstreet. That fall I got pregnant with you, and I was sick again. I used to get very, very nauseous and very tired. So I did quit. I quit at Thanksgiving time. We had our house, and I didn't feel like working. But I was such a good worker that they asked me if I would continue to work for them at home, so I did. Four months out of the year, when all the reports [were due] at the end of their fiscal year, then I would take the Dictaphone and typewriter and do all these reports. At that time in our lives, Dad was going to JC [Grand Rapids Junior College] to study to be an accountant. So, then, he would just drop off my work, because it was downtown, and pick up new tapes. I got paid a dollar an hour, and if I worked fifteen hours a week, that paid for the groceries. I mean, at that point in our life, it really helped out. So, I would work maybe a couple of hours here and maybe an hour here, like, three hours a day I would try to work.

After the initial three months of pregnancy, then I would feel great. I mean, I would feel wonderful. And I was always really happy again. Because I knew that I wanted more children than just one. And all my girlfriends were on their second babies, and I was starting to envy them. And I said, "Okay, now it is time." And then you were born. I think I told you the story about how you weighed exactly the same as Jimmy, and you were exactly as long. You weighed eight pounds and thirteen ounces, and you were twenty-one inches long. With Jimmy, I had a specialist, and for you I had a family doctor. His first words were, "You have a beautiful baby daughter, and she weighs" so much and whatever, and I said, "And I got the same size baby for fifty dollars less!" He just laughed. I was so doped up at that point—but, anyway, that was good.

But when I finally had you and I got to stay home, I just loved it! I mean, I didn't have a car, and I'd look out and it's snowing, and I had all these friends in the neighborhood. And it was, you know, just a healthy, good time—no one had any money, no one ever took vacations or did anything. We'd just get together and have coffee on the back steps or the front steps.

But when you were four months old, I was pregnant again. And then, it was this all over again—sick and tired and throwing up—and I was very unhappy that I was pregnant. I was just, like, "Oh, why is this happening to me?" I just had this little boy and this little girl, and my life is so perfect, you know. One in this bedroom and one in that bedroom. And I probably wouldn't have felt that way if I would not have always gotten so sick. But it is like you can barely navigate when you are throwing up and changing baby diapers, and I remember sitting on a rocking chair and looking out the window. That was that fall. And I would see a woman outside raking the yard and I was, like, "I don't have the energy to even move, hardly." Jimmy was only two. So I was just very, very unhappy.

But, probably after three or four weeks of knowing that I was pregnant, that all changed. I know [Jim] only wanted two children. He had a boy and a girl, that's it. [laughs] But then I wouldn't take birth control, because that was like a mortal sin in them days, and he wouldn't abstain. [laughs] We always say, "This is what happens when a hot-blooded Hollander marries a good Polish girl with morals. You have a house full of kids." [laughs] 'Cause I wouldn't give in, and he wouldn't give in. Way back then we knew that you had to be in control. [laughs]

And so, anyway, I said, "Well, okay, this is it." And Dad was always, like, "No, we will just do it. We'll just do it." He would never say, "Oh, God, you are pregnant again." My mother was the same way, and so was my doctor. He would always say to me, "If anybody could handle children, it is you, because you are just a very good mother."

But the only thing is, then [Diane] was born, and she was another easy birth. You know, just this little blue-eyed baby girl, and I thought every time that she would get sick that she was going to die because God was going to punish me. In my mind, I would always think, "This is it. I didn't want her, and he is going to take her away from me." You don't realize, like you say, you have to grow in this faith. But when she would get sick, and she was this good, sweet little baby, it was just like, "No, it's going to happen. He is just going to punish me, because I didn't want her." And then you realize at the time, these are kind of normal feelings.

And still everything is fine. I mean, we are just really happy in this house. He was working the second shift and going to school. He had to be there at eight AM, and he would be gone the whole day. I wouldn't see him until he came home at eleven forty-five at night. But this was something he wanted to do. But the only thing is, by the time he got through with his classes, I think we had four children, and there was no way he could have taken a job as an accountant versus what he was making at General Motors. I mean, we were barely living on what he was making, and then to take maybe a two thousand dollar cut in pay, because accountants at that time were making very, very little money, especially just starting out. He was not a CPA or anything, so he just kind of gave up that dream.

[ME: Did you have any say in what he would do? Did you have a strong opinion about it?]

I just encouraged him to study accounting. I thought he was very meticulous about things, just about everything. I think he would have been an excellent accountant. I think we both just agreed that it was not feasible at that time. At that time, he wasn't in skilled trade, so he was just more or less a factory worker. But once he got into a skilled trade and then went to school to study all the blueprint reading and all this grinding stuff, then he liked it a lot better. And I don't think he ever really regretted it.

So, anyway, that January I got pregnant again. And this time, I didn't have those feelings at all. I just thought, I'm not going to go through all these guilty feelings again. It scared me, and I thought, "No, this is fine." And my mother and my husband and my doctor were all supportive. My mother-in-law wasn't. I would always be afraid to tell her, because she would just say, "How are you going to do it?" Whereas my mother would say, "You can do it!" So David was born.

This was another thing. These are like times in my life where I was probably tired. But I lived in this neighborhood where everybody was pregnant all the time, so it was just, like, a lot of fun. I mean, this one was as sick as I was—this one wasn't as sick—and this one was having a girl—this one was having a boy. And it was just a lot of fun because the neighbors were all in the same position. There was only one lady out of all of us, Mrs. Racey, that worked. No one worked. So we were talking all the time, like in the summer.

In the winter we didn't. We would have a club where we would meet once a month and play—what was called the Bunko Club. But we got to know all the women up and down the street and all the kids. So, that was a lot of fun. When David was born, he was no problem whatsoever. Then I joined at Holy Name Church, St. Gerard Guild. St. Gerard is a patron saint of pregnant women—at one point there were fifty-two of us and thirty-three were pregnant! It was just a way of meeting all these young women—we would have a dance, and a Christmas party, or a fashion show—and they were in the same situation you were, and not anybody complaining or nobody trying to do anything about it.

But then, let me think. Then, after David was born, then Laura was born two years later. And the same thing then, too. "Okay, I'm pregnant, and we'll do it, and we'll manage." And like I said, I was totally blessed that I never had a hyper child or a real obstinate one. I mean, they were just like happy babies. I mean, they had colds and mumps and things like that, but we did not have any traumatic health problems. And when there is a multitude of children, they all play together. There was a baby always crawling around. And then I got pregnant when Laura was four years old. And I was sick. It was the same thing. This nauseousness and listlessness. And she [Laura] literally took care of me. And then Paul was born.

[ME: So, then you had three years of not being pregnant. (Note: between Paul and Laura, who are five years apart, she had a miscarriage.)]

Right! I don't know what happened there. [laughter] And I *did* want another child. I always thought I wanted a child that I could just sit and rock and play with and have to myself. There are years in my mind that I don't remember anything. I'm not kidding you. I mean, there are years, like when I brought the babies home from the hospital, there's just, like, total blank. And I think I should have kept some little memos or journals of how I felt about things, 'cause there's nothing. I think the years when I was always so tired was like a period of maybe seven years that my body was just, like, tired all the time, 'cause I never got a good night's sleep; and then I would be pregnant, and then this and that. And it was just like I remember saying to my mother once, "I'm just so tired all the time." I mean, not to the point of exhaustion, but you just, like, you knew you were just tired. And then, little by little, like when Paul started sleeping all night, then I got my strength back. But there's a period that I don't remember things at all. I mean, like Christmases, or birthdays, or anything, and it's really, really sad that I don't remember.

So, I wanted a child that I could just play with and have to myself. That

Fig. 24. Angel, Jim, and their six children, 1968

is sort of the way it was. Paul was born, and Laura started kindergarten that fall. So, [Paul and I] would have the days to ourselves. We would just go shopping and rummage sale-ing, and drink coffee in the morning. He would drink coffee with me.

But then, after Paul, I decided that was it. I just didn't want any more children. I thought this was just getting too much. And so, then, you know, I didn't. [Me: How? What'd you do?] Just using birth control. I went to Father McDuffy, who was very strict, and I said, "You know who I am, and this is what my situation is." And he said, "Use birth control, and don't be confessing it, because I understand where you are coming from, and someone else might not. As far as I am concerned, it is not a sin." And I said, "Okay." But he said also, "If you look in your dictionary part of your Bible, there is a word called 'probablization.' It's when the bishop and the pope do not agree on an issue." And so, that's what he says we will call it. He said, "You have a conscience, also." And I said, "I'm thirty-two years old. I could have eight more kids, and I am not going to be certainly saying no to my husband all the time. As much as it is, you still say no. But I'm not going to say that for years. We won't have a marriage left." And I said, "You know, the more my husband works, and we're trying to bring up these six children as best we could and educate them." And he said, "You're right." But I don't know what I would have done if he had said no, because in my mind the pregnancy wasn't bad, but [Paul's] birth was very hard, and the thought of going through all this again just frightened me. And I thought, "You know, this is what my conscience is for." Up to that point, except for that little incident with Diane, I had never felt that way. But after that, I thought, "Oh, I don't know." It just frightened me. And so I thought, "No." Some people probably feel that way after they have one or two or three, and some maybe after they have ten, I don't know. But I knew what I was going through.

Angel's narrative aligns with the master narrative for working-class mothers at that time whose husbands worked in manufacturing industries in the primary labor market.[13] She could stay home and conduct herself as a "good mother" (someone with a clean house and obedient children) because of government-backed loans that made it possible for the white working class to afford new homes in the suburbs, and because of unions that improved wages and benefits. That is, like other women in her race and class cohort, her ability to stay home with her young children was linked to her federally backed mortgage—which lowered interest rates, extended the repayment period to thirty years, and thus allowed them to have a monthly payment of only eighty-eight dollars, a third of her husband's monthly wages.[14]

Often, the story of having too many babies and worrying over money is told about low-income women of color dependent on federal funds, who are then directly and indirectly criticized for this "ghetto-related" behavior.[15] Angel narrates her life trying to justify why she had so many babies, arguing with the dominant paradigm that defines her behavior as questionable. Describing the good relations she had with her bosses at one of her jobs, she says, "I mean, they never chided me about [being] Polish, or Catholic, or all my kids." At another job, a coworker once asked her, "Why didn't you stop? Why did you have all those kids?" Angel answered, laughing, "I don't know. I'm glad I did. I mean, now, you think back, I'd like to have had a couple more." She says this in the same conversation where she talked about how the pregnancies nauseated her, and the children physically exhausted her (to the point that she lived whole years she does not remember) and financially stretched the family. She had the children because that was her career; she was a mother. She has no doubt about this. At least none she tells me. She absolves herself of the few negative feelings about the pregnancies by saying that she "wouldn't have felt that way had I not been sick." She understands the cultural directive that mothers are supposed to be happy with their pregnancies. Children are miracles, motherhood is blessed. To not want the child is then immoral, a slap in the face of a God who has given you the miracle of procreation. But if she had not been so sick, tired, and short of money, she could have enjoyed the miracle a bit more.

Her class position complicates her moral career. Children cost money. And yet, thinking of children as a commodity, which one can afford or not afford, seems wrong. Still, Angel jokes about this with her doctor after the birth of her second child: "I got the same size kid for fifty dollars less." She excuses her irreverent quip by noting she was "doped up." While gender and religion framed her decision to have six children, her class position influenced her choice to not have more. But she still needed permission from God— through his emissary the priest—to stop.

While her class position complicates her mothering career, her religious and class culture affirm her large nest. Her neighbors, church friends, sisters, mother, and husband all support her. They define her behavior as normal, which helps counter some of the nausea of being pregnant. Several families from her church had eight, ten, or twelve children, and her parents had come from large families (remember, her grandma Frances had thirteen children). Her experience of being pregnant was similar to her neighbors whom she introduces into her life history by telling me when they moved in and how old their children were. She also describes her friends in the St. Gerard Guild who were also pregnant, tired, and living paycheck to paycheck. Everyone she knew was having babies. That is what married women did, especially Catholic working-class women, what they rushed to do in their early twenties and then had to find ways to stop doing in their early thirties.

The culture of Boone Street helped her develop her career as a mother even though her working-class resources created complications. The stability of the neighborhood, the consensus regarding women's and men's roles, and the absence of absolute and even relative deprivation all encouraged her to continue having children. She said, "No one ever tried to keep up with anybody, or pretend they were somebody they weren't, because, I mean, you knew where their husbands worked, and you couldn't flaunt anything over anybody, there was never any of this. I never had to defend my way of life, or to defend my religion, or my having six kids." This is a privilege.

And yet, tensions between having babies and being able to raise the babies were evident.[16] The material conditions of her class position made too many babies a problem, while the cultural conditions of the class encouraged her to reproduce. Having children in quick succession—which she experiences as part choice, part obligation, and part nature—works to reproduce her own class position. Her husband finished an associate's degree to become an accountant but was unable to move into that white-collar track because they already had four children and could not (would not) take the two-thousand-dollar cut in pay required to start out in this field.[17] She does not regret (and doesn't think he regrets) his decision, which was offset by the fact that he moved into a skilled trade as a tool-and-die worker, rather than being "just a factory worker." The move from unskilled to skilled labor in a stable industry moved them from the middle to near the top of their social class groove; nonetheless they remained in the working class.

|||

None of the wives worked. . . . Well, Mrs. Racey always worked at Bill Knapp's. Um, then I think the next one to go, maybe, was Sarah. She went to work when Colleen was little yet. And Fay worked part-time, and I would baby-sit her children, her three boys; that was before she had Jodi. But JoAnne never went to work. Pat Reeder went to work years and years later. And I went to work back in 1970, so that was twelve years after I had not worked at all.

When Paul was one and a half years old, my mother was living with Aunt Mary [Mari] in Hastings, and she says, "Why don't you go back to work? You know, make a family room downstairs." It was, like, children all over this house. Three in this room and three in this room. And I don't want to go to work. I mean, I haven't worked for twelve years. I don't want to go to work. "You know, just for a few months, and just get your family room and then you can quit. I will come and stay with you and then I will go back there on weekends." But I don't know if she lasted six months. Dad was working the second shift, so he never cared if I worked or not. He was always so helpful. There was never any obstinance. He was, like, "Yeah, that sounds good." This was in 1970. You realize, it's 1998, and I am still working!

I remember I went to an agency because most of the time, in them days, to get a decent job you went to agencies. So, I went to ABC Employment. And I told her, "I'm really good at Dictaphone, and I like to type, and I want a job in this end of town. I don't like to drive." I was getting better, but I still don't like to drive. So, she sends me over to Meyer's in Walker, and I thought, "I don't want to drive way over here. I can't even find my way home." And then she sends me to work as a claims adjuster. I had, like, no experience. And so, then I see this ad in the paper, "Dictaphone operator on Eastern Avenue." [laughs] So, I went there and they hired me the same day, and it was eighty dollars a week; then it was two dollars an hour you were getting, but that wasn't so bad. So, I got a job just a few miles from my home, and it was Dictaphone work and typing, and they thought I was great again. So I had no problem there.

And I actually did not mind working. I mean, my mother was here. She had supper on the table. But all the children except Paul hated it. Everyone would come home, and it was just, "It's not the same. It's not the same. You're not here!" Everyone, Laura to Jimmy to you, everybody just literally hated it. "It's not the same when you're not here. You're not here to give us hugs. You're not here to give us some cookies." And that made me feel kind of bad. But I'd say, "It's only for a little while." [laughs] I did last for one year. Then my mother left after maybe five or six months. And then I would work, I think, until three PM. We had something worked out where I would drive in and Dad would be driving out. The only one that never minded me working was Paul because I went to work when he was so young. It never occurred to him that he should have his mother there every day. I worked full-time for one year at H & H, and I really liked it over there, they treated me really well. And then I continued to work there part-time.

[ME: Did you want to go back to work?]

No. No, I had no intentions of ever going back. Never, no, I was just very happy. Then we had to buy another car, and then [my mother] says, "Go back!" [laughs] "Okay, Mother." So then I worked at VanKuiken's [part-time], at that time there was no way I would have had energy to work full-time. The two days a week suited me just fine. But then, when Paul graduated from high school, and I thought "Ah, you know, I'm kind of tired of just doing housework," and I was just kind of laying around, and why not? I mean, why not earn some extra money? And Dad was working six days a week. So, then we bought that cottage, and shortly after, in '87, I started full-time. I only worked four years full-time. It seemed like a long time, but that's all. Then I quit, and now I'm back to one day a week.

Despite the long discussion about her work, brought about by my questions, Angel primarily thinks of paid work as something men do. After listing the jobs that men in the neighborhood had, she then states that none of the women worked, but has to correct herself because Mrs. Racey always worked and the other wives worked intermittently. In some ways, social scientists make the same slip whenever they talk about women "recently entering the labor force," a statement that ignores the fact that historically most women worked—as paid or unpaid labor—and that in industrial economies most women worked as paid labor at some point in their lives.[18] The situation in the United States in the 1950s and 1960s was an exception; it was an era when many working-class white women did not have to work because one income could support the household.

While women have always worked, there has nonetheless been a dramatic increase since 1970 in the number of women, especially mothers, working outside the home.[19] Angel and her neighbors did not start working until their children were older. Before then, they felt themselves fortunate to be able to stay home and be full-time mothers. Their husbands did not force them to stay home.[20] When I asked Angel if her husband ever objected to her working, she said, "Oh, never! Never, never, never, never, never, nope." This was true for her sisters as well. Caroline said that her husband didn't care one way or the other whether she worked. Mari worked regularly because her husband was in school, and Fran worked for a while even after her first child was born, as did Nadine after her daughter was in school.

Angel believes that it was her choice whether or not to stay home with the children or go to work. But choices are made within cultural frames. Her perceptions and dispositions are shaped by gendered messages, in this case the cult of domesticity that made motherhood "sacred" and housework a "privilege."[21] When Angel says she "got to" stay home, she is defining this as something she desired. But it is not a coincidence that her desire to stay home was consistent with the social expectations that she do so. The cultural messages that predispose her to be a career mom, however, make no less real her happiness at staying home to mother.

The women on Boone Street were able to fulfill their desires to parent full-time because their husbands had jobs that provided sufficient wages. This same luxury also gave them the privilege to choose to go back to work in the 1970s. These women did not have to work in the same way that younger working-class mothers found work necessary, in a contracting economy that required families to have two paychecks in order to make ends meet.[22] By the time the economic downturn began in 1973, the Boone Street mothers were halfway through their low-interest thirty-year mortgages, their husbands had mature wages, and their savings were accumulating. Good dental and health care plans meant they had fewer unexpected expenses, and they were not worrying about large college tuition bills (if their children did go to school, the parents' contributions would be minimal). When women like Angel returned to work, they did so to buy luxuries—the pool, the boat, the cottage, the trip to Vegas, the second car, the finished basement—not the necessities. As a result, they could work when and where they wanted. Angel recognizes this as a choice that her husband did not have (and that single mothers do not have).

> I always thought that I was so much freer than Dad. I could go to work if I wanted to. I could go to school if I wanted to. I could do this, and he had to go to work every day. He couldn't say, "Oh, I think I want to go to school for a while. I don't want to work." And so, in my situation, I never felt like I didn't have freedom. And so, I couldn't understand her [Betty Friedan], and I didn't agree with her at all. And now, they are just going back and saying that a lot of things she said weren't right. I mean, they are going back to saying that it's okay to stay at home. You don't have to work. This is a career in itself. And I can remember you saying once to me, "Oh, I think it's time now you went to school and got a career." And I said that I have a career and if you spend as many years in your career as I have in mine and loving it as much as I did, you are going to be pretty thankful. Because I think, you know, this is a career. It is not like a side job. I mean cleaning might be mundane, but it still is as rewarding as anything. But then again, when the kids got older, I don't think I would have been content, like when they are all in school all the time, I don't think I would have been real content just to stay at home every day. Because I've always just enjoyed working. So I think I've had the best of both worlds. Because I could work, and when I wanted to quit, I quit. Psychologically, I even still had freedom, and not like a single woman I work with, this single mom, or single women that don't have a husband. They are living in an apartment at fifty-five years old. When are they ever going to get a house? I mean, psychologically, I've never had that pressure. Dad would always say, "If you don't like that job? Well, quit."

Angel does not envy her husband going out to work every day; she appreciates the flexibility of working when she wants. Nancy Seifer points out that working-class women generally sympathize with their husbands, with the kinds of jobs they have to endure, and with the strain of financial pressure. As opposed to middle- and upper-middle-class women, working-class women see fewer advantages in leading "men's lives."[23]

Angel sees herself as part of a unit, a family unit, in which there is one permanent member of the labor force; Jim's work allows her more flexibility in terms of employment. More than anything, mothering influences where and when working-class women enter the labor market: full-time until the first children are born; not at all or part-time when the children are preschoolers; part-time and full-time when they are in school; and full-time when they graduate.[24] Clerical work helped Angel integrate employment and mothering because it provided easy entry into and exit out of the labor market, and she could work during the hours that her children were in school. The office setting helped her to manage the interface of the public (work)–private (home) spheres, which often bleed into each other. For example, Angel made it clear to her bosses and family that she would take phone calls at work. We children knew her work number by heart and called it several times a day for very mundane reasons: "Can I go shopping? What vegetables are for dinner? I'm bored!" In this way, employment and mothering were bundled together. In another example, she explains, "There are just some things that you don't want to be telling the whole office about. And then that time Paulie came to work and asked me about this money for this problem he was having, on my lunch hour, and I had to go back into work and pretend like everything is fine. It's very, very hard. But you can do it. I actually learned." Her emotional private sphere must be managed in the public sphere. This is often more difficult for women than men because the two spheres are not as distinctly compartmentalized. Angel's children called her rather than their father for at least two reasons: first, office work made her more accessible than factory work, because she had her own phone; and second, as the primary caretaker, she handled personal problems.

For Angel, the career is motherhood and the job is clerical. A job is a means to an end (money, status, socializing), but a career is a more self-consuming vocation that brings about a fulfillment and expression of the self. Most women participating in the labor force do not have occupational careers but instead have jobs. In 1990, secretary was the most common occupation for women, and the majority of employed women (52 percent) were in non-supervisory sales, service, and secretarial positions.[25] The tensions of the working mother are different for women who have jobs and are part of a "dual-wage" family than they are for women who have occupational careers and are part of a "dual-career" family. Unfortunately, scholars have more often taken the dual-career family as the model for working mothers, and in doing so they use the experiences of middle-class women with professional and managerial occupations as the standard from which theories and concepts about all working mothers are developed. Myra Marx Ferree argues that "the dual-career model has, by its idealization of middle-class family norms, led to a misunderstanding and denigration of working-class women and their families"[26] This occurs in two ways.

First, these models assume that professional occupational careers are more intellectually, financially, and socially rewarding than jobs, and that women who have occupational careers are more likely to want to work than women who have jobs. This assumption gives rise to the conclusion that working-class women's preference for staying home is in fact a rejection of secondary labor market positions characterized by low pay and low status.[27] This argument, however, contains a typical, but often invisible, middle-class elitism that one type of work is more rewarding (and perhaps more valuable) than another type of work. It overlooks the fact that many women like their jobs. There may be aspects of their job they do not like (e.g., low pay or long hours), but they often enjoy the challenge of the work itself, the social environment of the workplace, and the feelings of accomplishment, self-sufficiency, and satisfaction the job provides.[28] It is not the work but the workplace that can be alienating, as a result of nondemocratic settings, overcrowded work space, unmanageable work loads, and oppressive bosses (and this is also true for professional jobs).

Angel enjoys working; she sees her work as a craft, as do many other secretaries and office workers. Caroline also found it personally rewarding to cook lunch for the local elementary school, and she developed a stronger voice and a more positive sense of self as a result of this work. And Nadine continues to enjoy sewing and cooking. Whether cooking for priests, residents of a retirement home, or her guests at the bed-and-breakfast, her meals are creative expressions of her talents. Work for these women was not drudgery.

Perhaps one reason their work was satisfying is that they were "women" at work, engaged in traditional female caretaker roles—Mari as a nurse (in an obstetrics unit), Nadine and Caroline as cooks, Fran selling antique plates and dolls, Angel as a secretary. They made wages by being women in the public sphere. They entered the public sphere as women caring, cleaning, and cooking. And they found this work to be self-affirming. As Angel says, "It made me feel good about myself, because I always did a very good job, and I knew what I was doing, and I liked what I was doing. And so there was never, like, any reprimanding from anybody. It was always, like, adulation and praise, no matter where it was, you know, at Dun & Bradstreet, or at H & H, or at Auto Insurance, which was the very first place that I worked, and he called me back after five years. We laugh because every place I have ever worked, they have called me back." Caroline said her work gave her the confidence and strength which allowed her, at age fifty-five, to take driving lessons. And when Nadine went back to work after her daughter entered school, she took a lot of pride in the meals she prepared at an assisted living center and received a lot of positive responses for her gourmet cooking, her exquisite sauces and rich desserts. "They had really wonderful meals," she said. "But that's what I do, I can't do it any other way. And then, well, I made friends with all the people that were there. I got to like the people and they really loved me and we just got along so nice together." These women do not talk about their work as being oppressive or demeaning, but as engaging, fulfilling, and rewarding.

A second problem with using the dual-career model to explain the lives of all working mothers is that it overemphasizes individualism. When a woman has an occupational career to which she has devoted years of study, training, and practice, and then decides to drop out of the occupational career track and stay home with her children, it can easily be seen as a subordination of self-interest. But Ellen Israel Rosen argues that married working-class women do not work only out of self-interest; that is, their work is not just an individual strategy but instead a family strategy.[29] Taking the family as a unit rather than the woman as an individual, the woman who stays home is not subordinating her needs to a man but instead participating in a household division of labor. This division of labor is easier for women who have jobs rather than occupational careers. The decision to stay home does not require the abandonment of an occupational career that they spent years developing. Jobs are easier to leave, jobs don't require the same dedication or aspirations for advancement, and jobs don't relocate your family around the country. For these reasons, a mother's job is less threatening to the family than a career.[30]

This division of family labor, however, contributes to the reproduction of gender inequalities in the larger society. Paid labor has more economic and cultural power attached to it than unpaid labor (and the career more power than the job). Moreover, women may be less willing to leave a marriage when they are not wage earners themselves or when they are low-wage earners. The "family economy" argument falls apart when the marriage falls apart, as we will see in Mari's story in the next chapter; the mother who stayed home to raise the children often leaves the divorce much poorer than the father.[31] Nonetheless, as long as the family unit is working for the woman, when a woman stays home or leaves a job to take care of family needs, she is not necessarily subordinating herself to a man, but acknowledging the importance of the family. The family provides her with happiness and a career which gives her status and prestige within those circles that value motherhood. And those circles are more often found in the kitchen than in the boardroom.

|||

Between 1930 and 1970, an increasing number of women were educated and trained for professional and managerial positions, yet never entered the labor force because of early marriages, or left careers once they had children because of institutional regulations (e.g., pregnant women could not be teachers) and cultural pressure. Educated and trained to have careers, many of these women became frustrated when they found themselves locked out of the public sphere.[32] This frustration made them receptive to what has always been one of the underlying agendas of the women's movement—that women should have an equal role in the public sphere. By the late 1960s, Jane Mansbridge argues, women were hearing two conflicting messages. On the one hand, feminists (mostly white middle-class women) thought women should work outside the home, because only by being in the public sphere could women raise their status above that of second-class citizen. They argued that women needed to be independent breadwinners and have an autonomous identity in order to gain recognition, self-worth, and equality. On the other hand, traditional antifeminists and the societal status quo argued that women should stay home, especially if they had children.[33]

In contrast to middle-class women, working-class women were seldom promised or trained for an occupational career, so many did not expect one. What they expected to do was stay home and raise children. In doing so they resolved the conflicting messages by dismissing the feminist voice. Asked about Betty Friedan, Angel said, "I thought she was totally off the wall, because I thought she doesn't really know. I didn't think anything like her, so how could she be speaking for all these women if she doesn't even know how I feel? I don't feel that way. I mean, we didn't feel like we needed this freedom and say in everything. I felt like I did have freedom." For working-class women who did not expect to have an occupational career, who expected to either go into the convent or get married and have children, staying home with their children was the realization of their dream. They were happy staying home.

And yet, we don't always hear this voice of contentment when we write about women in the generic. Feminist scholars Myra Marx Ferree and Beth Hess write:

> For wives and mothers who steadfastly remained in the home, true happiness often proved elusive. Ultimately, as we know from events of the 1960s, a creeping sense of isolation in a daytime ghetto, of exclusion from the "real world" of power and prestige, led to vague feelings of discontent. Obliged to perform tasks once done by servants but now upgraded and mechanized, the suburban woman became a housewife in a more complete way than ever before. Many women began to perceive the restrictions of their lives, but until the emergence of the new feminism they lacked a frame of reference in which to interpret their discontent.[34]

Ferree and Hess are not describing the white working-class women of Boone Street. These women were not isolated in a daytime ghetto, these women did not hunger for positions of power and prestige, these women were not unhappy and discontented, these women did not know anyone in their long ancestry who had servants who did the chores that now they were required to do, and these women saw the new technologies, like washing machines and self-cleaning ovens that reduced their work load, as good things. How is it possible that we continue to write academic narratives on women that completely ignore the lives of the working-class women who, after all, represent the majority of women in the United States?

We need a more complex conceptual framework that allows us to understand women as both satisfied with their choices and yet longing for more, a framework that understands that we make choices that are both self-affirming and self-limiting, a framework that challenges both the patriarchal and feminist narratives on how women are or what women should be. We need a framework that allows for both happiness and sadness.

While not undermining their choice to be mothers, and without devaluing the labor they chose to perform as housewives, secretaries, and cooks, and in a model that accepts that these women were happy staying home, that their children were the most important and precious part of their lives, I nonetheless need to ask: were there any unfulfilled dreams?

Caroline feels something that cannot easily be spoken. Perhaps she cannot or does not want to name it, to make it real, to voice the dissatisfaction. Perhaps it is hard to speak the absence. Raising children was her career, but once they are grown, what does she do?

> Being just a mother taking care of three kids, I still think that was really great. I don't think—and no matter what profession you look at or what you think, there is nothing more important than taking a child and shaping it, and developing it. And I always thought that was such a big honor. That's why I never thought, "Oh, I wish I could do this or do that." I never did. I was always very happy doing what I was doing. But then, as I got older and the kids left, then I would have liked, you know, I wished I would have had something that I could have done.

I ask Caroline, with a little laugh after the question to suggest that perhaps this is sort of a joke question, "Did you always sort of think, uh, that, you know, that you were gonna get married? Did you ever have any ambitions of going to New York and being an opera singer?" "Nobody" she starts, pauses, and then continues:

> See, somebody has to tell you that, put that into your head. Nobody did. And that's my one thing that I'm sorry about. I would've liked to done something, to learn, because I love my books, and I'm interested in so many things. And sometimes I get really frustrated. If you have an inquiring mind, and if you don't use it, then it gets frustrating after a while. But I've always read, and I had books and books. . . . That's why I kept telling my children how important education was, how going on to college was good.

In this quote we begin to see how the "malaise that has no name" gets played out in the lives of working-class women. Unlike middle-class women who were frustrated because they couldn't use their education to develop an occupational career, she was frustrated because she did not have an education. Her dissatisfaction is not with choices she made, but with the choices not given.

Caroline allowed Mari to read the transcripts of her oral history. In doing so, Mari realized that she and Caroline shared the same frustrations that had not been voiced.

> I think when I was reading Caroline's stuff, and at the time I think I thought it was just me, but I see now that it wasn't, because she also mentions, which would have been twenty years earlier, that Mom and Dad never encouraged her to go on to schooling, to further her education. So, last night when I was reading that, I thought, "Gawd, she had the same feelings." Because, it kind of made a mark on you, 'cause you felt that you were so dumb that they didn't see [that you could go on to school].

Mari, the youngest Grasinski Girl, went to the Catholic high school in the city, with middle-class students, rather than the rural school. She did receive cultural messages that promised her an occupational career. Three of her close friends went to college, and a woman she worked with who was a bit older and divorced urged her to pursue more schooling. She states explicitly that this woman was "not like my mother, who said nothing," but instead asked, "When are you going back to school? You can't stay here [as a receptionist]." Mari was accepted into a nursing program, but never went because she got married instead. Of all the sisters, she was the one most frustrated without an occupational career. I asked her, "What would you change in your life?" She sighed and paused before answering.

> That's a good question. A lot of times, you know, I feel like, as far as [pause] sometimes I feel, uh, uh, that—my biggest disappointment would be not having the career, not being famous, something along those lines. Not necessarily being famous, but making more, uh, more, more of a contribution to society. I don't feel that I didn't [contribute], because I helped a lot of people, but I think I would have liked to have done it on a broader scale. And that's probably the one thing I would change if I could.

Between the starts and stops and loops to her speech, she articulates the choked idea that she would have liked to have participated more in the public

sphere. There is a person she could have been but wasn't. But that ⟨
mean she isn't happy with who she is.

The shimmer of dissatisfaction is not with what they have or who th ⟍ ⎺⎺
but with what they could have been. Not encouraged to continue their educations, these women find themselves in their sixties and seventies telling me
their previously unspoken dreams: Mari wanted to be a writer, Caroline reads
all the time and could imagine herself as a social worker, Angel believed she
would have been a good accountant because she is so meticulous. Caroline
thinks her mother Helen would have been good in sales, maybe real estate.
They could have been rich businesswomen, bohemian writers, compassionate
social workers, and analytical accountants, but instead they were mothers,
and secretaries, nurses, and cooks. They don't regret it. Motherhood was a rewarding career, but they also see, somewhat—or maybe I see—that the
choices they made were structured by the choices they were given.

Their lives are rewarding and at the same time limiting. Disposed toward
particular life grooves, they develop their potential within the spaces given
and feel happiness and satisfaction with being good mothers, efficient secretaries, and empathetic nurses. A pride accompanies who they have become.
Their structural locations provide both the space to create their lives and the
dispositions that direct them, and these dispositions are linked to social categories and not individual traits. They were predisposed to motherhood because of their gender, and not encouraged to continue their education
because of social class. The path of the professional career woman does not
represent a "path not taken" but a path not marked in their terrain. There was
no fork in the road at which point they had to choose.

Mary Marcelia

MARY, WHO RENAMED HERSELF Mari in midlife, didn't want to be interviewed. She welcomed my visit to Phoenix, but she wouldn't promise to talk with me. She is the youngest of the Grasinski Girls and has the raciest story—no convents or stay-at-home-mom roles for her. At the age of sixty-two she still has a Marilyn Monroe flair to her. She met me at the airport wearing khaki short-shorts and a black tank top, her bleached hair disheveled in an Andy Warhol-Meg Ryan sort of way. Like her mother, she wears hats, sometimes extravagant hats with big clumps of roses or violets on their brims, and, other times, especially nowadays, functional straw hats that keep the sun off her face.

Mari moved out to Phoenix several years ago from New York. The northern winters pained her arthritic joints, so she quit her nursing job and moved near two of her four children. As we pull into her subdivision, I comment on the profusion of flowers—bougainvillea, pansies, roses, azaleas—and Mari tells me in an excited voice about one particularly spectacular blooming cactus. She wasn't exactly sure where it was, but she wanted me to see it. We spent half an hour looking for it, driving slowly around the subdivision on identical streets of new single-family homes, elegantly landscaped in deep pink and burgundy flora. We never found the flowering cactus.

Mari followed the standard script of post–high school marriage, children, and stay-at-home mom until she was in her midthirties. At that point they had four children, her husband had a Ph.D. and a good job, and she wanted to go back to school. Then, well, then things happened, and when the dust settled she was out of the marriage and her children were living with her sister Nadine. I never knew the complete story. This part of Mari's life, and the ostracism she faced from the family for the divorce and her behavior, contributed to her unwillingness to talk with me for this project. But, despite the initial reluctance, once she started talking, she talked and talked and talked.

In order for her to feel free to talk, we left the house, because it was the weekend and her husband was home and because she loves being outdoors. She wanted to show me a lake in a nearby neighborhood park. In the warm but still gentle April sun, I spent two long afternoons listening to her confess her tumultuous life story in a very orderly fashion. The chronological order to her narrative was similar in form to Nadine's oral history. They both had major life events around which they anchored their narratives. They both had a "story to tell," and it almost sounded as if they had told their story before—maybe not to any one person, perhaps only to themselves. There were far fewer blessings in Mari's life than in Nadine's, and more sorrows and regrets. Yet, the sadness and poignancy in the narration was modified and transformed into something less than tragic by her humor and acceptance. Her narrative was littered with Kleenexes and laughter, a laughter that makes her sound just like her sisters, despite the fact that her story is so different.

I Thought I Was a Superwoman

So, it was at the end of senior year. Chuck was dating my girlfriend but he was passing me notes, and then, they kind of broke up. He said—of course, this probably was a big old lie—that he stopped dating her because he felt that he could use her, that eventually they would have sex and she'd give in. So, he was just kind of, was looking probably for the Virgin Mary, and there I was. [laughs] And I *was!* I mean I was that good Catholic girl. That image, I think, is what Chuck liked.

We dated, and after a semester or two at Aquinas College, Chuck joined the army. I was working as a receptionist. And then, Chuck [pause] I don't know what got into him, but [pause] he started writing all these gorgeous love letters. He was in Texas, and he started writing all these letters and how much he missed me and how much he wanted me, and then maybe we should get engaged, and this kind of stuff, and I was, like, "What?" But it sounded good, because at that time the thinking at twenty was, if you weren't planning your marriage, you know, life had passed you by, honey. So, you better get on the ball. I'm saying [laughs] that was the social climate.

And the fact [was] that I was also very sexually attracted to him, and my mother was in *love* with him, she just *loved* him because he was so funny and nice to her, but, um, he was really sexy, too—to me, not to my mother. [laughs] She never talked to me about the future and then one day all of a sudden she goes, "Well, you should really think seriously about Chuck as a husband." And I had been dating other guys, and I was, like, "*What!* Where's this coming from?" So, that was the only time in my life I had listened to my mother. So, then, he came home from Texas and we went to Lake Michigan, and the snow was falling and we walked out onto the lake and he got down on his knee and he proposed.

Well, then what happened was we went home and we showed the ring to his father and his father told me to take it off. He was right, actually, he just said, "You're both too young." Whereas my mom, it was fine with her, she didn't tell me that. The only thing my mom said, "You should really seriously consider him." You know, because of all these good qualities and things like that, he's responsible, and he was nice to be with, he wasn't rude, he was fun. He was always really good in school. He was a manager of a grocery store when he was nineteen. He was mature, looking back at it all now. We did get married, and I got pregnant on my wedding night. [laughs] *Dumb!* The Catholic Church said you couldn't use birth control, but we were so dumb, it didn't matter what they said. We were nineteen and twenty—you don't think. You looked like a grown-up, but really your experiences don't prepare you for getting married and getting pregnant on your wedding night. *Dumb!*

Our marriage was great, a love story. There was no abuse, there was no screaming. There was no fighting. We had a lot of really happy times, especially with the children, they added so much. They were healthy, beautiful children. And when the divorce came, our children must have been totally confused, because our whole life together, we never fought. I mean, he wasn't controlling or anything like that, he wasn't. He never said, "You'd better be home," nothing like that. In fact, we made a pact. I said, "You go to school first and I'll do everything I can to help you get through school, and then when you get your degree you'll do everything you can to help me get through school."

So, I did my part, but when it came time for me to go to school, it was okay for me to go to school, but he had his own world already, and "If you can manage four kids, keep a nice house, work part-time, keep your grades up and go to school, then that's fine with me." But it wasn't like he said, "Okay, I'll quit my job so you can go full-time." You know, I was working nights in a nursing home so he could feed his children and still get his masters and Ph.D. and all that, so. And then I think I was thirty-six and I woke up and I said, "All I've got—" Not "all I've got," but I have four kids, and that's it, and he has the degrees. So, that was kind of like, "Okay, now it's my turn." But my turn never came, because now he was involved [in his career]. He was flying to Florida and working on projects being written up in newspapers and I was, like, "Uh, what about me?"

I definitely—talk about choices—definitely, I made the wrong choice. So, what happened was [laughs] I don't even know. Throughout our marriage, even though he was very charming to me and everything, it seemed he always had woman friends who were like his ideal. She was always the smart one, she was the one getting the Ph.D. He always had a female friend like that. Different friends, from college or work, I mean it wasn't like it was hidden. He would bring them over, in fact, he would talk about them. "Sofie did this, Sofie's getting this." I mean, he didn't say, "Oh, I wish you were like them," but it seemed to hang in the background. It wasn't like I was jealous of these women, it was just that it wasn't me he was talking about and how important my accomplishments were. And I was there with four kids, and I was working, I would work all night and then come home and sleep for an hour or so and then get up and take care of the children all day, and then I would repeat that again. But it wasn't like I did that straight for seven years, it was, like, on and off, because I was getting pregnant, but I always continued to work. But it was nice for me, too, because, you know, I was with my children, but it was just that I wasn't getting anywhere. It was kind of like, if he really did love me he would make my education a number-one priority like I did for him, which was really unrealistic when I'm thinking about it. I mean, he was the major support of four children, so what did I want him to do, quit his job? [laughs] But, going through that experience, it was like you don't count. [Here she writes into the draft of the manuscript, "It made me appreciate the doctrine of feminism."]

I was confused at this moment in my life. So, when you're confused you tend to make wrong choices. You know, instead of going into counseling at that time and bringing all this out, I didn't, because in my mind I was convinced that if he loved me he would do something, something more than what he was doing. He was out there enjoying his degrees, his family, and where was I going, no place.

So, then I met this guy and it seemed whenever I was at the pool he'd be there, if I was taking a walk, he'd be there. He wasn't putting a lot of pressure on me, it's just that he was there. I told him to bug off, I wasn't interested. We moved away for a year but came back because we owned a house there, and I started seeing him. So, instead of doing the smart thing, which would have been to go into counseling and get this all straightened out, I had an affair. I'm not excusing my behavior, it was a terrible choice. I had no idea of the hurt and cost to lives when betrayal happens. After the divorce the kids were totally wiped out.

I think when we're talking about choices, I think that the choice to have an affair played to my romantic instincts and the essence of a woman kind of thing. It wasn't like Chuck didn't make me feel attractive, because he did, but he didn't make me feel *that* special or that attractive, mainly because his life was more exciting. I suppose it was a better life, opposed to staying home and cooking, which I never found exciting at all. Boring as shit. After everything, all I really thought was Chuck didn't really love me.

I mean, it was just a bad choice. The really sad thing is, it wasn't continuous. It wasn't that I was even in love with him. It was just more of a diversion kind of thing. And that was what was really, really sad. I told Chuck [about the affair] because I never lied to him, that's how close we were. I never lied to him. I couldn't lie. And then he started not coming home. Like he wouldn't come home till three in the morning, or whatever kind of thing. And then he said he wanted to go for counseling at that point. And I was, like, "You didn't do anything wrong, so what good is counseling gonna do?" But that was wrong on my part, because at that point maybe the marriage could have been saved. But, since I said, "No, I have to work this out—" You know. I mean, I didn't even think that much of it, really. I guess you're just young and you just don't think of the consequences. And he just kind of withdrew and I withdrew.

Six months later, [Chuck] came one Saturday morning with Greg [their eldest son], and he just took the furniture he wanted and he moved out—no long discussions, never said anything about it. I think what happened was, up to a certain point he was willing to work at it, but then after he started going into counseling—at that point I no longer existed to him.

So, he moved out. In the divorce court, [his new girlfriend's] brother was his lawyer, the judge was a male, there was Chuck, my lawyer, which was a male, and there was me. It was horrible, it was like a slaughter. Everything I asked for—I asked for money, you know, to put me through school, because I helped him go through school, no such thing. I asked for joint custody, no such thing, the facts show that the children should go with their mother. He was making the money, I was making fifty-five dollars a week because I was working part-time. Child support, yes, I got that. It was like pittance, even back then. It was a hundred dollars, bimonthly. I didn't get the house, because he said that you can stay there, but if you want to sell it you have to split the proceeds. I couldn't afford the house. I walked away with absolutely nothing, absolutely nothing except the child support. And then, at one point I was so distraught, and Chuck threatened me with, "Well, if you don't want the kids, I'll take them." You know, it was like, "No." I was afraid he would take them. At least I was quick enough to know that I want them—if you want the house, fine, but just give me the kids. My lawyer said just take what they offered and walk away.

I was making, like, fifty-five bucks a week, and now I wasn't getting any child support, he wasn't paying it. He was living in a nice apartment in East Grand Rapids with his girlfriend living on another floor. So, I called him up, you know, he wouldn't let his secretaries put me through, it was just like that [gestures as though shutting a door], he just, like, closed the door. It was nothing like, "Are the kids happy?" *Nothing!* It was nothing, *nothing*, no phone calls, no nothing. So, anyways, I wasn't getting child support, even. I went to apply for welfare and it wasn't enough, it was like three hundred bucks a month, so I'm, like, "Oh, my gawd, what am I going to do!" You know, and so I said, "Okay." So I called a lawyer at Legal Aid, and I said, "Look, he's supposed to be giving child support and he's not. What can I do?" He said, "Well, we can put him in jail." So they did put out an order for him to appear in court, and they ordered him to start paying child support.

But then, in the meantime, Nadine and Bob offered to take them, Elizabeth, Charles, and Jean Marie [three of her children], to become their guardians. So we went to a lawyer, through the courts, and legally they became their guardians, you know, with the option that they would come back to me if it didn't work out, you know, if it was too much for them, then they would come back to me. And then, in the meantime, they started garnishing his wages. And that's how I got child support. And they kept garnishing until they all turned eighteen. The money came to me. [Nadine and Bob] were so very generous, because now I was poor working class.

[Chuck] had moved to Lansing now, and he was head of some department in a big hospital in Lansing. I went to see him and I didn't tell him I was coming. I had only seen him once after the court session. I wanted to find out why he refused to see his children. He just, like, totally cut them off, totally, no way. We could not figure him—his sister, his family couldn't figure that out either. If he wanted the divorce from me I could understand that, but certainly the children didn't do nothing to him, so why take it out on them, it made absolutely no sense whatsoever. He didn't know I was coming, right. [laughs] I walked in with one of my Marilyn dresses. [laughs] I mean, I just had short blonde hair and I was 117 pounds and this dress was, like, little spaghetti straps, with these high, clunky heels—I mean, these were the seventies. [Pause] So. He didn't have the decency to take me into his office. He took my arm and he shoved me into the chapel. [laughs] Smart, right! [laughs] Figuring there would be a big old scene. [laughs] He shoved me into the chapel. I, being a Grasinski, true to the bone, started weeping, "How could you do this to your children," blah, blah, blah. That got absolutely nowhere. Somehow he maneuvered me back outside. That was terrible. That was so humiliating—not inviting me into his office to talk but instead shoving me into a chapel where no one could see me! I had just spent sixteen years of my life working to make him a success and now I was being shoved into a dark corner! [She writes in the manuscript, "To borrow someone else's words, and I forgot the author: In her bid for freedom she pays the highest price. The man, even though he relinquishes his responsibility for his children, never calls or guides them. And she is the one in the family to be stigmatized."]

So, after that I was, like, okay, this guy's out of my life. I mean, you can only try. I mean, it was kind of good in one way because it saved me a lot of emotional "well, maybe he'll come back" kind of thing, but in another sense it was, like, heartbreaking. But it was really funny, because it wasn't like my own personal self was devastated, it wasn't. It was that, it was about the children, and how are they gonna grow up without his guidance?

I was living in Kalamazoo, and I went to JC [junior college] in Grand Rapids [in the mid-1970s], and I thought this was very cool. I applied for a women's grant and they gave me enough to start at Western [Michigan University]. So, I was going to school at Western and then Jean Marie [her oldest daughter] and Nadine were having problems. She was rebelling. In one sense, along with Nadine, Jean Marie became the mother for Charlie and Elizabeth, and that just kind of, like, messed up her whole teenage years. She went from being thirteen to twenty-five in probably about nine months. She was like the mother—she would remind me always of Elizabeth's birthdays, Charlie's birthdays, gotta do this or you gotta do that or whatever. And she wasn't getting along with Nadine. But she did spend, I think, a year with them, which was good because I was not in any emotional shape to deal with those kids. Or it wasn't even the emotions but it was the money, the financial—even if I didn't go to school, even if I worked full-time, I still couldn't take care of them because I was making, like, seventy-five dollars a week.

And then, in the meantime, Jean Marie said [crying]—like Elizabeth says, *"Get over it!"* [laughs, crying, laughs again] This is like a therapy session. Now is the time that you're supposed to hand me the Kleenex, like they do on the talk shows, and murmur some words of pity pretending that you care. [laughs] As if they care! [laughs] It's just like, Jesus, when's she gonna get done crying, I gotta go to lunch. [laughs] So, anyway, Jean Marie said, "I want to be with my mom." And so, since it wasn't working out and that was our agreement, then she came back to stay with me. So then I had her to take care, and go to school, and that was like, "Oh, my gawd!" [crying, laughing]

She's, like, fifteen years old, and that whole previous year she was like their [Charlie and Elizabeth's] mother, with Nadine, and so now it was, like, "Don't tell me anything!" [laughs] And then, her looks, she was really beautiful, she didn't look like fifteen, she looked like maybe eighteen, so everybody she was attracting was twenty-one, twenty-six, twenty-seven, and she loved it. She isn't getting the attention from her father, you know, so she was getting it from wherever she could. And I wasn't giving her the structure she needed to do well in school.

|||

The time I spent in college was probably one of the happiest times in my life. In a different sense. Not that I wasn't happy with my children, or being a mother. How do I say this? My mother, throughout my life, made me feel like I brought joy into her life whenever we were together. I experienced the same thing with my children. They gave me pure joy and so much support. I was in love with each of them at different times in their lives. [But when I was in college,] it was just that I could do all these things. I was finishing my degree in fashion merchandising. My courses were photography and art, so you had to produce things. I would go [to] downtown Kalamazoo and I would shoot pictures, for example, of boots. And then I had to make a slide show out of that, present it to class, put it to music and write the thing, tell about fashion, what was going on that year. You know, I would do that, and then I would jump into my car and drive to Detroit, and Bob and Nadine would take me to this really beautiful restaurant, we'd eat, and then I'd spend the weekend with my kids, run back, and then I would go to work that whole night, and then the next morning I would be in class till twelve o'clock. And I was writing

a lot, and I was meeting people in my classes and at parties from all over the world, from other places, with other perspectives. It enlarged my world.

But then, I guess, probably I had everything I wanted kind of a thing. It wasn't like I had this fantastic dream that I was gonna become something fantastic, it was that I was doing what I wanted to do—I wanted to get my degree, I wanted to raise my children. Beth and Charlie stayed with Nadine and Bob three years during that time. And then, it was kind of like Nadine thought that

Fig. 25. Mari during her college years, 1978

ﹶeeded to be with their mother. So, it was, like, okay, you know, you helped me
﹵h. I was just about finished with school, and so then they came back, and then I
had all three of them. [The oldest son was living with her sister Fran.] And, uh, I thought
I was a good mom, but if you listen to my kids, like Beth, oh, my gawd [laughs] it's a
totally different picture. But to me, it was very cool. I was working, because now I was
taking care of them again, when they came back. But I was getting child support also.
And also by that time Jean was already working, she had a little job, she was taking care
of herself, and, you know, even though the bananas were a day old, there were bananas.
So, to me, you know, I mean I survived the whole male thing, and I'm not saying I didn't
ask for some of it.

Now my children are with me. And, uh, my relations with my sisters and my brother,
they're not that great, because no one ever comes to see me. No one calls. Or writes.
Well, actually, my brother came one time to see me, once. Chuck's grandparents [sic]
never called or came to visit their grandchildren, not once. My mother wasn't into
condemning [me] about the whole divorce, you know, nothing like that. She was very
quiet. She did offer to come and live with me and take care of the children after they
came from Bob and Nadine's. And I was, like, "No, I have to do this myself," because
now I was really—I thought I was a superwoman, that I can handle this. But, obviously,
my family let me know how stupid I was. It was just, like, "How could you do this to your
children!" It was like that. They just thought that I wanted to go back to school and I
didn't want to be married. And all this stuff, it was the farthest thing from my mind. I
mean, I wanted everything. I wanted the degree, I wanted my children, I wanted a
husband, I wanted lovers, I wanted everything. [laughs]

|||

And so, then what happened after that was, "So, now you got the great degree, now what
are you gonna do?" It was partly my fault, partly what was happening in the economy. It
was now the recession of 1980. There was nothing open around Kalamazoo. I mean, there
was places, I'm sure, like Kmart or something, but I didn't want to do that. I went to
Chicago, I interviewed, and they offered me a job. But the salary was, like, twelve thousand
dollars. So I'm like, "Okay, how am I going to raise three children and live in Chicago on
twelve thousand dollars?" I couldn't. I'd have to take them and put them in a ghetto or
some really dangerous place, so I figured I really can't do that. And then, also, some of it
was my fear, I couldn't take that risk of not being able to pay the rent. I mean, it's one
thing when you're by yourself. So, I continued working where I was. I had worked with a
geriatric population, I worked with the developmentally disabled as a paraprofessional, and

I had worked with the severely retarded. And the place was a for-profit organization, private, and so it was run very, very poorly. It was fine while I was going to school because I had the school, it occupied me, but when that was all I had, it was, like, "Ee-ew." [laughs]

I made another choice, which was a dream of mine. It was then I decided to go to San Francisco. My goal was to go and live in California. I didn't know anything about it. I made one trip before I moved there, just to see what it was like, and, well, of course I fell in love with it. I liked San Francisco because it wasn't as big as L.A., but I didn't actually do a job search. [laughs] I was really naive, compared to today, how people go about getting a job. And I didn't have anyone helping me. Anyway, Elizabeth wanted to be with her dad, so we set it all up, I wrote him and went to the courts and everything, we got his signature that it was okay for me to take the children out of the state of Michigan, and, yes, he would take Elizabeth. Greg was being taken care of by my sister Fran, things had thawed a little, and he was in his last year of high school before he joined the Air Force. And Nadine was gonna take Charlie because he was already used to the school up there and stuff, and then Jean Marie was going to come with me.

So, we, we did it. [laughs] We sold everything. She was, like, eighteen, but she wasn't ready for what I was asking of her to do. But we were cool, like Geena Davis and Susan Sarandon [in the movie *Thelma and Louise*], we sold everything and we took off, just the two of us. [laughs] I had my Datsun, and we were sleeping in the car at rest areas outside of Chicago and Idaho, and stuff like that, because we didn't have any money. We had a little bit, but we didn't have a whole lot. And then, we had so much stuff our car started breaking down. [laughs]

[Jean Marie's] ex-boyfriend was living in San Francisco at the time, so when we got to San Francisco, we stayed with him for a few nights, and then he took us around and we found an apartment, a basement apartment that wasn't registered. But it was in a beautiful old part of San Francisco, it's gorgeous there—the ocean, the music, the food, the arts. I was supposed to be interviewing for my job at last, but then Jean Marie started seeing [the ex-boyfriend], and so, what happened then, she got pregnant. And I was, like, "Ooh." I'm supposed to be interviewing for all these jobs, but it was so emotionally overwhelming. I had no insurance or job and I became a sounding board for all her irrational fears. It was just a terrible, terrible few months. I in turn felt so guilty for putting her close to him [her ex-boyfriend]. I felt I had put her in harm's way. And then, after all that pain, she had a miscarriage.

Then I received a letter from an attorney in Michigan stating I had to appear in court and I was, like, devastated, because it was just a legal paper, and there was no letter stating what his intentions were. So I went to a lawyer and they said, "Well, he might try to take Charlie away from you," because Elizabeth was turning eighteen and he didn't want to pay child support anymore. But I didn't know that. Nobody told me. I was just told that I had three days to appear in court, they gave me three days. [laughs] Okay, so I called the Legal Aid Society. And they sent a woman lawyer and she represented me, just so that I would have a voice there. So, what had he done? She called me, and she goes, "Why didn't you tell me that you were doing drugs?" So, he made me out like a druggie and all this kind of stuff. And, basically, he just wanted to get so that he wouldn't pay child support for Beth anymore. Then, in the meantime—that had messed me all up because I didn't want to lose Charlie—and, I mean, to me that was, like, horrible for Charlie. But, like I said, it didn't turn out that way because he just took it to court to make sure that he no longer had to pay his child support.

And so, in the meantime, my job search—"Oka-ay, now what am I gonna do?" Also, it was the recession, so the places I did go to weren't hiring. I went back to school, then, and I got my California license. So, I did that, I graduated. It was, like, six months. And in the meantime, I got a job at a community hospital.

And so, also in the meantime, Jean Marie got pregnant, again from Billy [the ex-boyfriend], and they got married. And she was, like, I don't know, maybe six or seven months pregnant, but she wanted a wedding, and when she puts her mind to it she does what she says. So she got this whole wedding together. She had a white dress, I bought her camellias for her hair. She had flowers. Billy had a white jacket. They had people standing up for them. The wind was whipping our umbrellas backwards and they went to the courthouse and got married before a woman judge. Afterwards, we went back to the house, and we were sitting on the couch, Elizabeth, me, and one of Jean's old boyfriends, we're sitting on this couch and we cried and cried. I don't know, it wasn't what we had planned. I guess she was intent on having this child.

|||

And my life then was nice. [Charlie had moved out to San Francisco.] I was just dating, and the-en, there was this one woman where I worked and she said she wanted me to meet her aunt's ex-husband because he was coming out to California for a vacation. And so, then Raphael showed up, and we were riding cabs up and down the streets of San Francisco and it was fall and he was very kind of intense, maybe that's not the right word, he just seemed more available. I was, like, "Okay." So, what I should have really did was continue on my job search [for a position in fashion merchandizing]. I mean, I was doing fine, and I think eventually the job might of worked. But it was really hard to find a niche for somebody starting out with no experience. And I sort of realized that. And

Fig. 26. Mari and
Raphael at the
Chateau Chantal
Winery, 1993

then, here's Raphael, and he lives in New York. And then we started writing, and he started calling three times a day, and that's what I meant when I said he was intense. And so, I was just, I don't know, I wanted to go to New York but I didn't want to leave Charlie, and Jean was with the new baby and stuff like that. So I said no. But then, I didn't want to continue what I was doing either. So, then he kept saying, "Just come to New York." And it wasn't like pressure, I was starting to fall in love with him too. And I always wanted to live in New York, it was like a dream. I wanted to live in New York and California and Italy. So, you know, you want to do certain things. So I thought, "Okay, here's my chance to get to New York." So-o.

We went to Reno and got married. [laughs] So. Um. Some people say they're risk takers. Some people are just stupid. I guess you have to make up your own mind. [laughs] One of the reasons I [married Raphael] was [here she described in detail a date-rape that she later edited out of the manuscript, writing in its place, "After being date-raped by someone I worked with"]. I think that was another reason why I said yes to Raphael, because I wanted some security, because I felt up until that point, I felt that I could be anything I wanted in this world, and after that experience [trails off]. Psychologically, for me, he [the rapist] showed me that, I don't know, he took something away from me. And now I needed someone, someone to help me or protect me, whereas before I never thought that way. [Quoting a source she doesn't remember, she writes on the draft, "My thinking that I was strong was just an illusion. Violence had not stopped because of the feminist movement."]

So, anyway, he flew down, and we got married and we flew back to Brooklyn, and it was wintertime, and we got in this cab with this woman with bleach-blonde hair and she yells [in a rough, masculine voice], "Eh, what you want me to do with these suitcases?" And I remember it was snowing and it was cold. [laughs] I was, like, "Oh, my god, I think I made a mistake." I mean, Brooklyn is not San Francisco.

When I met Raphael, I remember writing on a picture he gave me, "You're like a never-ending holiday." But he could be very confrontational at times, which I didn't see when we first met. [She edits out some scenes she described in the oral history and writes, "His behavior was non-negotiable at times so I moved out with my daughter and grandson only to find the apartment we rented was in a pocket of poverty. Eventually he moved out and we came back to live in the same house." They then got a divorce.]

In the meantime, here again I'm starting to get emotionally overwhelmed, but it also may be I was not very into the career thing at that time in my life. I liked working with people. I was very good at observing people, instinctively knowing what they wanted and needed in stressful and painful situations and helping them feel more at ease. I had been in New York only three months, and I just happened to walk into the employment office of a large New York hospital and was hired. My starting salary and benefits were much higher than in retail, plus things always happening at a clip. I stayed for twelve years.

At the hospital, a strong union was in place. I was a *working*-class woman. [laughs] You found me. I even belonged to a union. Nonprofessional working woman. [laughs] But I learned a lot, I really did. It made me change my perspective about management. How organization means strength. I seen how management could not enforce at-will contracts, like they do in Arizona, because of arbitration. Because of the leadership, the years I belonged to the union it grew and grew. Sometimes I marched in the streets of New York and other times in a different place. When you have three hundred thousand people supporting a new contract, you get results.

And then they wanted me to get involved in their union affairs, and I was kind of, like, I really didn't want to be working class. [laughs] And it wasn't that there's anything wrong with working class, it was mainly that my father was working class and I sort of thought that it was a failure on my part that I didn't accomplish more to bring myself out of the working class. But at the same time, a lot of non-working-class women weren't making four or five hundred dollars a week! [laughs]

||||

Beth had left Chuck [her father]. She graduated from Lansing. And then she took off with her friends, they said that they wanted to move to Arizona and they wanted her to go with them, so that's how she ended up in Arizona. And so, she liked it, she loves it. She was just, like, nineteen or something, and they were probably having a blast.

And Charlie had not graduated from school. So then we said, "Okay, you better come on out so you can finish school here." We put him in school. He didn't like the school. This was in Brooklyn. So Charlie disappeared on me. [pause] In New York. [laughs] He never told me about his experiences. Well, he did a little bit. Enough to make you shiver. Some were good, some were not. He was a kid out there, on the streets of New York, are you kidding? So, anyway, eventually he came back, and at that time he got his GED, and we sent in the application for an apartment using the lottery system. I sent in the application fee thinking nothing was going to happen, right? Well, they picked his name. And he went down, and we paid the money, and he got that one-bedroom apartment on the tenth floor overlooking the ocean and stuff!

Raphael kept in contact after the divorce, he was trying. We went to counseling, it helped. The most grievous behavior, he changed; that he was in denial about some of his thinking about what constitutes a real man, didn't. I think the counselor would have to be God to get underneath the denial system. But by that time, we learned to discuss before screaming. I was looking for security, so I moved back in, on the seventeenth floor overlooking the East River. So, that stayed that way for ten years. [laughs] He was involved with his kids and his jobs. He went to NYU and graduated with a certificate in computer programming.

[Mari concludes her life story with this paragraph she wrote:

Raphael changed and I fell in love with him again. New York, what can I say: bicycling across Brooklyn Bridge in the fall; rowing in a boat in Central Park in the spring; walking on the boardwalk at 6:00 AM the air is fresh, the beach has been cleaned from the previous days assault; swimming in cold, cold Atlantic ocean water; eating raw clams and drinking white wine at Coney Island in summer; celebrating Christmas with a party on a boat going slowing around Manhattan, under bridges with music tinkling sound in the night. At the same time, assaults on my heart with hopes changed into unfulfilled dreams. But always choosing life!]

5 ⫾ The Importance of Being Mothers

> I had always thought I would have children. I am 41
> now. . . . I try to keep the grief hidden from other people and
> like to deny it to myself, but it is there. It has the power of a tree
> buckling concrete as it forces its way to the surface. I scuttle
> around as the ground seems to shift and bulge beneath my feet,
> and children are everywhere. Babies loll in the pew ahead of me
> at church. The littlest ones squeak when they cry. I see little
> girls in scratchy dresses and boys with oversized feet. My
> friends get pregnant and become round and full and hormonal.
> As I am talking to them, their babies move inside their bellies,
> like the earth moving under heaven during creation.
> Childlessness is a strange kind of pain; different from the
> pain I felt when my mother died. This grief has no pivotal mo-
> ment, no death, and no end. I don't miss a person; I miss what
> that person might have been. . . . And I think, I could let the
> grief I feel over childlessness rise to the surface. When the grief
> rises, I could try not to bury it anymore. I could find a way to
> talk about it to other people. I could say, I always wanted to
> have children.
>
> Nancy Tester, "Missing Person"

I ALWAYS THOUGHT I would have children. It was a natural thing to think
if you grew up surrounded by women who were mothers. Grandmothers
were mothers, neighborhood women were mothers, nuns were mother superiors, aunts were mothers to my cousins, aunts not married were sorry
aunts because they weren't mothers yet, and we young girls were mothers-
in-waiting searching for men, not to be husbands, but fathers to our children. I was so sure that I would have children that I gave away my first one

because I was not ready. I was sure I would have more. But, I am not sure I ever really wanted children. It is very, very hard to separate desire from destiny. How does a young woman conceive of *not* being a mother? Motherhood is so deeply engraved into our female charm bracelet that we seldom ask ourselves if this is what we want, but instead accept it unquestioningly as one of our primary gendered routines.

I don't regret that I gave away my first child, who turned out to be my only child. He is alive, somewhere, I believe. And happy. I believe. That's what I have to believe. He is happy and loves his parents. This is a rational belief because I have met lots of happy adopted children. When I meet them, I often have to repress the urge to hug them and tell them that those women who gave them birth remember them. Always. But I don't tell them, because we are not supposed to talk about that. Mothers who give away their children are not considered mothers. They don't usually get Mother's Day cards and no one expects them to contribute their birthing narrative at a baby shower.

Having a child does not make me a mother. My sisters, mothers themselves, remind me of this, in that special way that mothers let nonmothers know they are not mothers. They can do this by moving some dangerous thing that I set in reach of a child—like my steaming-hot cup of coffee. Mothers sometimes do this to fathers, as well, when they redress, rediaper, reclean, rearrange the play area, and in doing so nonverbally say, "No, no dear, you are doing it wrong. Mother knows best." So far I have heard only one father loudly resist this by saying, "This is how I watch the child." But I could never say that to my sisters because I can't claim any parental authority.

By not being a mother, and not feeling a lot of grief about not being a mother, I sometimes feel like I have done something wrong, akin to denying my Polishness or renouncing my Catholicism. It is as if I have refused to collect my inheritance. My tugging of wrongness is different from my friend Celia's, for whom not being a mother seemed to violate some sort of natural order, and so she adopted children. She knew she was meant to be a mother, it was a part of her destiny, her emotional self, her soul. Motherhood made her a more complete person. And so it is for the Grasinski Girls.

Motherhood is one of the primary weaves of the Grasinski Girls' identities, yet it took me a while to understand and appreciate this. Halfway through this project, I sent each of them a biographical sketch I had written about them based on their oral histories. After reading them they quickly let me know that I "got it all wrong," because I had underestimated, underplayed, and undervalued their role as mothers. As Nadine told me:

> And then, you kind of emphasize that I was so happy being free in my apartment [this was after she left the convent], but you didn't say anything about Marie Chantal being—that was, like, I had beautiful, beautiful days of my life, when I became the nun, black veil, white veil, the day I got married, absolutely beautiful, but nothing can compare to the day that I held her in my arms. That was, like, the most beautiful, that was my high point in my life, that was above everything and she still is. I just wanted you to emphasize that more than being free in my apartment. [laughs]

After Caroline read her biographical sketch, she informed me that I had not written enough about how happy she was being a mother. "Most of my life was with my kids. I thought it was such a special thing to be able to mother children. I had the privilege of having children and raising them." And Fran wondered why I had not mentioned her being a mother. Despite the fact that at that point she had not given me her life story beyond her eighteenth birthday, she assumed that I would construct a biographical sketch of her that included her three children.

Why did I miss this? Why did I not see the centrality of motherhood in their life stories? Was it because I wasn't a mother that I wasn't interested in motherhood and therefore did not see this in the transcripts? I went back and reread them to see how much they talked about their children, motherhood, and family. I found two things. First, while their life stories were not children-centered, they did talk about their children. Caroline told a long story about her son's sickness and talked about her daughters' struggles. She also said she "never thought about anything" except to be a mother. Nadine did say Marie Chantal "was my life," and even after Marie Chantal started school she continued to be Nadine's "main attraction." She really did talk more about Marie Chantal than she did about being "free" in her apartment; I was the one who chose to emphasize the freedom. Angel actually had a lot to say about her children, even if it was mostly about their births. In the first biographical sketch, however, I focused mostly on her one year in the convent. It was only after revisiting the transcript that I wrote about her as a mother on Boone Street. So it was I who initially glossed over the motherhood aspect of their lives in those first biographical sketches. In fact, they talked quite a bit about their children, but often these stories were only about their children, and I left them out of the narratives because I thought, "Well, this isn't about Angel (or Caroline, or Mari), this is about David (or Eddie, or Jean Marie)." I figured they were their children's stories, not their own stories. I was wrong. Talking about their children, they are also talking about themselves.

In a later taping session, Angel shows just how central her children were to defining her own life. I asked her what her turning points in life were. She replied, "Turning points are probably the children growing up, you're losing the little children and they're going to grade school, and then there's the stage of high school, and these are all like turning points in your life because you have to deal with a whole different set of problems and joys. And then you see them getting married and going on to college, and then having children. These are all probably just natural turning points." But this was in a later taping session, when I asked her to talk specifically about being a mother.

In the initial sessions, their motherhood was not as well articulated. And this is the second point. Given the centrality of children in their lives, it is interesting that when they told the stories of themselves, the years they were most likely to gloss over were those years when they were primarily occupied with the tasks of mothering. Their narratives were more detailed and descriptive when discussing those years before they were married and after the children were grown. In the first session, Fran talked exclusively about the first sixteen years of her life; even in the next session, when I asked specific questions about her children, she spent more time talking about religion, which was most central to her life at that time. Both her and Caroline's stories were more detailed and vivid when describing their pre-motherhood years and their present lives as compared to those in-between years when they were raising the children. It is this missing chunk that also does not get detailed in Angel's narrative. She remembers the births, and she tells her life in relation to the births, but there was very little in her story about those twenty to twenty-five years when she was raising children. In all three cases, the mid-adult years (from about twenty-five to fifty) were very sketchy. Nadine talked a little more about her child than did the others (maybe it was because she only had one, and it was more recent, that she could remember more clearly those early years), but in the overall narrative it did not take up a lot of pages. Even with Nadine, there is more discussion about the pregnancy than about raising Marie Chantal. Only Mari, the mother who relinquished the daily mothering tasks for a few years, framed her life story in relation to what was happening with her children. The children don't enter her narrative as central characters, however, until the divorce, that is, until her motherhood has to be negotiated because it can no longer be taken for granted. (Her children are not so prominent in the final text because she edited out their stories to protect their privacy.)

In subsequent interviews I asked specific questions to try to make mothering visible. Mothering includes caring for the physical, psychological, emotional, and spiritual development of the family members as well as engaging in the kinship work necessary to keep the family together.[1] But motherhood is a being as well as a doing. It is an identity, a psychic paradigm, a dominant status. When asked what it means to be a mother, these women do not describe the tasks of mothering but instead talk about the privilege of motherhood, the vague emotion of motherhood, the depth of attachments, the primacy of the identity. They *are* mothers; it is a *being*ness. Children and motherhood are as much a part of their life as breathing—and perhaps because motherhood is so much a part of their personhood, it is hard to see.

Motherhood is also hidden because it is sacred.[2] Regarding jobs and work in general, Caroline said, "You have to have something that satisfies your soul, and if you don't, it's not a good thing, whatever you're doing. I mean, you have to have something that, while you're doing it, it's soul-satisfying." For Caroline and her sisters, raising children was soul-satisfying. Fran wrote to me, "I thank God for giving them to me." Angel also defines motherhood as a gift from God: "I like my life and I like all the people I produced, and the grandchildren. I think I'm blessed." For Angel, the six children were acts of creation that gave meaning to her life after she was rejected from the convent. I asked her when she got over this feeling. "Oh, this feeling that I had, that I was rejected? I don't know, maybe after I had them all. Yeah, I think so. Then I just, I realized that what I was doing was really important. I mean, I was creating little bodies, and little babies, and bodies, and more bodies, and more bodies. [laughs] But I always felt that each one child was like a real special gift." Motherhood is a part of the act of creation, and this makes it sacred. Angel was called to be a mother, she is doing God's will, searching out that which will give her the highest place in heaven. Sacred identities are revered more than they are articulated. The sacred is unexplainable, and it preserves

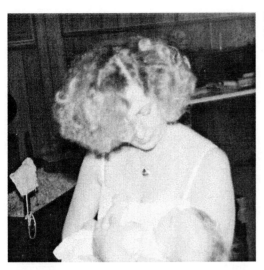

Fig. 27. Nadine and Marie Chantal, 1978

some of its sacredness by being shrouded in mystery. The divinity of motherhood loses something when forced into words.

Mothering is also hidden because it is embedded in the routines of our days and often taken for granted and overlooked.[3] In this way, mothering just *is*—what's there to talk about? Which could explain why, when I asked Caroline about the twenty-five years in the middle of her life she said, "Well, then I was a mother." Women (and scholars) have a difficult time articulating the everyday routines of women in domestic settings. When Angel says "there are whole years I don't remember" and "life was a blur," it could indicate that raising children was tiring, but also that everyday chores run into each other as a bleary stream of washing, cleaning, nursing, storytelling, feeding, bathing, ironing, vacuuming, wiping noses, wiping bums, dusting lamp shades, picking up dirty socks, folding clean socks. Rather than being itemized, the physical tasks are lumped into a monolith of mothering. And it is even harder to talk about the emotional work of mothering, the hard, exhausting, but extremely fulfilling emotional work that taps into the beingness of motherhood—listening, consoling, touching, encouraging, soothing, laughing, supporting, and loving.[4]

Perhaps this particular methodology did not lend itself to making mothering and motherhood visible. Maybe because I was "family" they did not feel the need to tell me about the family—it was obvious and they took it for granted that I knew their biographies as mothers. Moreover, it could be the public nature of the oral narrative that fails to elicit the routines of motherhood. While mothering is a private-sphere activity, the interview itself is a public activity, and the interview material will be used to make a public narrative. So, when I ask them what they did in those child-rearing years of their lives, they tend to describe public activities: their jobs, their volunteer work, their religious activities. For example, I asked Caroline, "So, what did you do between the time you were thirty and fifty-three?" She replied, "I was just, um, I was just a housewife, and kids—I did a lot of things in church. I mean, I worked on bazaars, I volunteered, and stuff like that. I still do a lot at church. I volunteer at the blood bank, and I work in the pantry. I still do that, and I work at the bazaars and stuff like that. And I like to do stuff like that, I mean—what did I do? Just the—doing regular stuff, I did not do anything eventful or anything like that." She tells her niece, the college professor who has no children, about her church involvement and her craft displays. She doesn't narrate her children's lives and she doesn't detail the tasks of mothering.

Fran answered my questions about mothering by pointing to activities in the public sphere. I asked her how she would "define herself as a mom."

Ooh. I just, this little guy over here [referring to her youngest grandson], I'm telling you, I almost eat him up. But I mean, I've always, I've always felt that way, they're just so special, and so innocent, and you can make them all beautiful if you do it the right way. [giggling] You know? And I think that, anything you'd ask me, what I'd been able to do, what I would have liked to have done, I would have liked to have taught little children in the Catholic school. There is nothing I would like better than that, you know, to tell them who Jesus really is, and how much He loves them. I see these little kids when we go to church here sometimes for children's mass. Most of them don't genuflect, or, you know, it's like they're going into a theater or something.

Then she told me how she had been an assistant catechism teacher and had thought about becoming a kindergarten teacher after her second child entered school (she was not yet pregnant with the third), but that didn't work out because the certification process changed.

When Anita was in school, you didn't have to have a degree to teach in the kindergarten. And then you had to have a degree, so, then, that's where it kind of left me out, if I had to go to a school. So, then, that's why I guess I got into Boy Scouts. [laughs] Fifteen of them in my kitchen every week. And Campfire Girls for nine years, about sixteen girls, going all around, to the beaches and everything with all of them. So, sort of always there was children involved. And then I was a teacher's aide there for a while at Holy Spirit. That's when you did it for volunteer. And then I also went for noon hour, watching the kids at noon hour, lunch time. I did that too for a couple years, two or three years.

Like Caroline, Fran does not talk about the private tasks of mothering, but her public role as an educator, as kindergarten teacher, Scout mother, Campfire leader, and religious instructor.

To summarize, mothering is one of the most important aspects of their lives, yet it did not occupy a significant portion of their narratives, at least not proportional to the significance it has in their lives. Why not? First, motherhood is deeply rooted in their being and it is a sacred identity that may be difficult to voice. In addition, mothering tasks are such commonplace, everyday routines that they are fused together in memory. Moreover, mothering is done in the private sphere, and, as women give oral histories, they shape them around their public-sphere activities. It may also be easier to talk about concrete experiences than relationships or connections. What could they say? "Well, for those twenty to twenty-five years I just loved my children"? (In fact, this is exactly what they are saying when they say, "Well, I was a mother.") In addition, their narratives were offered to a listener who perhaps could be seen as an "anti-mother" (or at least someone who chose an occupational career over motherhood) and might be perceived as just not understanding. Or, maybe it was because I knew them personally that they felt no need to tell me about something I already knew. And, finally, perhaps the narrative of self is clearest during those periods of life when they are not consumed with mothering, that is, the years before the children are born and after they are grown.

It is understandable why Mari's narrative was more centered around her children. First, Mari's identity was complicated by the divorce. She did not have the resources (especially financially) to mother. She had to negotiate her occupational career and her mothering career, which could no longer be taken for granted. None of her sisters shared those same tensions. Nadine and Caroline only worked outside the home when it did not interfere with child raising.

Fran worked only before the children were born. Angel did feel some tension during those periods when mothering and paid labor conflicted, but Angel, like her other sisters, depended on her husband to provide basic needs—shelter, food, insurance, clothes. Being financially stable makes mothering a lot easier. Second, Mari's pursuit of a professional career was complicated by her mothering responsibilities. Several of her occupational career choices (e.g., the decision not to relocate to Chicago) were made in relation to the needs of her children. It was often in describing the competing needs of work and motherhood that her children entered into her life story.

|||

It was Mari's desire for both motherhood and an occupational career that made her receptive to feminism, and it was her sisters' almost exclusive identification as mothers that made them resistant. After reading the draft, one Grasinski Girl said, "You got that word 'feminism' on almost every page"—as if it was a nasty word. While they conditionally accept the idea of gender equality, they do not see themselves as feminists. In their minds, feminists are women who are unhappy staying home with their children, women who are pushy and selfish, women who are not feminine. In contrast, the Grasinski Girls enjoy being mothers and they like being women—which for them means they enjoy being responsible for the household, being emotional, dressing up, and taking care of their family. Feminists, they believe, are contemptuous of these gendered routines. As a result, as Nadine said, "To me, 'feminist' doesn't really have any special good thoughts in my mind."

The Grasinski Girls are not alone. According to a national survey in 1996, 83 percent of working-class women and 75 percent of middle-class women did not think of themselves as feminists.[5] And yet, most women, of all races and classes, are in favor of gender equality. Even women who resist being labeled feminists often agree with the goals of the movement, such as equal pay, day-care provision, and shared domestic responsibilities (e.g., parenting and housework). Nancy Seifer interviewed working-class women in the 1970s who said, "I'm no women's libber, but . . . ," and then went on to talk about the need for equal pay and equal jobs.[6] Twenty years later, Lillian Rubin also noted that, on issues of pay equality, sexual harassment, and women in politics, working-class women "have decidedly feminist opinions."[7] But these same women would not call themselves feminists. Feminists might support their needs, but not their identities, not their values. Talking specifically about white working-class women (who differed from women of color[8]), Rubin notes, "I only had to mention the word *feminism* and the talk turned quickly to caricature and stereotype. Feminists, they said repeatedly, are 'too hard,' 'too aggressive,' 'too pushy,' 'too loud,' 'too demanding,' 'not soft and feminine enough,' and 'not like women.' 'I'd never be a feminist because they want women to give up being feminine and soft.' . . . 'I like to be able to cry, you know, and they talk like that's being weak or something.'"[9] The stereotype of the feminist contradicted their identity as women.

Many women, the Grasinski Girls included, value those traits that make them good mothers—altruism, selflessness, the capacity to nurture, the ability to hold without possessing, working for the collective (the family unit and local community). They listen and console and help to mend broken egos. Their rejection of feminism is a rejection of aggressive, domineering personalities better suited for the competitive labor market than the nurturing domestic life. As Nadine puts it, "Feminist, to me, means a woman who is really strong, who is almost obnoxious, who wants to announce that she's superior to everybody. And that's not me. It doesn't really bring out good thoughts because it seems like she wants to be powerful, but only just for herself, that's what I think. Everything is for herself and she's selfish, and everybody should work around her and proclaim her to be the best. And that's not me." Nadine rejects those traits that are antithetical to mothering.

Mari, in contrast, applauds the feminist pursuit of equal opportunities in school and work.

> Well, like I said, when I made that pact with Chuck, that "I would work for you till you got your degree, and then you're gonna work," that was before Gloria Steinem, that was before Betty Friedan. As far as once it [the movement] happened, and was I interested in it? Yes, very much so. I just really admired a lot of what these women were doing, and I supported them wholeheartedly as far as the job situation, as far as the education situation. And even now, I think I'm a hundred percent right, because they did a study on women and they asked what's the one thing that they would change to their life, and 80 percent said it would be to have more education. Being a feminist, it means a lot, I think, in terms of becoming what you want to be. . . . [But not] to the point that I don't want any men in my life, no, I'm not. I think my relationships, some of my relationships with men

have been magical. And I wouldn't have gone through my life without experiencing some of those relations. But basically, as far as work goes, as far as women excelling or fulfilling their dream, I would be a feminist. But it's like I said, it's a contradiction. I mean it's not where I hate men, where I'm gonna put them down.

Mari is typical of most feminists. They do not hate men. What they hate is the fact that they have been denied the rights that men have: opportunity, choice, freedom to move about in the public sphere. And, like Mari and her sisters, most feminists also value egalitarian relationships and collective ideals.

Mari wanted more power and an identity in the public sphere. As her husband's career was taking off, she saw her homemaker life as less rewarding. She defined his life as "more exciting," and, in comparison, "staying home and cooking" was "boring as shit." Comparing herself as a stay-at-home mom to the career women at her husband's workplace (where he spent an increasing amount of time), Mari says, "It was like you don't count." And she is right. The domestic and childcare work that most women do is not valued in the United States. Economist Ann Crittenden, in her book *The Price of Motherhood*, outlines in detail the lack of cultural, social, and economic rewards for mothering. Examining maternity leave policies, divorce laws, earning potentials, and career tracks, she comes to the conclusion that in our society, mothers don't count very much. And yet, she argues, mothers do some of the most important work for a society. Mothers educate and raise the next generation of citizens, workers, and leaders. Mothers produce the human capital necessary to power modern high-tech economies. Unfortunately, the work mothers do is often invisible, underappreciated, and at times penalized (for example, with derailed or stunted careers, lack of Social Security accruement for those years when the mother is out of the paid labor force, and lost earning potential).

Many women feel "the price of motherhood" when they go through a divorce. After the divorce, the mother who left her career, worked only part-time, or did not pursue a career because she was the primary caretaker is left more disadvantaged than the father who continued his schooling and career. Mari's case exemplifies this. At the time of the divorce, Chuck had a Ph.D. and the beginning of a successful career. Mari had just started to work on her bachelor's degree. She spent the previous decade helping him get through school, managing the house, raising four children, and working part-time.

When they divorced, they did not split the family assets, meaning she did not get a share of Chuck's career. All of the people making decisions about Mari's future—the judge and both lawyers, who were all men—told her to take what Chuck offered, minimal child support payments and no alimony. The years Mari spent as a mother meant lost Social Security benefits later in life, lost time on the career track, and lost wages.

After the divorce, Mari's standard of living dropped dramatically. While married, she could afford to live in a comfortable house and provide for her four children as well as attend college part-time. After the divorce, she was forced to live in a rented apartment and had to choose between her children and college. Even if she had chosen to forego college, she still would have had a hard time raising her four children on the wages she could earn without a degree. Mari survived as well as she did because her sisters stepped in and helped care for the children, the state provided welfare, and Chuck paid minimal child support—but only after she fought for a court order forcing him to pay. Financially, Chuck's standard of living improved after the divorce and Mari's dropped—at the same time Chuck's responsibility for child care decreased and Mari's increased.

None of the other Grasinski Girls experienced divorce. Staying married, their domestic work was better rewarded. They shared in the assets of the family unit and their standard of living was equal to the standard of living of their husband. They had access to their husband's pension funds and social security benefits. The informal contract that puts the man in the public sphere, earning wages so that he can support the woman in the private sphere doing unpaid work, is binding as long as they are married.

|||

Mari and many other feminists wanted an education and an occupational career. A career outside the home would necessarily decrease the amount of time they spent in the home, and this became one of the reasons critics defined feminists as antifamily and antimotherhood. Phyllis Schlafly, a politically conservative Catholic, made her public career denouncing the Equal Rights Amendment for its threats to religious traditions and families, and "women's lib" because it undermined women's roles as wife and mother.[10] According to Schlafly, feminists see husbands as exploiters, children as an evil to be avoided (by abortion if necessary), and the family as an institution which keeps women in "second-class citizenship" or even "slavery."[11] Schlafly got more than her fifteen minutes of fame, and a large number of women heard and agreed with her message—especially women who were mothers, and those women whose beliefs placed them in opposition to abortion. Historian Elizabeth Fox-Genovese and the women she interviewed for her book, *Feminism is Not the Story of My Life*, also denounce feminists for being pro-abortion, encouraging bisexuality, and criticizing men. She argues that feminists' fight for the right to have children outside of marriage may protect women's sexual freedom, but it is ultimately an antifamily platform.[12]

At the heart of many women's antifeminism is the inability to reconcile with feminists on the issue of abortion. Fox-Genovese's book is almost entirely a critique of the pro-choice agenda and she frames reproductive freedom as the centerpiece of women's liberation. While some feminists have made this the litmus-test issue, in her book *Feminism is for Everybody*, bell hooks argues that economic, political, social, and cultural equality are at the heart of feminism, and reproductive rights is one of many issues. She also notes that the abortion issue per se is much more a central concern for white middle-class feminists than for feminists of color and working-class feminists. Moreover, feminists' pro-choice activism has alienated women of color and working-class women from the feminist movement.

This is one of the key stumbling blocks as well for most of the Grasinski Girls, who are openly hostile to abortion. Fran runs the pro-life group in her parish, she organizes the distribution of pro-life roses to women at church on Mother's Day, and she sends pro-life messages with her Christmas cards. Angel collected signatures for a pro-life campaign in the 1970s and worked the church doors on Mother's Day distributing flowers with pro-life messages in the 1980s. Angel said, "I probably am the strongest, on any issue, against abortion. I just think it is just killing something. They say it is not a human, but it is. If you believe what we believe, it is. I mean, it just is. It's a sin. I strongly oppose it."[13] As long as being a feminist means being pro-choice, they have a hard time being feminists.[14]

|||

Mari, and many women like her, wanted not only equal rights, but liberation from domestic chores. The women's movement itself has long included both the struggle for liberation from traditional gender expectations and the fight for equality. Ann Crittenden describes these two currents within the women's movement at the beginning of the twentieth century as "one that denigrated women's role within the family, and one that demanded recognition and remuneration for it. The first argued that only one road could lead to female emancipation, and it pointed straight out of the house toward the world of paid work. The second sought equality for women within the family as well and challenged the idea that a wife and mother was inevitably an economic 'dependent' of her husband."[15] The first path valued more the public sphere, the second path the private.

Charlotte Perkins Gilman took the first path. In her book *Women and Economics,* written at the end of the nineteenth century about middle-class white marriages, she argued that, to achieve a fairer distributions of goods, greater equality, and hence greater democracy, it was necessary to liberate the wife from the husband. Because a woman does not produce for the market, she argued, the wife's primary role in the market is as a consumer. While this traditional marriage arrangement (woman as consumer, man as producer) impels capitalism, the privatization of both consumption and production is inefficient because only half of the population is contributing to production; dependent wives and mothers become parasites on the system. For Gilman, only work outside the home was considered productive labor, and as such her arguments trivialized the unpaid domestic work of mothers and wives.

Throughout the twentieth century, most feminists followed Gilman out the kitchen door. By the 1960s, full-time motherhood lost its appeal for educated middle-class white women who wanted careers in the public sphere and had the resources (education and child care) to pursue those careers.[16] These women formed the backbone of the women's movement and pushed the "throw-down-the-apron" agenda. Political scientist Jane Mansbridge states, "The very existence of full-time homemakers was incompatible with many goals of the women's movement, like the equal sharing of political and economic power."[17] If women continued to be primarily homemakers, it would perpetuate the belief that women *should* be homemakers. Ann Crittenden writes that even while she was arguing that housewives were undervalued and underpaid, she herself looked down on them for being "just" housewives. "I realize now that my deeper attitude was one of compassionate contempt, or perhaps contemptuous compassion. Deep down, I had no doubt that I was superior, in my midtown office overlooking Madison Avenue, to those unpaid housewives pushing brooms. Why aren't they making something of themselves? I wondered. 'What's wrong with them? They're letting our side down.'"[18] This gender message was embedded in class relations. Mansbridge suggests that being a homemaker "lost status primarily because high-status women abandoned it."[19] The departure of middle-class women reinforced the dominant culture's devaluation of the private sphere. When middle-class women left, homemaking became just another dirty job relegated to immigrant maids and child care workers.[20] Women like the Grasinski Girls heard this contempt in the voice of these educated middle-class feminists and felt no strong desire to join a movement that devalued the work they did as homemakers and mothers.

Martha McMahon asks, "Does resisting patriarchy mean resisting what is patriarchally defined as the 'essence' of womanhood—motherhood? Or does resisting patriarchy mean rejecting masculinist devaluation of women and motherhood, not womanhood and motherhood themselves?"[21] Moving into the public sphere to claim power is in some ways accepting the patriarchal devaluation of the private sphere; working instead to empower women in the private sphere, to appreciate tears and laughter and the multitudinous, though often invisible, tasks of mothering represents resistance to its devaluation.

Ann Crittenden argues that if our society truly valued motherhood, women would be compensated for their work done as mothers (e.g., with Social Security benefits), more resources would be allocated to the private sphere (e.g., better subsidized child care programs), and institutions would make more room for mothers (e.g., with flex time).[22] The Grasinski Girls, I believe, would agree with a feminism that pushes for equality without devaluing the private sphere or their role as mothers. While they may not accept the label of feminist, while they are staunchly anti-abortion, and while they would like to preserve the modern family structure, these women nonetheless want to construct a more just society wherein women have the same access to power and resources as do men, and they want to do this without devaluing women's traditional gender roles or harming men. They define men and women as being equal but different, and they appreciate the special gifts of women. Caroline says, "I'm very strong for women being treated equal. But I do not think that they have to be into every job or everything that there is. I mean, I like some things just being for women, I don't want anybody else to be in, and I think there could be things that are expressly just for men. And I mean, I think each one should have some things that are just their very own that they can do." She and her sisters argue for a "separate but equal" gender division of labor. There are some things men are good at and some things women are good at, and they value those things women do well and don't desire to be like men.[23] They like their female softness, their laughter, their caring for the emotional details of life, caring about how one feels rather than what one is doing or accomplishing. They see a need for this personality, especially as it complements the male personality. Nadine spoke about the gendered division of labor in parenting.

> He is a strong figure because he is very important to her and she respects what he's got to say to her, and it's always, "I can talk to Dad," and so it's always about business or schooling or what classes to take or anything that's serious side. He handles all her expenses, pays all the bills, tuition, et cetera. And, uh, what problems do I have? "Ooh, Mom, I'm so sick." "Ooh, I'm going to the *concert* tonight!" "Ooh, I had so much fun." [said with emotive tone] This is what I get, and he gets all the serious things. We're a good combination, because I can't do the things he does and he doesn't do the things I can do. So we are, really, we're a good, good pair, because he's different than I, he can't do what I do and I can't do what he does. So we get along.

Nadine appreciates the differences between men and women without directly demoting women's culture (though she sees his role as "more serious"). Rather than trying to imitate men, she instead affirms her own identity as a woman, and respects the emotional work she does in the home.

Next to this quote above, Nadine wrote on the draft manuscript, "We are two halves making a whole." Similarly, Angel sent me a newspaper clipping announcing a lecture reconciling Catholicism and feminism. It read, "Is it possible to be a Catholic and a feminist? The answer is 'yes!' says Dr. Pia de Solenni, a theologian. . . . Pope John Paul II maintains man and woman are different, but equal. 'True feminism, therefore respects women's identity as an image of God. Where she differs from man, a true feminism understands these differences are constructive and complementary.'" Attached to the clipping was a small note: "I didn't know I was a true feminist—but I guess I qualify!" Feminists they could be, as long as their domestic sphere was not devalued, and as long as they were not expected to act like men or put down men. They wanted to complement and compliment men.

|||

It remains an essentialist argument to say that men and women have different skills and personalities, unless we can show how these differences were socially constructed. What is evident is that some patterned differences still exist (and certainly did for the Grasinski Girl generation).[24] Women often develop personalities based on attachment and connection that preference relationships, while men develop more autonomous personalities that preference occupations. Nancy Chodorow, a psychoanalyst and sociologist, argued in her book *The Reproduction of Mothering* that these differences are not biological, or innate, but socially produced as a result of women being the primary caregivers and men being more absent from the household in modern industrial societies. When mothers are the primary caregivers, boys have to detach from their first love object in order to identify with their own gender. This process of detachment produces more autonomous personalities in men, which makes it easier for them to pursue more impersonal means of satisfaction and better prepares them for the capitalist world of alienated work. Girls experience identity development differently because their primary caretaker is of the same sex. Girls first develop a love relationship with Mom and later develop an attachment to Dad, who in modern industrial societies is often unavailable, physically and emotionally. Because Dad is not as accessible, it is not as necessary for a girl to sever her relationship with him in order to develop her female identity. Because of the strong identification with Mom and the less accessible relation with Dad, girls can maintain attachments to both Mom and Dad in a triangular relationship which is re-created later in life when they have their own child. Chodorow argues that, because they are mothered by women, "girls come to experience themselves as less separate than boys, as having more permeable ego boundaries. Girls come to define themselves more in relation to others."[25] As a result, the female personality is more empathetic and its capacity for relations is also more complex. "Masculine personality, then, comes to be defined more in terms of denial of relation and connection, whereas feminine personality comes to include a fundamental definition of self in relationship."[26]

The female personality, according to Chodorow, does not develop as a result of being mothers, but develops as a result of being mothered. This fact also explains why women continue to mother. Gendered inequalities are built into the modern institution of motherhood. The capacity to mother is reproduced in these institutions, which then produce different gender personalities, one that makes women more suited for the domestic life and one that makes men more suited for the labor market. This creates an inequality, however, when power is more exclusively located in the public sphere. To eliminate these gender differences, she argues, would require that we transform the traditional family by encouraging men to take an equally primary role in nurturing and caring for children.

Of course, what Chodorow leaves out is that the capitalist institutions must also be transformed so that child-caring women and men have flex time, part-time work, and paid paternal leaves.[27] Charlotte Perkins Gilman, a socialist as well as a feminist, argued that gender equality required more collectivist practices like socialized child care. Marriage, she says, cannot be a partnership of equals if one person is left home to pick up the socks and clean the toilets. Moreover, it is inefficient and costly to have individual homes, just as it is inefficient to home school. It is better to move toward public utilities so that through economies of scale we can reduce the costs of child care and food preparation.[28] She argues that as we move toward more communal living situations, women's role in the private family will diminish, freeing up their energies to engage in the public sphere.

Each of the Grasinski Girls had special talents that they were disposed to develop because of their gendered identities. Society benefited when they contributed their skills and talents to the larger collective. Caroline cooked and provided emotional care to hundreds of elementary children at St. Stanislaus school in Hilliards. Not only did she serve nutritious and delicious meals, she also tended to the emotional needs of children. She said, "There was always one child that was having a really bad time, and somehow or another they would find their way into that kitchen," and she would give them the necessary hugs and attention. Caroline's talents as a mother and a cook were extremely useful when employed by the school. In the same way, Nadine cooked gourmet meals in a retirement home, creating a community kitchen that respected the dignity of the elderly. These women found ways to bring themselves into the public sphere. Their participation, however, came only after their own children's needs were met.

Women who spend years caring for others will not agree with a platform that promotes self-interest alone. Nancy Folbre writes that women "have a legacy of commitment to caregiving that should make them suspicious of the 'every man for himself' principle."[29] But an agenda that promotes gender equality and liberation is not necessarily based solely on self-interest. Charlotte Perkins Gilman worked for the individual liberation of women in order to promote the collective good (democracy). African-American feminists encourage women to "lift as they climb," to raise the status of the group by improving the self.[30] While the pursuit of individual liberties and achievements can elevate the collective, for the Grasinski Girls, caring for the collective dignifies the self.

PART III

Learning to Sing

Agency and Resistance

THIS LAST SECTION looks at the sociological masonry of the Grasinski Girl. If structure is our metaphorical social house, then we live in a house that we are constantly constructing.[1] Our active participation in creating and recreating these social structures is expressed in the notion of human agency.[2] We work with what we are given (both the tools and materials), but we can choose to knock out walls, open windows, or go live in the shed. The potential to challenge the social order and change conditions does not mean change will always take place. Sometimes we throw ourselves at brick walls that refuse to budge. Other times we accept the brick walls and hang colorful material over them to make the rooms more comfortable. Still other times we drink bourbon so that we no longer see the wall. Or we close our eyes and pray. The absence of structural change does not signal missing agency, but the power of the structure. Even our unwillingness to challenge structure does not represent missing agency, but the power of ideology and objective conditions to shape our subjective perception of what is possible.

All social actors have agency; we all contribute to producing or reproducing structural conditions and we all have the potential for resistance.[3] This means that there is no completely powerless group or individual but only people with more or less power. There is a sympathetic tendency on the part of many well-meaning people to believe that oppressed groups are powerless. We fear that if we acknowledge that people contribute to reproducing their structures of domination, that we are blaming people for their oppression. Yet recognizing that social actors have agency does not make them responsible for their own liberation nor their victimization.

Agency operates within the parameters of social structures that constrain our ability to act. The structural parameters vary by sociohistorical period as well as by social location (e.g., race, class, and gender), and these parameters, or grooves, define both our confinement and our resistance. For example, in *Where She Came From*, Helen Epstein writes that at one time she admired the liberation of her grandmother, Pepi, an independent business owner who lived openly with her lover in Prague in the 1920s. But when she started talking with women of her grandmother's generation, she learned that they did not see Pepi as "a heroine, but as an object of pity, a woman forced by circumstance to work and by a recalcitrant man to remain unmarried, outside respectability."[4] Pepi had neither the status nor the resources to make being unmarried or working for a living an act of resistance. However, the structures of class and gender which confined her also defined her room to maneuver. Pepi, forced to work, owned a dressmaker's *salon.* The *salon* represented space uninhabited by men and therefore provided women with the opportunity to claim some authority. "The *salon* was a rare institution that allowed a woman to acquire expertise and authority at a time when few women had authority over anything. It was, along with the convent, the brothel, the birthing room, and the all-girls school, a feminine realm, where women could speak."[5]

Similarly, Gene Grasinski's unmarried status was certainly not an act of resistance. She wanted to make it to the marriage altar and create a family. For the Grasinski Girls, the convent allowed singlehood to be acceptable (but, even there, one was spiritually married to Jesus). The convent provided women with space and resources to pursue an education and an occupational career. Nadine emphatically reminds me that this was not why she, and the nuns she knew, went into the convent. Yet, even though she did not choose it for that reason, the convent nonetheless allowed her to have (in fact, insisted that she have) an occupational career, and this helped her develop a more confident public persona. Talking about the major changes in her life, Nadine said, "I think probably the biggest change for me was when I went out to teach, because I was a very quiet person, not a very outgoing person. And that changed, as far as my personality. I can laugh. I always laughed a lot, so maybe I really was that kind of person, but I never had the opportunity to stand in front of people and talk a lot." The *salon* and the convent represent spaces where women could develop their selves, where women could have a voice. While they did not directly challenge the existing order, their acts of accommodation helped them to live more fully within the structures of inequality. They found spaces for freedom within the system.

The space where the Grasinski Girls could maneuver was in the house of God and in their domestic homes. Caroline's presence dominates the front rooms as her hobbies overrun the dining room table. Fran has taken over every closet, cupboard, and nook of the house with her antiques. Angel appropriated the only single bedroom for herself when the last child left the home. Nadine has her own sewing room and a large, deep bathtub with a view of the vineyards. The space appropriated by each of the sisters also represents differences in class levels. While Nadine was living in a large chateau, Mari was sharing a studio apartment in New York. Obviously, class situates us differently in the matrix of domination, and as such affords us different abilities and reasons to challenge (or reproduce) the social structure.

The Grasinski Girls did not resist their gendered roles in a modern family (with Mari always the exception). As a result, there is a tendency to see this group of women—homemakers who did not join the feminist movement and who were parochial and apolitical—as reproducing gender inequality.[6] I challenge this interpretation for two reasons. First, the absence of collective resistance against institutions of inequality does not mean there was no resistance. At the most private level, they resisted through the practice of self-love. Self-love, for a member of a subordinate group, represents a resistance to the dominant ideology that defines the group as less worthy. To not want to "be like men" represents a rejection of the dominant culture. Moreover, internal struggles for self-definition and self-valuation countered internal scripts of self-blame. For example, even those who were not college-educated refused to label themselves as stupid and understood that this was not a choice offered to them. For those given the short end of the stick, learning to live with dignity is resistance. Swallowing pain and responding in song is resistance.[7] Their resistance (refusing to psychologically succumb) is also not resigned acceptance, which is more likely to result in socially induced depression. Mental resistance is also not Pollyannaish optimism. Instead, it represents a personal struggle to not let the world get you down, to do whatever you need to do to continue to laugh and enjoy your hours, so that at the end of your days you can say, "I lived a good life."

Second, in order to better understand what effect these women had on the larger social structure, we need to look at what they passed on to their daughters and to what extent they encouraged or challenged the reproduction of gender inequality in the next generation. What may appear to be fallow fields for one generation become the seed beds for activism when understood within a historical and generational context. For example, Ann Moody's autobiography, *Coming of Age in Mississippi*, describes the civility and docility among rural Southern blacks who accepted a doctrine of Christianity that helped them survive to bear children who took up the struggle for equality. Perhaps this was all they could do: refuse to die before birthing and raising the next generation. In many ways, the Grasinski Girls did for their daughters what they did not do for themselves. Caroline encouraged her daughters to go to college so that they could support themselves. Angel produced me, in some ways a gender rebel—an aggressive feminist who refuses to remain quiet in the private sphere, a woman who refused motherhood when it was first offered.

Sociologist Charles Lemert writes that agency represents "the hidden power of the less powerful," which is the ability to resist and challenge social structures.[8] In this section I examine this hidden power in the sacred and the secular. Chapter 6 looks at the role of prayer as a means of petitioning the Lord to change both external conditions and subjective perceptions. Caroline's story illustrates the strength of a woman in both the everyday routines of building a home for her children and the more extraordinary measures she took to keep her family together. Chapter 7 examines agency in the domestic setting and makes a distinction between power and strength. Power derived from status, authority, and income is located in the social structure, but strength belongs to the social actor. Strength is the ability to be happy even in sad conditions. These women are strong women, and it is their love for Jesus and their families that makes them strong. They passed their strength on to their daughters, who took it with them into the public sphere.

6 ⫼ Fate and Faith

AFTER A PARTICULARLY fierce argument with my partner, I storm off in the car and head out of town to an abbey for Trappist monks. As I approach the stone chapel, built on a hill away from an already remote road, I smile for the first time that day. I have come to a silent place where I won't have to fight. I have not been to church since Christmas, even though I live across the street from a Gothic basilica that overwhelms our second-floor picture window with its golden-orange stone masonry and its androgynous statue of Jesus looking right into our living room. I went to mass there once and didn't like it. It was a parish church, and people talked, babies cried, and the organist played too fast and too loud. The priest lectured about money, while I thought about my weekly schedule. Most unappealing, the Our Father was prayed in a rapid staccato, and no one crossed themselves after the miracle of transubstantiation.

In contrast, the abbey is in the middle of hills green with summer wheat. Silence permeates both the exterior and interior; prayers are said deliberately, slowly. Handsome celibate men chant rhythmic psalms. The few outside attendees are reverent, the solemnity is graceful. I realize I am here more for the silence and the chanting than the Love of the Lord. In fact, I am a part-time nonbeliever. In this way, I am not at all like the Grasinski Girls. Yet, by going to mass, even if it is for aesthetic reasons, I am, as Kathleen Norris found herself, "engaged in my inheritance."[1]

Not until I am kneeling down in the abbey and swooning in the notes of Psalms do I realize that they are venerating the Corpus Christi. I participate in this adoration and I have in my purse a book about the Blessed Virgin Mary. Mother Mary and the Blessed Sacrament, the dual devotions of Polish-American Catholicism.[2] My mind shifts back to a summer when I lived in a rural village in Poland, going to mass almost every day—in May for Mary, in

June for the Blessed Sacrament. The century-old church bells would ring a quarter hour before mass, and I would put down my pen, slip on my sandals, and merge with the trickle of older women walking to church.

If I believed in the Lord the way the Girls believe, I might think that He called me to the abbey that day, to vespers in adoration of the Blessed Sacrament, to help me write this chapter on religion. But I don't believe. At least not always. And not in the same way that they believe so completely in Jesus. Fate and faith are the prisms through which they understand the world. God is their reason for being. Religion orders and explains their lives, but religion is more than a routine, just as the convent is more than a career.

Religion is the lifeblood of the Grasinski Girls; they drank it from their mother's breast. It is the aroma of the mass, the beads of the rosary, the prayers they learned as little girls and recited decades later over the dying body of their mother. Their religion is not an abstract course in miracles but something concrete that operates in the present moments of their life to help them find parking spots, bring their children home safely, and accept the grief of death. They pray daily, thrice daily, pray as they breathe, to God and His entourage of angels, saints, and dead relatives. Nadine prays to her brother Joseph every time she gets in the car, and Angel prays to her mother-in-law for good weather on special-event days. When they get what they want, they are grateful and thank the Lord; when they don't, they concede that God knows best, and accept His will.[3]

When I ask Nadine what role religion plays in her life she tells me, "Well, religion is, I think, number one, and then there's money. [laughs] Religion, our whole life, was very important, from what we had when we were growing up—you went to mass, you prayed. It's kind of hard to say, but to me it's everything. It's your whole life, your whole life is your religion. It's kind of hard to explain, but I know that I love it! I love everything that's religious—the singing, the hymns, and the churches, and being good. To me, it's like I said, number one."

|||

In a religious framework of fate, God is the Master Planner. This worldview is in some ways similar to a sociological understanding of social structure. Fate, like social structure, is a force above and beyond the individual that directly influences the course and content of an individual's life, and the fated hand of God, like social structure, is often mysterious and always salient.[4] Moreover, a framework of fate, like a sociological understanding of structure, does not blame individuals for their circumstances; rather, it accepts that extra-individual forces slot people into particular social locations. This worldview is well illustrated in a discussion Nadine and Angel had about their position in life relative to others.

ANGEL: But then I think, this is easy for me, to [thank the Lord]. I have this nice house, and this nice family, and I think of the people in Ecuador, like with the earthquake. Now, how can they have, like, these same feelings toward God and Jesus? Their house is gone, their families are gone, they're living in dirt, how can you look up and say, "Thank you, Lord?" I mean, that always confuses me. I can see where I can be thankful, and things are beautiful for me and I don't never go hungry. Or people that have to live on the street, how can they look up and have the same feeling that I do? It's very confusing for me.

NADINE: Confusing. It's confusing, why are some people here, and why were you born into this, and why were they born into that?

ANGEL: Like, why were they born in Africa?

NADINE: And why were they real rich, where you never even think of, I mean, why? Who knew where to put, place who?

ANGEL: You don't have no choice. Like the Kennedys, they didn't have any choice being born there, and we don't have no choice being born here.

NADINE: I know, but why do some people have such horrible lives and other people have had pleasant, beautiful lives, like ours? We don't want anything.

ANGEL: Right. Right.

ME: The reason we have really poor people is the same reason we have really rich people. The rich people get rich off the poor people.

ANGEL: But all rich people are not evil.

NADINE: No! And all poor people can't really help themselves for being poor.

ANGEL: I don't think so. I think of these people, like they have these lost boys of Sudan, I don't know if you heard of them. They told in the paper how they escaped from all this terror and they come to the United States, I think seventeen thousand of them have come already to the United States.

> Their families have been killed and they were fleeing this country and many of them got killed trying to get away from this terror. And I thought, you know, it's too easy for us. I think sometimes we'll have to be accountable for a lot. Those people might not have to be, that much.

While Angel and Nadine's analysis of inequality is not based on economic and political systems that produce differences in power, their worldview is similar to a structural analysis in that they attribute inequality to some larger force (even if they don't understand it) rather than blaming the individual. They see their own privileges and others' disadvantages and they neither praise nor blame people for their social position. It's fate!

So where is human agency (our ability for self-propelled action) in this worldview of a fate whereby God does things to people and for them? In the Gospel according to John, chapter 15, Jesus states, "You did not choose me; I chose you." Mother Angela, founder of the Felician Order, wrote, "Now I see that it was pride and because of this God disrupted my plans . . . God Himself took this work from my hands."[5] Mother Mary Monica, the superior of the group of five Felicians who went as pioneers to Polonia, Wisconsin, wrote in her diary that "we felt grateful that Our Lord was pleased to choose us."[6] Nadine wrote, "Generally speaking, my greatest happiness can be accounted for by the fact that God has chosen me, a very unworthy and poor creature, to work for Him in His vineyard." Nadine says, about having been a nun, "I had nothing to do with it." That was God's plan. And, about leaving the convent, she said, "The ball started rolling and just rolled and rolled, and, like, she said no, and this one said yes, and things just kind of fell in place." This external control appears to stand in opposition to human agency. Yet, we sociologists are as adamant as religious folk in believing that forces external to the individual are responsible for the conditions of the individual. They call it God, we call it social structure. So, if we can allow for human agency even while believing in the powerful influence of social structure, we must consider that, even with a meddling God, there might still be room for human agency. And there is.

The human agency in their framework of fate is prayer. Prayer provides them with control and acceptance, active and passive processes. As a passive process they come to rely on God for those things they have no control over, but prayer is also an active process that provides them with some power to set the conditions (if only psychologically) of their lives. The Grasinski Girls believe that only God can bestow blessings upon them, but God's love is a matriarchal love. He is not a vengeful, punishing God, but a kind and benevolent God in whose lap they can dump their troubles.[7] Worried about a grandchild, Angel said, "I started praying. 'Okay, I gotta deal with this now, what am I gonna do, and You take care of him.' And it was just like, then I became more peaceful. Then I knew, okay, it's gonna be okay." Fran said, "He just really always knows how to take care of everything."

They pray for concrete things like finding a good job or losing twenty-five pounds. They pray that a son will sell his house, that a daughter will quit smoking cigarettes, that new babies will be healthy, and a wife's grief will be bearable. To get these things, they pray to dead relatives as well as saints and the Holy Trinity.[8] Anthony Bukoski writes of a Polish-American character, "He whispered a prayer to Poland and one to the priest, who'd been dead twenty years, and to the nuns who were all gone, and to Stanislawa Rozowska, his niece."[9] Nadine prays daily to her brother Joe, who died of lung cancer in his late fifties: "I keep very close to him, and always, I get in the car, 'Joe, help me!' and he does. I know he's around and I pray to him a lot to help me and take care of me, and I need this and that, and Marie Chantal needs, and he always does help me." They pray for themselves and for those they love. They pray for character adjustments and mortgage adjustments, and they pray to those who have died to help those who are still living.[10]

They believe that through prayer they have some power to control the situation. In one interview where we were discussing prayer, Nadine and Angel simultaneously broke into a prayer that they learned when they were little girls. "Remember, oh most Gracious Virgin Mary, that never was it known, that anyone who fled to thy protection, implored thy help, or sought thy intercession was left unaided. Inspired by this confidence, I fly unto thee, oh Virgin of Virgins, my Mother, to thee do I come, before thee I stand sinful and sorrowful. Oh Mother of the Word incarnate, despise not my petitions, but in thy mercy hear and answer me. Amen." Angel said the prayer "thousands of times in the night, waiting" for one of her six children to return home safely. And Nadine repeats the mantra while she is walking, especially if her daughter needs something: "'Remember, oh most Gracious,' I keep saying it over and over." They powerfully, consciously, and resolutely petition the most Gracious Virgin Mary: Hear me! Answer me!

They pray to Mary, the suffering Mother of the crucified Jesus, who becomes their model for strength and womanhood, the Virgin superior who accepts the will of God, gains strength through her agony, and thereby turns sorrow into a greater love. Not only is she an inspiration, Mary is also a primary intercessor to God. But so is Jesus, who stands beside Mary in their prayers and adoration. Angel said, "My favorite prayers are all to the Sacred Heart of Jesus, it's like my best person in the whole world." Their devotions to Jesus as well as Mary are reflections of Polish Catholicism, and more specifically the Felician sisterhood, whose motto is "All through the Heart of Mary in honor of the Most Blessed Sacrament." In this Eucharistic-Marian spirituality, these "two devotions are inseparably united" and together they remind us of suffering and redemption.[11] The mother of the Grasinski Girls nurtured their adoration for Jesus. As Fran said, "From a very little girl I can remember her talking to me about Jesus." And it was in the family that they learned to pray the rosary, a Marian-based prayer that involves contemplation of Jesus (two of the three mysteries, the joyful and sorrowful, are entirely devoted to the god-man).

Praying empowers them to change either their life conditions or the way they experience these conditions.[12] They try to influence external situations to protect themselves and their loved ones from potential harm. Fran tells the following story of being with her father: "One time we were in a boat and it started to storm and thunder and lightning, and, oh boy! He was paddling and he says, 'Now, you better start praying. You pray and we'll get this boat back there, but you pray hard!'" Prayer also works to change subjective conditions, so that if harm does befall them, they pray for the strength to endure. In this way, prayer helps them control themselves even if it does not control external events. In both cases they are actively working to change something—either the external situation or their internal perceptions and feelings.

Many prayers to God are said during times when they need extra help or need the external conditions changed. Angel talks about praying while her husband was on strike and when their seventeen-year-old was out late in the car. Nadine said, "And I pray the rosary. You pray whenever you're troubled. Whenever you're afraid, you pray, whenever you're hoping for something, you pray." When Caroline's son Ed got sick, the whole family prayed.

That time when he was sick, that was the most troubled time of my life. This little boy, he was so, I mean, he was so sick and they didn't know what to do with him or anything, and we're running with him to the doctor. He'd fill up with water, just like a nine-month-pregnant woman, and his little eyes were just like the same thing. He spent a couple months in the hospital and after that we'd just take him and they would stick him and then that water would all go out. And then, finally, he ended up in Ann Arbor. They didn't think he was going to live, so they sent him home. They thought that whatever happens, happens, that they couldn't do anything for him. So they took all the medicines away and everything, and, as you can believe, everybody prayed, we prayed like crazy. Anyhow, we brought him home, that was around November, we brought him home for Christmas. While he was in Ann Arbor, there was an old doctor there, and he says, "When you're coming home, you find the first church that you can find, and you take that little boy in there and offer him up to God." Well, that's what they did. I was pregnant, so I couldn't be there, but Mom was there. And little Ed, they took him into that church and they were praying there, you know, offering him up, offering him up to God. And then, in January, Helene was born. Well, on her baptism day, when she was baptized, he just got *well.* I mean, he just got well. I mean he just sat there and he played, and he was never sick after that.

Prayer is a way of believing that you have some control in your life and then acting on that belief. Prayer does not make you passive. Fran's father rowed hard in the boat and Caroline took her son to numerous doctors, but they also prayed for help. While dependent on God's benevolence, they can also petition the Lord, and their faith gives them the courage to take action.

The Grasinski Girls see their privileges (blessings) as God's grace; they seldom take credit for their actions that may have helped to produce the desired results. They don't always see their own agency in making their life what they want it to be, but instead credit God for performing mini-miracles. God may indeed find Angel a parking spot, but she is the one who drives patiently through a crowded lot looking. Fran tells a story of one Christmas Eve when she and her husband drove to Milwaukee for midnight mass at a large cathedral they had attended when their three children were students at Marquette University. They drove three hundred miles in snowy weather, and when they arrived they opened the door to the church and the ushers, reminiscent of the innkeeper in Bethlehem, said, "There are no seats left."

And I said, "There's gotta be seats for us." And he says, "Well, we'll take you down this aisle and we'll take you down that aisle." So they did, and they took us down this aisle and took us back, and we could see that every seat was full. And he says, "Sorry. You can stand in the back." And I says, "We drove all this way," and I say, "I'm gonna find us a seat." So I took both of them [her husband and her daughter], and I went down the center aisle, and there, three rows from the front, were sitting three empty seats. And I said, [crying] "You knew we were coming, Jesus, and saved those three seats." Because we drove all the way from Grand Rapids, and here then all the priests come in, and they were all at the communion rail, and there were about fifty priests in their red robes that were kneeling and sitting just these three rows from us. So we seen this throughout the whole mass. So not only did He find us a seat, but He put us right down front. And it was just like, you know, "I wanna shake your hand or something." You know, it was just like I could just feel it, you know. "You did this for me." You know, there's just a lot of times that are like that.

And there are. The stories of the Grasinski Girls contain numerous life events where it appears to them that Jesus stepped up, took them by the hand, and was there for them, like a good friend.

Their God is a personal God, a loving, kind, laughing God. The love the Lord provides is a maternal love. He hugs them, brings them near to Him, cares for them. But note, Fran was the one who took her husband's and her daughter's hands and led them down the center aisle and found the seats. She was not passive in this story. Not taking "no" for an answer found her those seats. I don't know whether God saved those seats for her (she is absolutely sure that He did), but I do know she actively searched. And she also initiated this beautiful experience by getting in the car and making the effort to drive the three hundred miles. Fran grew her own metaphorical rose garden—God may have provided the sun and the rain, but she certainly picked up the hoe.

|||

Their faith is not something they found, it is something they were given. It was something passed down through the generations. They learned to say the rosary from their mother and father; they learned to sing in St. Stan's choir; they learned how God was personal when their sister Gene died suddenly and they comforted their grieving mother. They all say their faith "came from Mom and Dad." As a young girl, Fran remembers her mother as "very religious. I say my gift of faith and everything came from her." She qualifies it by saying her mother was not someone who walked around all the time "being religious." And yet she says her mother was "very religious. And she laughed a lot. She laughed a lot and she sang a lot." This is how their relationship between happiness and religion was formed: their mother was happy, even during bad times, and they attribute her ability to be happy to her strong faith. They inherited their recipe for happiness from her. Explaining the role of religion in her own life, Angel tells me,

> I used to think that if you had your health, that was the most important thing in your life, and for the last twenty years I've never thought that. I thought, what if you become a paraplegic? You don't have your health, but if you have faith, you can survive and be a happy human being. So I don't think health is, like, number one. I think it's wonderful, but I think, faith in God and faith in somebody that's there for you. That's how I think of my faith, there's this God who is gonna help you if you ask for it. And I think that is my most important thing, that saved me through a massive amount of things. It helps me now.

Their faith mediates their experience of life conditions and thereby provides them with the possibility for happiness.

Neither the girls nor their mother lived in conditions that always inspired happiness, but their faith helped them manage the conditions. For example, faith helped them accept the sorrow that accompanies death, especially unexpected deaths. Their mother Helen lost her daughter, husband, and mother, all within an eight-month period. Nadine believes that Helen's ability to cope was rooted in her ability to accept these misfortunes. "She could never have handled this the way she did without accepting it as a sorrow, as a pain. She had to accept it. You know, what do you do? You say, 'Okay, Lord, take it, help me, help me.' What else can you do when you have a great sorrow?"

God does not take the sadness away. This is important. God is not an opiate for their sadness. In fact, just the opposite. Opiates numb the body and the emotions. Their religion, however, gives them access to a full range of emotions, from joy to sorrow, gladness to sadness. Sadness is one emotion, one way of feeling the world. Their faith allows them to feel the sadness without the sadness overwhelming them. When their mother died, the sisters stood around her coffin singing "Amazing Grace," her favorite song. They sang all six verses and cried through all six verses. One niece wondered why they would "put themselves through that pain." And even ten years later, as Fran was telling me this story, she started to cry gentle tears, but then said it was "okay, because sadness comes along. And Uncle Joe [her brother] always says the same thing with loneliness. He always says there are times he likes to be lonely, you know, it's just like joy—there's nothing wrong with being lonely, or feeling sad over different things." Their ability to be happy is related to their willingness to be sad. They don't dismiss but accept the sadness or the loneliness. And this acceptance comes through faith.

|||

Sadness brings them into prayer, which brings them closer to the divinity. Nadine said, "Great sorrow really brings you closer than anything else. You are really close to Him at the time of great sorrow, like nothing else, like no joy or no music or nothing, there is nothing like pain that brings you closer to Christ." Through faith, pain further connects them to the benevolent provider, and it is this relationship (and not the material rewards it brings) that is their ultimate source of happiness. Any notion of the instrumentality of prayer is mere frivolity compared to the deeper understanding of prayer as connection.

Prayer is conversation with the Lord. While they may pray for things in the abstract or the concrete, the real benefit of prayer is that it helps them develop a relationship with the Lord. Nadine said, "When I went to the convent, I thought that that's what I wanted to do, to spend my life praying and being in touch with Jesus." In this way, prayer is also an end in itself. Sitting with Him in church, praying the rosary with the Holy Mother, contemplating her passions of joy and suffering for her son Jesus, this is why they pray. It is not just to make things happen, but to share the moments of their day with Jesus, Mary, and Joseph. As Kathleen Norris writes, "Prayer is not doing, but being. It is not words but the beyond words experience of coming into the presence of something much greater than oneself."[13] Nadine tells me,

> I prayed all my life. It's something I love to do. I loved to do it when I was a little girl. I loved these holy hours and benedictions and these masses in all of these big churches, especially in the big churches. [laughs] I really love it. I

just love it. And I love to pray. . . . How do I pray? I pray when I go to church. I pray when I drive to town, when I go for a walk, I always walk down to that water and there's nobody there and I pray there by the water. And it's kind of like being by myself, the way it was when He first called me, when we were close, when I was just all by myself and nobody's around.

Fran also described how praying created a close, almost physical relation. "When you say the rosary you're going through the whole life of Christ, whether you're doing the sorrowful, or the glorious, or the joyful [mysteries]." And when "you go through the Way of the Cross in your mind you can feel the stones and the gravel underneath His feet, and I can just really feel that He's right there." Prayer creates an affective relation. It is not a cerebral exercise, but an intimate connection.

Because one purpose for and result of prayer is that it builds and maintains relations, prayer reproduces familiar gender routines. They talk about the Lord using the language of relations—Jesus is an old friend who calls out to them, and prayer is like sharing morning coffee. Nadine describes this personal, intimate relation.

They have a little chapel at St. Francis where they have the exposition of Blessed Sacrament, and during the day when I'm driving by I'll try to stop in there. And if I try to slip by the church, I hear that little guilty voice, [laughing] it's drawing you. He's there, [laughs] and He's saying, "Come." And I just keep going. [laughing] And sometimes it's just, like, "Leave me alone!" [laughs] And like, now, you always try to make the presence of Christ, you know, you try to bring Him close to you, with the things around you, when you go for a walk, take Him into your heart, and hold Him in your heart.

This friendship is strengthened through prayer. Nadine said, comparing her present life with her convent life, "I don't pray as much as I prayed when I was in the convent, and I don't feel, sometimes, that close to Him either, because I don't put that time into it." Like any good relationship, what you get out of it depends on what you put into it.

Angel refers to Jesus as her "friend" and talks about how she learned to understand His love in this way from her mother.

I probably learned the most religious thing I could ever learn in my life from my mother, at that point when Gene died, [crying] and she took this crucifix, and she said, [crying] "I never thought He would ask this of me." [crying] It was like Jesus was her, her friend, and she was saying, "I never thought He would ask me to sacrifice my daughter." When I think about it now, this is, like, my whole religious life, thinking that Jesus is your friend, that He's not somebody so far away that you can't talk to Him or pray to Him or anything. So, [crying] He wasn't like some God. It was like, here, He's my friend and He's gonna help me, St. Joseph is gonna help me.

God, the benevolent giver, does not sit high above them like some patriarchal figure, but beside them on a park bench.[14] He walks with them along the lakefront in the white light of sunrise, and whispers comfort into their ears when the darkness of night feels lonely.

Another way that their religious identity is intermingled with their gender identity is that the church building, while a public institution, is remade into a private domicile. Not only are women responsible for cleaning and decorating the churches—the main task of every women's altar society— but going to church is like visiting God in his home. For Nadine, a church is home.

> I go to the church as often as I can. I'd go every day if I could. I would love to just start off the day like that. I'd love to live in the city, walk to church, instead of driving twenty miles to church. Church is one of my most favorite places in the world, like you just walk into a church and immediately you feel at home, you know, this is where I belong. No matter where I go, that Blessed Sacrament is there and He's so real. It's just like, now I'm home. And like I said, the more you go the closer you become.

The relationship with God is something that requires time and effort, something that has to be nurtured, and they play an active role in maintaining that relationship by visiting Him often in His home.

Prayer is also a gendered act for these women because it reproduces the other-centered orientation of their female personalities, in that their prayers are often for the benefit of others. This is most evident in Caroline's favorite prayers, the Prayer of St. Francis ("Make me a channel of your peace . . .") and a prayer to St. John Newman, which she read to me.

> Merciful Father, you have given me all that I have in this world. Even life itself. In all my daily needs, help me to remember the needs of others too.

Make me aware of the need to pray to you. Not just for myself, but for the Church, the Pope, for clergy, and for people who suffer any need. Make me as selfless as St. John Newman was. Throughout my life, give me the grace to direct my first thoughts to the service of You and others. Make my prayer Your will be done, knowing that in Your mercy and love, Your will for me is my sanctification. I ask this through Jesus Christ our Lord.

Asking for help to remember the needs of others, her prayer to a man nonetheless reflects her gendered caretaking role. The Grasinski Girls feel a responsibility to care for family and friends, but also the poor, unborn babies, and the lost boys from Sudan. As such, prayer is not simply a selfish act of directing God to change their own external conditions or subjective experiences, but an act they undertake to make their immediate and global world a better place.

|||

The question that begs to be asked is whether or not the prayer works. About prayer, Kathleen Norris writes, "God only knows if it does any good; I am certain it does no harm."[15] But what if the prayer does harm? What if prayer stood in the place of more effective ways of bringing about change? While they do take some action apart from praying (e.g., working for the pro-life movement and donating money to charitable organizations), they do not challenge the conditions that create inequality. Sending money to feed the poor is not the same thing as trying to change the conditions that produce world hunger. However, when someone confronted Mother Teresa with the same criticism, she said something like, 'I hope someone finds a way to end hunger and disease, and until they do, I will continue to feed the poor, minister to the sick, and comfort the dying.'

Prayer itself does not prevent the Grasinski Girls from engaging in action to bring about broader social change. Many people who work for social change also pray. And, in many cases, prayer and religious doctrine have been used to support social justice movements.[16] In general, however, the Grasinski Girls do not use prayer to challenge structural inequality.

Whether or not prayer can change the world, it does empower them to change themselves. Angel believes that her faith, as manifest in prayer, has made her a stronger woman.

I think my faith, my *trust* and my faith have grown by leaps and bounds as I had children. . . . The thing that I see changed more is that my faith has grown. Before, I would worry about every little thing, and now, sometimes— it's just, through the years you seen things sort of taken care of by praying, and the strength, you become stronger in yourself when things do happen. And sometimes, you know, you get a kick in the teeth and you're right back to square one. [laughs] It's like, "Okay, now why did this have to happen?" But you just sort of pick yourself up again. I just think the same with our mother. I don't think she started out being this really strong person. I think it was through this whole journey of her life, day by day, what she's gone through, that she ends up really strong.

But what is the strength used for? To endure? Then doesn't their faith become the proverbial opiate? It makes it easier to accept the hard knocks of life, numbing them so that they do not feel the bruises, so they can get up again and face the punches. Can prayer be empowering if it is used to help them accept bad conditions rather than change those conditions?

Learning to cope with bad conditions does not mean that they accept the conditions as justified or legitimate, only that they refuse to let the conditions sour their hearts. And it is this refusal that allows them to be happy. A strong faith that helps them to survive can be a personal victory over oppression without lessening structural oppression. Caroline, talking in general about her life, said, "It wasn't very easy, but I've never been unhappy in my life. I've never been, you know, I've never been unhappy, like that." "Why do you think that is?" I ask. "I just think I was—well, I think that my life, my kids—I have a deep, really strong faith in God. And it holds me up through a lot of stuff." Faith in God helps her live with dignity and grace and joy, even when external conditions do not provide these for her. Caroline said about faith, "That's one thing that you must have, because life gives you things that, you know, if you don't have it, it's hard to handle. And if you have a good, strong faith, and strong trust in God, it can get you through everything." Talking about someone who did not go to church and recently lost a child, she said, "And now she's having a very bad time. . . . If you have this religion, this love of God and this strength in God, it's hard, it's a terrible, terrible thing, but somehow or another you pull through it. I think, if you want to live on Earth, you need the structure, you need some structure in your life, and that's your religion. Put that on there!" (The last command directed at me and the tape recorder.)

Religion is their structure. It gives them direction and power; it helps them find church pews and save errant daughters driving through rainstorms in the middle of the night. Angel said about faith and praying to God in hard times, "It's not like you're never gonna have tragedies or problems, but somehow you get the strength to cope with them." The strength comes from their God and their connection to God. God alone does not supply the strength. The connection to God gives them strength, which means that by nurturing the relationship, they are active producers of their strength, not passive recipients of strength. They have to make the effort to maintain contact with God; they are responsible for their own empowerment. While prayer does not inspire them to take action against the larger structures of inequality, it does help them live through the days with some joy. Their lives are better because of this faith.

Their fated worldview is not based on passivity, though it does describe a life where things happen to them—God calls them or rejects them; God gives them children and takes away siblings; God gives them grumpy husbands to manage and children who give them gray hairs. Their job is to count their blessings and thank God for their heartaches because it gives them a chance to connect with and be closer to God. They are active players in the drama. Their strength comes through endurance that allows them not only to suffer but also to enjoy life. Their efficacy is rooted in consciousness; it works because they know that it works.

Caroline Clarice

CAROLINE CLARICE, THE OLDEST Grasinski Girl, was born on June 1, 1923, in Grand Rapids. When I interviewed her she was seventy-six years old, but looked ten years younger. She is a pretty woman with a gentleness to her beauty, a soft voice and kind personality coupled with a resolute strength that is both physical and mental. She still lives in Hilliards, in the family house on Walnut Hill Farm with the old-fashioned wraparound porch framed by two blue-green pine trees and clusters of bearded purple irises. A spiky rhubarb patch perpendicular to the driveway is left untended, and one remaining walnut tree out back produces grocery bagfuls of thick-shelled nuts for Christmas fudge. The house is old, drafty, often messy, but always colorful. Caroline creates pleasant space in the house: jade-painted walls and bunches of dried mustard-colored flowers, piles of books scattered next to chairs, an old baker's hutch with cut-glass figurines, and, every year, a Christmas tree with large white birds and little blue lights. She is often in the middle of some project, and that means the dining room table is covered with pieces of cloth, dried flowers, and small bottles of paint.

Caroline lived a privileged life, she says. She has three healthy children, eight grandchildren, and a husband who worked in a union position as "a journeyman, a tool machinist. He worked thirty-seven years, and being that, our life was fairly easy. We couldn't do everything we wanted to, but it was a good life. We traveled a lot. And I was a good person that could hunt down sales." One of the most important facets of Caroline's life is her ability to hold the family together—both the extended family, through annual re-unions, Easter celebrations, anniversary parties, and summer bonfires, all held at the old family house, and her immediate family, which is more difficult because her eldest daughter lives in California. Caroline overcame her fear of flying in order to maintain a close relationship with her daughter and granddaughters. Of all the sisters, she is the most engaged in Polish traditions: she bakes *babka* and *makowiec* (poppy-seed cake); she makes *pierogi*, and *czarnina;* she pickles long yellow cucumbers (something her aunt Sophie taught her); and she sings *kolędy* (Polish Christmas carols).

She was eager for me to interview her and arranged a time for us to talk when her husband and her adult daughter would both be out of the house. The house was clean and she made us a wonderful lunch, chicken salad with apples and walnuts. She was nervous at first. There was no crowning event to shape her narrative—nothing like her two sisters' nun stories, or Mari's divorce drama. She started out chronologically. Up through her teen years, the storytelling was detailed, thorough, and self-directed; I asked no questions and she left no questions to be asked. But then she started jumping around from then to now: the past was in the present as her mind snaked through free-flowing reams of thought that twisted and turned to embrace some memories and to recoil from others. She often got her point across without saying anything directly. Her speech was punctuated with numerous "you knows," half-finished sentences sometimes restarted, often unfinished, and a litter of "whatchamacallits" in place of fully articulated feelings. Where there were holes, I began to ask questions to fill in the blank years and feelings. She would answer the question, drift into some other topic, and when she came to a lull she would say, "Okay, now ask me some more questions, I like that." In this way, she got me to direct her story. She gave me control, and that worked for her.

Two years later, I was back for a third taping session. By this time, she had read a section of an earlier draft and she let me know that I didn't get it right. I had not talked enough about how honored she felt to be a mother, nor did I mention that reading is one of her "mainstays, one of the things that I most enjoy. I like history, not history itself, but novels or stories that have to do with people from history, and women from history, and things like that, and books on flower arranging, dried flowers, and wreaths. I have a ton."

Most importantly, I had missed entirely her whole creative side, the soul of her life. She was ready for me this time. She said, "I would like you to know about my love of music and my working with the flowers, and all my church work. Here! This is just a little to show you what I did," and she pulled out her photo albums to show me the quilts, banners, Advent wreaths, crocheted snowflakes and angels, appliquéd sweatshirts, and hundreds of bread chicks she bakes every year for children on Palm Sunday. She loves the

colors of winter "and going out into the fields in the wintertime and picking
dried milkweed pods and teasel and coming home with a big bouquet. I enjoy
that almost as much as a big bouquet of fresh flowers in the summertime."
And she "just wanted to show this" photo she took of "Lake Michigan, my
most favorite spot that I love to go to."

Not only had I left out two important parts about her—her mothering
and her creativity—but I had also dwelt too long in the valley of darkness.
She took out more than half of what I had written about her, and she continued to take out large pieces from the final draft. She told me that she is
"glad I said those things out loud," but did not want to see them in print.
Okay. I had to respect that.

Caroline is a listener, a watcher, but she is not passive. Her images of her
childhood are frenzied with the activity of running; in adulthood she continues
to search for something, often not knowing what it is. But she continues to
seek, to innovate, to find ways to create a life that is satisfying. She showed
me a yellowing scrap of paper that she has carried around for decades with
these typed words:

Don't ever feel sorry for feeling, for caring as deeply as you do, the tops of
the mountain peaks are ever so breathtaking when you climb them from a

valley. Feel, care, and don't give up simply because the majority of the people are too shallow or too busy to really feel. Don't ever let anyone take away that inner wondering, searching, and dissatisfaction with the ordinary. Don't be too hurt over someone not understanding you. Too many wounds make scar tissue, and scar tissue is numb and insensitive to pain or pleasure.

She does not know who the author is, but at the bottom of the paper are her own initials: CM.

So I Learned to Fly

My birth certificate said I was named Clarice C. Grusczynski, and I was born on June 1st, 1923, at 322 Cass Avenue in Grand Rapids. When I was only seven years old, [my mom] let me take Gene, she was five and Fran was three, to John Ball Park, and I took care of 'em all day. I knew that park. We were in the bandstand, we were up to see the monkeys, then we were in the pavilion, we sat on all the little chairs, and after that we went and fed the swans. [laughs] That's what we did. Then we came home. After supper I would take Joe in this great big green stroller and walk around the block several times. I was only seven years old.

And I also was the main grocery shopper. Every day I went to Lewandowski's for a bag of groceries. I was running all the time. I would go to Miner's Pies on Butterworth and get the day-old pies. Then I came home, and I would take this shiny black oil bag and I went again. I used to stand in line to get bread and milk during the Depression. And we played and played. We had all my mom's old hand-me-downs: a big round muff. That's what she'd give us. [laughter] That was new, and I don't know why she give it to us, but I played with that, and a red fox fur. We were poor and didn't know it. We didn't have much of anything but it didn't bother us. To me, those were the best years of my life, those first ten, twelve years.

One time, when I was at Sacred Heart, I was about eight or nine, and eyebrows were important to Mom, and so one day she took this old-fashioned hard lead pencil and marked little eyebrows. And I went to school that way. And pretty soon the nun came along and took me by the shoulder out of the room and asked me why did I do that to myself. And I said, "I didn't. My mother did." And that was the last time the nun ever spoke to me about that.

I remember when they lost their home. I remember the day we had to leave that house. I still can hear it. Mom had Joe in the green stroller and Fran sitting down on the bottom and Gene on one side, me on the other, and I still can hear the wheels on that stroller. We were walking, we walked from Valley Avenue all the way down to First Street. And that's a long ways.

And then we moved out here [to Hilliards] when I was sixteen. There I met Edmund. I started going with Edmund when the war came. And I asked myself a lot of times, again, would I get on the train by myself and go down there [to Georgia where he was stationed] and get married? Would I do that again? I don't know. You know, that war was a different war and it was a different time period. And when somebody said he was lonesome and he thinks he's going overseas and that, to come down, and—I can't imagine myself never being anywhere, going anywhere by myself—getting on an old train and going down, all the way down to Georgia. I remember I got in the station in Chicago and I left my ticket on the sink [laughs] where I was washing my hands, and I had to run back and get the ticket, and I was so afraid I had lost it.

We were married at Camp Wheeler, right in the camp, in the chapel, on November 7, 1942. Georgia was nice. I mean, all these little southern houses and stuff like that, I liked that. It was just around Christmastime. Well, I had to have my tree. I didn't care. So I walked downtown and I bought myself a big tree. I carried that tree home, and I'm knocking on the door, and the man who owns the home where we were renting the room says, "We have a tree already." I says, "But I have to have *my* tree," so he let me in with that tree. And, um, there was another Christmas, I wanted a tree again, but no car. So I asked the bus driver if I could come on with a tree. "Sure, I'll take you home!" I bought one that was almost half the aisle of the bus. They let me on with that tree; they took off and I had my tree again. I'm never without a Christmas tree.

And I remember one time we rented this small place that was out in Kitchen Corners [in Georgia]. One evening I'm home alone when suddenly something is banging on the house. I was terrified. I slowly looked out the window, and there was a big old goat banging his horns on the house. We did not stay there very long! And then we moved to Jefferson Road, it was very nice. The house was on a hill and across the street was a Negro Baptist church. And every Sunday you could hear them singing, I used to sit and listen to them.

And when I was down in Georgia, I don't speak too much about it, but that was a very good learning experience. I saw the town of Macon before the civil rights came to being. I saw all the colored always standing in groups by their self. Or, the white were always up in front and the colored were always somewhere in back by themselves. And I even

Fig. 29. Caroline and Edmund in Macon, Georgia, 1943

witnessed, when I was there, a man with a horsewhip was whipping one black man. And that man was rolling on the floor and that man was after him with that whip. And so, when all this came about, with the civil rights and Martin Luther King and that, I kind of knew what was going on, what they were talking about over there. They were everybody's maid. Everybody had a black girl or woman for a maid over there.

After the war was over, we had to bring all of our stuff home. Ed found this old car, a little Essex. We piled all our stuff into that car, and you couldn't stop because if you stopped it wouldn't go again. [laughter] So we came all the nine hundred miles never stopping, never doing anything until we finally got home with that car. [laughter]

Anyhow, we came home, and we moved in here [her family's house in Hilliards where she lives today], which I felt, when I think about it, was really bad. I mean, there was six kids [her brother and sisters], and we moved in. But we stayed there until Annette was born. Exactly about four years after we were married. And then Ed decided it was time to move. So, he walks out there, and the next thing, he's building this little house [on the same property as the family house], just three rooms, so we moved into that. And then, Eddie was born in there. We stayed there for seven years, I think, and then when they [her parents] sold the [house and the] farm, then we moved into here. I thought I was in heaven, you know, after living in that little place with no room or anything, I thought, "This is great." Then Helene was born.

I was about fifty-three years old [when she took a job cooking lunches at St. Stan's grade school]. They had no program, no outline, no nothing. You had to start everything from scratch, all your menus, and I remember taking a paper and a pencil and my recipes, and then, quick, multiplying everything by fifty, by one hundred kids, multiplying. And those pans that I used to cook in, they seemed this big, like big vats, when I started. [laughter]

Oh, that first week, I came home, it was on a Friday, and I laid down on the couch to rest. I did not wake up until Saturday morning at ten o'clock, they couldn't get me to bed, I just laid there and slept. Then it kept getting easier and easier for me. And I learned a lot of good things there. I can organize a big bazaar or dinner, I can organize a big party. I cooked dinners for bishops and for priests and nuns.

And I liked the kids, there was [pause] very often there was always one child having a really bad time, and somehow or another they would find their way into that kitchen. They would come in that kitchen, and then the teachers would chase them out and get mad. And I remember one little girl, she would come in and get a hug every day. She would watch the teachers there, and she would crawl in on her hands and knees, and come up in there to get a hug. I was really glad I did that, because when you work around little kids and teachers it's a positive thing. I'm not that good with older people that sit and complain about constipation, or this hurts or that hurts, or don't wanna do this. I do a lot better if I'm with younger people. And then when I stopped, then that wasn't a good thing either, because I missed all these positive experiences I used to get. I stopped working when I was seventy-one.

I'm this person that has always thought that, if you have no challenges, no mountains to climb, you die. I have to have goals, working, thinking, creating—and if I don't, it doesn't work. I took my driver's training, let's see, I wasn't very old. I was working in school, I was already working in school, so somewhere in my fifties, about fifty-eight, somewhere in there. I did everything. I mean, when I got to be about sixty or something, I got really strong. I don't understand what took me so long, but it, um, but that's the way it was.

I always wanted to hold our family together. Annette moved to California; our oldest daughter, and I worried that our family would fall apart. I thought Annette was so far away I would never be able to see her and she would not be able to come to me. So, I just decided, every year I would go and visit her. So I learned to fly.

So, the first time that I went it was to see Elizabeth [her granddaughter], and that was to New York, to LaGuardia Airport. Scared stiff! But I went. I've been scared a lot of times in my life, but it never deterred me from what I wanted to do. They were in New York a couple of years and then they moved to California. And so, that's when I decided I was going to go and see them. Again I got on the plane, scared to death! [Me: Were you by yourself?] By myself, all the time! And scared to death, but I made it and it worked out real good. I've been doing this for thirty years.

Being in California, I spent time with my grandkids, I was close to my daughter, and

Fig. 30. Caroline, Edmund, and their children Helene, Eddy, and Annette, 1955

after thirty years I still am close with my grandkids and with my daughter. And I also learned to love the West Coast. I love Carmel, Monterey, Montego Bay, San Francisco, Berkeley, I've been in all those places several times. And I love Tahoe. I love the oceans and the cliffs. I love the flowers. I love the West Coast. But I'm also glad to come home. But I still want to do it again, even though I'm almost eighty years old, I'm still planning on taking another trip to the West Coast. I'm planning on taking my twelve-year-old granddaughter with me.

The other thing that was important to me was to keep the Grasinskis all together. I had so many family reunions, I had Easter, I had bonfires with hot dogs, all the years. And our last gathering was July 13, 2002, for our sixtieth wedding anniversary that we celebrated. Keeping my family together was important. I was the caretaker, from the time I was a little girl, I was the only one who could give Mary [Mari] her bottle, and now I have the family reunions.

I made a commitment, and I'll keep that commitment if it kills me. And I mean, that's what I did. I wanted my family, I did it for my family, so that they would have a home when they got older. Now they got a home, anybody can come here. I made a commitment, it wasn't an easy thing, but like I said, I make a promise and I don't break promises like that. And it's okay. I look now, and I see that I'm the strong one, [laughs] that I am not the dumb one, or the stupid one, or the no-good one. And I see that I am a very strong, good person.

And things weren't always the way I would have liked, but I made a good life for us. And I never was unhappy. So, that's got something to do with them Grasinski girls laughing and crying. You know that goes with the Pawlowski girls [cousins], that goes with the Iciek girls [cousins]. Everyone is laughing. I remember Annette used to call up from California and she'd say, "Mom, I just called to hear you laugh." I still laugh.

7 ⫯⫯⫯ Kitchen Table Resistance

I USED TO PLAY basketball. I played when I was a girl, in the dark early evenings of Michigan winters. Out on the driveway court, fingers numb with cold, we played three-on-three driveway ball, suburban ball. At that age, six kids fit easily on the two-car-driveway court—take it out behind the crack, out of bounds is Veldman's garage and the chain-link fence. "Don't be jumping that fence to get the ball, walk around!" my father would yell. We jumped it anyway, trying not to rattle the chain-link.

In ninth grade I was still playing basketball, now on my first organized team. At about the same time, I developed an obsessive crush on Eddy Westerhof, a neighborhood boy who went to the public school. I had known Eddy for several years but only saw him in the summers, when the kids from the Catholic school, the Christian Reform school, and the public schools played together. In fact, when I was twelve, he was my summer boyfriend. That was after he knocked me to the ground playing baseball. I had challenged his "no girls can play" rule and went and stood between first and second bases on the diamond we mowed on the field behind our houses. Eddy came up to bat, hit the ball, rounded first and deliberately crashed into me, knocking me down. My glasses flew off and my world became disoriented for a few moments. I remember having my breath knocked out of me, but I also remember that it was okay. I knew the worst was over. I had no thought of crying, no tears welled up in my eyes, I didn't even think of the hit as being unfair. I stood up, not even bothering to brush off the sand, crouched over, put my glove on my knee, ready for the next batter. When the inning ended, I took my place in the rotation behind the last batter. The girls were in. Later that summer, I became his girlfriend and he rode me around on the handlebars of his Stingray bike. He kissed me once, but he had braces and it wasn't a good thing.

I lost track of him for a few years and then met him again in ninth grade, after I graduated from the Catholic grade school and went to the public high school. Eddy was a junior. He had grown a lot (so had I, by that time I was six feet tall) and he played basketball. Too embarrassed to actually talk to him, I stalked him instead. I watched him from my living room window while he shot free throws in his driveway. I learned his class schedule and knew when he would be walking down which halls and arranged it so I would pass him several times a day. I stole all the signs that the cheerleaders put on the players' lockers—"Whip the Huskies, Ed!" and "Sink the Sailors, Ed!" I went to every one of his games and recorded all his stats: shots attempted, shots made, offensive and defensive rebounds, assists, free throw attempts and completions.

That year, I also played ninth-grade basketball. The entire season consisted of four games and about as many practices. We had no real uniforms, just gym shirts with masking-tape numbers on them. One game we lost 20 to 4. We had no plays, we didn't pass the ball, we couldn't shoot well, we couldn't play defense, and no one taught us how. We were terrible. I was too aggressive for the referees and often fouled out early.

The following summer I finally talked to Eddy—and it was on a driveway court that I found the courage. It was the eve of my fifteenth birthday. He was shooting hoops with his friend Jim. My girlfriends and I rode over on our bikes and asked to play. Later that night he asked me out. We started dating. The kisses were much better without the braces, and pretty soon we were a couple. (He was called "pussy whipped" and his buddies "gave him his walking papers." My friends were impressed that I was dating a senior.)

As a senior, Ed started on the varsity basketball team, and as a sophomore, I started on the junior varsity team and moved up to varsity for tournament play. The boys did well that year, finishing second in the conference. But it was another bad year for us girls. Title IX had passed a few years earlier, but the girls' sports program remained underfunded. We had a coach who did not know how to play the game. She read to us from a book about how to dribble: "Look straight ahead and bring the ball up waist high— Mary, demonstrate for the others." We lost a lot of games, had no concept of strategy, didn't learn to do something as basic as a pick and roll, and once again I fouled out of a lot of games. Driveway ball with the boys had not prepared me for organized girls' sports. I was frustrated. It wasn't fun.

And then there were the catfights between the girls. The varsity players didn't like my having replaced one of their friends when I moved up; *i* over, the girl I replaced was someone who had a crush on Eddy. It was decided by the informal girls' "committee" that Eddy should be with her and not me. They sabotaged my locker, taunted me, excluded me, told stories about me that insinuated I was "putting out." I have no fond memories of playing basketball—the bad coaching, the silly girls, the lack of any good players, and the damn fact that I kept fouling out. One more thing: I never saw myself as "pretty" when I played basketball. My mascara always ran and the sweat left streaks in my foundation. I never thought of my six-foot-tall body as beautiful or athletic but only as something that was big and awkward and committed fouls.

I had more fun being the girlfriend of a basketball player than I had playing basketball. "Girlfriend" of the starting center was a great role, and it made for fond high school memories. Thinking back, I still can feel the flush of status when, after the game, Eddy came out of the locker room, still in his uniform, sweaty and red-skinned, looking so desirable to me and (I assumed) every other girl milling around, and he would toss me the keys to the car and yell, "Go warm it up!" I loved that. I was Eddy's girl, and that was so cool.

I played basketball one more year and then I quit. I tried out for the cheerleading squad and made it. If you were a cheerleader you couldn't play fall or winter sports. My father, I believe, always disapproved of that decision. At the time, I didn't regret it one bit. I didn't sweat my makeup off and I liked how I looked in the short skirt of the cheerleading outfit much better than the basketball uniform (and so did my math teacher, who made a point of commenting on my legs whenever I wore the short-skirted outfit).

I didn't play basketball again until I was forty years old. My partner Tim invited me into a game with mostly middle-aged men who wear knee braces and protective eyewear. He taught me how to post up, to finish my shots, to roll after the pick, and that a moving screen is a foul. Today my body feels strong and beautiful, and it works. This is what amazes me most. I can do a turnaround jump shot (though it seldom falls in), I can pull down a rebound, and I am learning to do a head fake. I feel like a girl again, a kid, back on the driveway, playing three on three.

It took me more than twenty years to feel that I had lost something when I stopped playing basketball. I was well into my midthirties when I presented a paper at an academic conference that began with the sentence, "I am not a feminist." Why would I say that? I knew gender inequality existed, and I even took action to change it in the small world within which I lived. On the block, I forced the boys to let the girls play baseball. In grade school, I challenged the nuns' rule that only boys should be on the safety patrol and was subsequently elected lieutenant captain. In college, the traditional "Suicide Stomp" at Notre Dame (a keg and an ounce at ten different houses) was a completely male-dominated affair until we lobbied to include a girls' house and became the kick-off house the next year. Because of these actions, I did not feel powerless or constrained by my gender.[1] And if women (e.g., those feminists) did feel that way, then I figured it was their fault. Change it or stop whining. I was a postfeminist "girl," someone who had benefited from the struggles of the women before me, someone who believed in and expected gender equality but did not see the need to get "all political" about it.[2]

At college in the late 1970s I was introduced to white middle-class feminist theory. I remember taking an assertiveness training course for my psychology degree. The white male professor kept emphasizing how women are passive, submissive, and get their power through manipulation. While I did not accept the stereotype of woman as weak, I did mistake structural subordination for behavioral submissiveness. I think this misperception was one reason I rejected white woman's feminism, as well as the fact that I did not see myself (or the role model/archetypal women in my life, the Girls) as being submissive, powerless women.[3] I did not see women as victims. Moreover, white feminist literature promoted a middle-class set of expectations and values that were critical of my mother for "just" staying home, for not having a "career," and for taking care of my father's needs. My mother rejected these criticisms of the life she had chosen, and I was somewhat reluctant to accept a framework that undervalued my mother.

My feelings about feminism began to change when I was introduced to black feminist literature, in particular Patricia Hill Collins, bell hooks, Paula Giddings, and Audre Lorde.[4] Each of these writers presents strong women acting within and against the constraints of the matrix of gender, race, and class domination. Patricia Hill Collins, in *Black Feminist Thought*, reconfigures power to be connection with someone, not control over them, and, as such, women are powerful. Paula Giddings, in *Where and When I En-*

ter, talks about slave women reclaiming their lives by aborting their ch as a protest against slavery—the ultimate act of self-denial, portrayed more graphically through the character of Sethe in Toni Morrison's *Beloved.* Audre Lorde, in *Zami,* presents an image of a black lesbian resisting efforts of whites, heterosexuals, and blacks to define who she is. Strong women. Tough women. Tina Turner type of women. Women who pushed back against the structure.

These black feminists wrote about women differently than the white feminists I had read.[5] Black feminists depict women as powerful, as actively pushing against the structures that press upon them. Their writing is liberating, aggressive, in-your-face writing that reminds me of how I played driveway ball with the boys. Their women are self-reliant, resourceful, and autonomous—not dependent, weak, and submissive. Aida Hurtado, a professor of psychology, argues that "Feminists of Color have theorized from a position of strength rather than a position of victimhood."[6] In contrast, she argues, white womanhood has been constructed as frailty and weakness.[7]

Of course, many white women do not define themselves as frail and weak. Certainly, the Grasinski Girls, bearers of children and keepers of family, do not. When I ask Caroline if she thinks "men are stronger than women" she answers, "Maybe physically, guys are maybe stronger, but I don't think that they are, no, I think women are strong. Just looking around me, I think that women are strong. They can hold up to adversity, that's what I'm talking about, mainly." Sociologist Susan Krieger believes women are strong because they have to survive the ridicule, the objectification, and the subordination of their status. "Women are often depicted as weak when just the opposite is so. I think only very strong individuals could absorb as much pain as women do."[8] And journalist Natalie Angier writes, "If the world's women went on strike, the world of work would effectively stop, and you cannot say that with certainty for the enterprises of men. For the vast majority of women, the injunction to be strong would ring silly. They are strong of necessity, by sweat and callus."[9]

Working-class women in particular are strong because they have to be, and they tell heroic tales about each other being strong. They have a "Buck up!" attitude. This is what it means to be a good woman—you don't kill yourself or run away when things are tough. You stick with a marriage because you made a commitment. You make it work for your children. You take care of others. You work to be independent. You learn to drive when you are fifty-eight years old. You carry a Christmas tree onto a bus because it is important that you have one. Angel learned to mow the lawn at the age of sixty-four, when her husband was recovering from an operation, despite the fact that she has three sons and two sons-in-law living close by who would gladly have done it. She did not want to "bother" them, she said, she could do it herself. Caroline admires her mother, who got on top of a table to hang curtains when she was nine months pregnant. And when asked to name women she respects, Caroline spoke of her aunts.

> My aunts, my Aunt Rose Iciek, and my Aunt Sophie. My Aunt Rose Iciek was left with these children. [Her husband] committed suicide and left her with these nine or ten children, and she just pulled herself together, went back to college, raised all these kids—you just have to respect somebody that does that. She went to school in the day, at night she was sittin' there sewing clothes for all them girls, and crying and everything. But she just did it. She never took "no" for an answer. She was such a strong lady. No matter what, you could find a way to do it, you could fix it. And then Aunt Sophie was just as strong of a woman. She was just as much a woman of integrity, she raised her family of ten children and nursed her ailing husband, and kept her house and cleaned it until she was almost into her nineties.

Caroline admires strength in the face of adversity. This is also evident in the respect she has for her daughter, Annette, who raised her two children alone after she divorced their father. At the age of fifty-two, Annette, already a registered nurse, went back for more schooling to protect her occupational position in a changing health care system.

Strength is a form of power that originates in the self. Power is also located in the structures of domination. When we concentrate on structural inequality, we portray women as victims of gender oppression denied access to resources in patriarchal systems of power.[10] But when we look for women's resistance, we find their strength. The focus on structure emphasizes powerlessness; the focus on resistance emphasizes agency, the hidden power of the less powerful.

|||

Because the Grasinski Girls spent most of their lives in the private sphere, it is in the domain of the home that they struggle for power. My father had front-stage power, but my mother had veto power that she exercised backstage and executed in the kitchen. If we could convince her, then she would convince him. We never argued our case to him. He sat at the head of the dinner table and said, "No, no, no"; she sat at the side of table and did not contradict him. Later, we would make our private appeal to her, sitting on the toilet while she soaked in the bathtub. In the morning she would slip us the keys, or the ten dollars, or give permission to go to the beach. How she managed to do this escaped us, but if she assented, then he consented.

She said she knew from the beginning of her marriage it was about control, and she fought hard to have the control. "I always thought it was the men who needed the liberation. I never felt like I didn't have power. I control the money and make all the decisions. So did my mother." Angel refused to cede control over certain household chores, even after her husband retired and she continued to work full-time. What looked like an unequal division of labor was in fact her desire to exert her authority.

> Because, even though he would fix supper and do the dishes, I still had the job of paying all the bills, buying all the presents, picking out everything, planning everything. And then he would always say, "Well, I'll pay the bills." But I didn't want to give up that control, so it was my own doing. Or he would say, "I'll buy all the birthday cards and mail them." But I knew he would buy, like, cheap ones, and so I didn't want to give up that control. And I'm in control of the social life or the trip planning. But I think he likes that I get out the map and say, "We're going here and here and here." I really think that he does like that. He may not admit it. But certain things like that, I'm in control of it. So, the same with the finances. I've always done that and now it's just easier. But he looks at the checkbook, and it's not that I'm spending something that I'm not supposed to.

Nadine has similar control during vacations. She said she follows the philosophy of Mae West: "A cowgirl gets up in the morning, decides what she wants to do, and then she does it." And her husband now has his own version: "A cowboy gets up in the morning, listens to what the cowgirl wants to do, and then he does it."

But what happens when the cowboy doesn't want to do what the cowgirl does? Angel said that, on issues that mattered to her, she stood her ground.

> There are just things that I had to fight for, and I wasn't about to give in. And most of the time he did! I don't think I ever lost an argument. And

once in a while, if I did, it ended up that it was better that I didn't get my way. I don't remember instances, but I can remember at the time thinking, "Yes, this is better," that I didn't get what I wanted. But generally, if I fought hard enough, I got it. [Me: How would you fight?] Just talking. Yeah. I had no secret weapon, I was just, like, "No!" Just being stubborn. Crying, maybe, I don't know. Trying to get through to him. Wear him down. We always talked a lot, a lot, in private. We didn't swear or anything. It's just like, when I would get him alone, it was, like, "Why did you do that? Why did you say that?" Blah, blah, blah.

Their power might be hidden—negotiations are done behind closed doors or between the sheets—but the end result is that they had some control, over some things. As Angel said about her own mother, "She was in control, and I never really realized this until I got older." From the fact that she "gave the spankings" to the fact that she decided to move them back out into the country, Helen was an active player in the household. Fran agrees: "She ran the whole household and everything. Oh, yeah, all the bills and everything. She was a good organizer and a good mathematician. She contacted all the insurance men and everything. Whatever they had to do, she always did it. I don't remember if she bossed my dad, I don't remember, I don't think she did that. She kind of bossed her own, but you know you have to have discipline." She did not have power "over" Joe, her husband, but she had a powerful presence in the household. She was the matriarch, and while she did not rule the kingdom, she did rule the castle, which was typical in Polish-American families. Helena Znaniecka Lopata writes that, in second- and third-generation Polish-American families, women were often in control of the checkbook and were the top authority in matters of the house, including consumer behavior, discipline patterns, and recreation.[11]

But are these actions—controlling the checkbook, organizing the social schedule, disciplining children—representations of power? Judith Andre distinguishes power from authority. She defines authority as the right to exercise power, and argues that women often have power without having authority.[12] Women often have power without having authority, she argues. This is sometimes called "feminine wiles," and refers to power through manipulation. Women can get their way, but they have to get their way without people knowing they get their way; they cannot announce their power, they cannot claim their power. They hold a sneaky sort of reign from the side of the table.[13]

Deborah Tannen disagrees with Andre. She argues that covert ways of getting your way are not deceptions of power, but a woman's way of being in the world. Women seek connection. Control from the head of the table in an authoritative position may represent higher status, but it is not the best way to nurture relations. Forcing the issue or demanding your way often ruptures connections. "But if you get your way because others happened to want the same thing, or because they offered freely, the payoff is in rapport. You're neither one-up nor one-down but happily connected with others whose wants are the same as yours."[14] Being one-up from others is less desirable to these women than being side by side with them. Thus, sitting at the side of the table is a preference, not a sign of powerlessness.

Building relations rather than declaring dominance works better for people in subordinate positions. Subordinates have limited access to power, but they are not necessarily weak or powerless. Power is found in the structural relations, it is conferred by racial, class, and gender structures. But individuals also have power as strength, in their agency. In fact, their strength derives from their position of subordination. Women have to be strong to survive. Women rule from the side of the table and reign from the bathtub because they are smart enough to know that this represents the best chance for them to get their way. To aggressively push their agenda is less likely to bring the desired results. And the desired results are not only to get their way, but to do so without threatening the relationship.

And yet, Aida Hurtado argues that "white women have been *seduced* into compliance because they needed to reproduce biologically the next generation for the power structure."[15] This seduction leads white women to seek intimacy with white men, the dominant group, and this intimacy requires white women to be coy, indirect, and manipulative in their pursuit of power so as not to disrupt their intimate relations with men.

Both Andre's and Hurtado's understanding of power grows from a male-centric definition of power which, in its simplest terms, can be defined as the ability to make someone do what you want them to do. It is, in a real sense, power "over" someone. In contrast, Patricia Hill Collins redefines power relations not as control "over" but as a connection "to" someone, so that power is energy and strength.[16] When power is seen as connection and not domination, as strength not oppression, then we can develop models of power that resonate more with a woman's understanding of the world, one that values connections with people rather than autonomy and independence. Deborah Tannen agrees. She asserts that, because women are oriented in the world to promote connection, they are more likely to value equality and resist hierarchies of power.[17] This was evident in both Caroline and Nadine's discussion of equality in an earlier chapter. Strength is found in community, through connections. Even in prayer, strength is derived not from the omnipotent power of God to deliver the goods, but from the relation established with Jesus. Empowerment for women is done in the group, not by the self. Mary Field Belenky and her colleagues also noted that women believe that "they can strengthen themselves through empowerment of others. . . . Through listening and responding, they draw out the voices and minds of those they help to raise up. In the process they often come to hear, value, and strengthen their own voices and minds as well."[18] Similarly, Collins's understanding of empowerment is that the self and the other both benefit when we "lift as we climb."[19]

Rather than imposing one's will on another, these women understand strength as the capacity for compassion, the ability to care for another, especially in adverse situations. When I ask Nadine, "who is stronger, men or women," she rejects my either-or dichotomy and says "both are strong." She then defines the internal, emotional strength of women.

> I think women are very strong. Women have always been very strong. [Me: In what ways?] Starting with the Blessed Mother, you know, how she was chosen to be the mother of God, Christ. She had to be a strong woman to do something like that and to watch Him being crucified. I mean, how much stronger can you get? And I think of all these pioneer women. I think women have always been strong. I think women in motherhood, you have to be a strong person to be a mother, you have to be strong for your husband. I think women are very strong and I don't think that men are stronger than women, I don't think so. They may think they are, but I don't think they're stronger. I can think of a lot of women who have gone through a lot of troubles and sicknesses and yet came out. I think men are not as emotional as women—well, some are sensitive and some are not very sensitive—but that is not strength, not being emotional is not strength.

Susan Krieger explains this strength to which Nadine refers as an artifact of women's subordinate position. Because women have few external resources, such as physical strength and armies, "we have learned to use internal resources well" in order "to absorb the hurt and misery others feel and to convert these internally into the strength needed to help others. . . . Part of being female is to weather adversity, to persevere despite what is asked of one, because one must."[20]

As Nadine pointed out, Catholic women are shown how to be strong through the example of the mother of Jesus, who carried the world's burden of grief.[21] These women absorbed the grief of their children and smoothed the way for the family functions; they were the peacemakers, the menders, the ones who stayed awake long into the night praying for their children's safety. They comforted the class wounds of their husbands, cried with their neighbors when they experienced loss, and cleaned, cooked, mended, and listened and ministered to those who had emotional, physical, and social needs.

|||

Black feminists raised my consciousness and helped me to see the structures of gender inequality. What I saw angered me. I saw gender inequality everywhere: in the everyday misogyny of salesmen, the exploitation of women in television commercials, the masculine bullying of academic administrators, the absence of women leaders in the wake of 9-11. I saw it in the market, the political arena, the academy, in church, sports, clothing, income differentials, and the domestic division of labor.[22] Arguments in my household became overdetermined because everything was "gendered." I could not do the dishes without this being symptomatic of the overall unequal division of labor. My anger and gender rage fit the image of crabby white feminists captured in the title of Wini Breines's book *Young, White, and Miserable.*[23]

Yet the Grasinski Girls are not troubled by their gender. They are not miserable; they love being women. They are happy mothers, not angry feminists. What is there to be angry about? When I see their happy smiling faces, I have to wonder if they are oblivious to gender inequality. But when discussing the issue of equality at her worksite, Angel knew that the men had higher status and larger paychecks, and that the secretaries, all women, made less. She did not think these differences had much to do with intelligence or ability. In fact, she implies the secretaries are perhaps smarter and work harder than the men.

I think that the field that I worked in, office work, that women always worked harder than men and got paid way, way less. This is the secretary part. It wasn't like you were top secretary, but you always did so much, and kept everything in order and everything, and they just figured you'd do this. And you'd catch their mistakes, and rectify them, and have everything done, and they expect you to do that, but yet you weren't compensated. The man is getting these five thousand a year raises, eight thousand, and you see them, and they're just sittin' there with their feet up, and it's like, "What the hell does he do to earn that?" And here you're working from the time you get there and you're not making nothing like that.

Well, so they say it's the higher-uppers, management, account executives [said sarcastically], yet you couldn't see them actually really earning this. But maybe by who they were, the companies they represented, they were doing a good job, or otherwise we probably would have lost the account or they would have been out. So I'm sure they were doing their job, but it's just how we sort of perceive them. Everywhere I've worked it's been that way. But they must have brains to do what they do, because we don't run companies, we just do the servitude, the typing and things. . . . I've never had a hand in the running of the business, so I might not be good at that. But as far as finding errors in what they do [I can do that].

Sometimes when I do the payroll, I think, "Well, I should be making more money." And then you look and every other woman is making what you're making, and you think, "Well, this isn't fair." But then, you're not an account executive, and the woman that is, she makes as much as the men. So there, you can't say anything against that. And I never would want that position. Anyplace I have ever worked, I was always content to do exactly what I was doing. I never wanted to move up, to be office manager, and in fact at Van Kuiken's they asked me to be office manager and I declined. I didn't want to be in charge of anybody!

Angel moves between structural and personal explanations—men make more money and this must be because they do their jobs well, but she can't really see exactly what it is that they do. In fact, what she sees as a secretary are their mistakes—accounting mistakes, spelling mistakes, grammar mistakes— and she has to correct them.[24] But even though she doesn't know exactly what skills they have that command a higher salary, she assumes that the world is fair, and that if they are making more money they must surely deserve it, they must have some knowledge or skills that she is not sure she has, because she never tried to run a business. However, she does not want power over (or to be in charge of) anyone.

But Angel does not examine why she did not want to be a manager. She does not articulate how her class and gender location influenced not only her structural choices but her desires and values as well. She values motherhood over occupational prestige and income, connection over authority. Gendered expectations allowed her to be content as a secretary in ways her male bosses most likely would not have been.

Angel does not blame herself for her low salary. She sees herself as smart and believes that she could have been a manager if she wanted. She can see the inequality when she does the payroll but she does not respond with bitterness or overt anger toward her boss and male co-workers, even if she does think she should be better compensated. Being aware of inequality and not being upset about it is not always what Lillian Rubin calls "resigned acceptance of the limits of the possibilities."[25] Angel resists the inequality in her mind. Believing she is worth more than she is paid, or that the labor of secretaries is as valuable as the labor of managers, is an idea that challenges and redefines the societal valuations of clerical workers.[26] Her redefinition does not change the objective conditions (she does not narrow the wage differential), but it does challenge the authority of the dominant group. In this way, self-definition becomes an act of empowerment; resistance is manifest in her happiness, which represents a refusal to allow the oppressive structures to control her affect. It takes emotional strength (not delusion) to live in subordinate positions and continue to smile, sing, and treat people with respect.

|||

My chest used to puff out and I'd smile and swagger whenever some guy told me that I didn't "throw like a girl" or that I played ball "as good as the guys." But the statement "I don't play like a girl" devalued myself, because I was a girl. What did it mean that in order for me to be good at sports I had to deny my gender? I don't throw a softball like a guy, I throw like a girl. This is how a girl throws a softball. Look at me, watch me, I scoop it out of the ground, my mitt hard against the dirt, I am on the run, my left leg in front holding my weight, and then in one smooth movement I reach into my glove with my right hand. Automatically, unconsciously, I pull out the ball with my palm. It fits perfectly, like it has always been there, and then I lean back onto my right foot, my back arches as my right shoulder dips back and down, I cock my arm, bringing it straight out almost behind my back, and then, with elbow-leaning, wrist-snapping velocity, I hurl the ball, releasing it when my arm is directly in front of my shoulder, my hand pointing at the glove of the first baseman. I release and the ball sails, hard and straight, over to first. Out! That is how a girl throws a ball.

On the first day of my seminar entitled "Interpreting Women's Lives" at the College of the Holy Cross, I asked my students to recall when they first became aware of their gender. Most of the women told stories of discrimination and denial. In many cases it was a story of wanting to play with trucks or wanting to wear jeans instead of dresses with bows. One girl told how she secretly ripped the lace off of her little white socks. Others told of desiring Matchbox toys and Transformers and hating to play with dolls. Their stories were narrated with much bravado. These are "antigirl" stories, and the message is "I was a tomboy and didn't want to be a girl." Mari also tells this sort of story of her childhood. "I don't remember liking to play with dolls. I had this big old fat doll that I pulled its arms off. I didn't like them. It almost seems like from day one I loved to be outdoors, I didn't like being inside, it was, like, too cramped." These girls wanted to play "like the boys" outside, with trucks, in an active not passive mode. They have accepted a value system that defines girl things as bad and boy things as good.[27] Internalizing the message that girl things (and later, women things) are inferior contributes to reproducing systems of oppression.

To resist the act (of dressing up, playing with dolls, becoming a mother) because this act is devalued in society is one form of resistance, but to resist the devaluation of the act is another form. Both forms of resistance—resisting the label and resisting the label as negative—occur in the realm of consciousness. Revising and improving negative self-images empowers women; rewriting the script, learning to value "girl" things, is a lesson in self-love. When we refuse to believe that we are dumb, or don't throw a ball well, then we resist owning a set of beliefs that tears us down, devalues us, mocks our ways of being. When we defiantly insist that being "silly girls" is an okay way to be, because it is a fun way to strengthen our connections, we resist the denigration of girl fun as trivial. When we define what we did "as girls" to include throwing softballs and shooting hoops, we resist eclipsing our girlhood from our childhood.

We more often think of resistance as public and collective acts, for example, as social movements for change that challenge institutional structures of inequality.[28] We give much less attention to resistance in the private sphere because it is less visible and at the level of the individual.[29] As a result, we can miss much of what is resistance and mistake non-action for resignation. One of the ways the Grasinski Girls resisted was to refuse to accept a devaluation of their lives and their womanhood. They liked being women; in fact, as Angel explains in regard to herself, they preferred to be women.

> I would describe myself as a nice person, a person that people like. I would describe myself as someone who laughs too much. [laughs] I would describe myself as someone people can depend on. I would describe myself probably with more positive things than negative things, from the fact that I do like myself. I like what I stand for. I feel really lucky that I was born a woman and not a man. I've always felt that way. I've always felt that I'm really glad I'm a woman. Women can have friends they connect with, and not only the part about having children, but I think they have these really close inner feelings, and they're free to express them, and they can just bond with other women, and I just always loved that part about being a woman. But I see men in the office [lowers her voice and makes it gruff] talking about sports, or talking about this. Women get together [voice raises, there is a lilt and joy] and we're just, "Aagh, *your* sex life! I haven't done that in the last year!" [laughing, talking fast and excited] And you're not ashamed, and you can joke about womanly things and about your children—and men will never say nothing bad about their children [lower, gruff voice], "My children are always really good," and women [laughing, high, excited voice], "Ooh, you won't believe what this one did, I can't stand this one," and you're, like, free to express yourself. And someone else will understand you. So I've always just been really, really glad I was born a woman.

Angel, like her sisters, sees herself as a smart, interesting, and beautiful person. She once said, "They told me at work that I was very analytical. I knew that was a good thing, even if I didn't know what the word meant. But I knew I was good. I could do anything they asked me to do." She may recognize there is inequality in the world in terms of the paychecks, which she does not think is right, but she does not have to denigrate the women's world in order to liberate herself. She values her range of emotions, her laughter, her rich connections with others, and rejects the ambitious, status-seeking, non-emotional role expectations assigned to men. Nadine is the same.

> I like myself. I think I got a lot of good qualities. I think I'm relatively attractive. I always try to look the best that I can. And I like to dress up. I like

people. I like to pray. I think I'm a good person. And, uh, what else about myself. [pause] I guess I'm a person who is artistic, a person who loves music, of most any kind, a person who's generous, a person who loves to do things for other people, to make other people happy. A person who is happy and thankful for the many blessings. A person who loves every phase of my life.

While these women may be constructing a positive image of themselves for the sake of the sociologist niece and her public document, we nonetheless must ask, why the positive construction? Why the happy face? How the happy face? How do they manage to have such strong feelings of self-worth when they live in a society where they are second-class citizens, treated unequally, and, as Ann Crittenden documents, when the work that they do as mothers and housewives is undervalued? How do they manage to continue to love themselves? Caroline said, "I was blessed with a pretty decent personality—a little laid back, a little generous. I don't get upset over every little thing that's said or if something doesn't go right." Why not?

We live our lives between our mothers and our daughters. It was from their mother that the Grasinski Girls inherited the wealth of woman-love. Helen gave her daughters a strong sense of self-worth. While she may not have encouraged them to pursue their education, she did teach them to value who they were. This is evident in Nadine's story, when Helen's voice stands as a corrective to the Felicians' preaching that novices were only misery and sin. Helen told her daughters they were good mothers and good nuns and that they had soft skin. She not only raised them, she raised them up and rejoiced in their being. Mari recalls:

> We grew up with this really strong sense of value, of being worthwhile people, and yet, as far as words went, it wasn't like they ever sat down and said, "Now, I want you to learn to do this." But yet, throughout her whole life, and I find this with my children, it's like a joy every time you see them. And that was the kind of feeling I got from my mom, that every time she saw me it was, like, a good thing. So, I grew up thinking I was special. That I was destined for great things. [laughs] It's like, yeah, that was the feeling she conveyed, joy is the only word I can think of, and even more so as I got older.

As Mari said, they feel the same way about their children, and in doing so they pass on woman-love.

Fig. 31. Angel and Nadine with their mother Helen, c. 1985

But the Grasinski Girls also gave something else to their daughters, something that they themselves did not have. They encouraged their daughters to get an education. In fact, several of them fought to make sure their daughters went to college. Caroline describes one such struggle.

Kids show talents in certain directions. I mean, nobody fostered that or did anything about that before. They clothed you, fed you, loved you, and made sure you loved God. Those were the things that you did. And then, sometimes, maybe when you're thirty-five, forty-five, then, then the stuff just starts coming out of you, like that. And if somebody would've fostered this, like to go on to school, and your good points were brought out and everything—[but] they didn't do that before. And that wasn't a very good thing. 'Cause then you had these people, as they got older, then all these things would come out and they got frustrated and stuff like that, you know, they would've liked to have done something like that. They just assumed they're just gonna go work on a farm or go to the factory. Nobody stopped to think that there was something else that they were capable of. When Annette [her daughter] was wanting to go to school, I was after all them to see they got good marks, which they did, but [her father], all he wanted for her was to get a job working in Hilliards, in the tavern. I couldn't, that's not what I thought it should be. We used to argue every night before supper that she's going to be a nurse, that she must go into nursing. And I couldn't see not wanting any more for them than to go into a tavern and be a waitress there or something, be a barmaid.

And for Angel it was the same.

Those years [raising children], it was hard, because we didn't think alike. We might have thought alike on discipline, but there was a lot of things that we didn't think alike. Like, he didn't think that women should go to college, and I had to fight so hard that you had to go. And when Diane wanted to go, he said, "Why don't you let her get a job in a factory? She will make so much more." And at that point, even women couldn't get good factory jobs anymore. . . . It was like we fought each other tooth and nail. But I had to. I had no choice. I wasn't going to not let you go to school! I mean, there are just things that I had to fight for, and I wasn't about to give in.

It is important to remember that both Angel and Caroline married husbands who were skilled laborers, while the other three married men with professional careers. This is a class struggle as much as it is a gender struggle. Those from the middle class had an easier time going to college. In the next generation, of the eleven granddaughters of Helen Grasinski, nine of them have post-secondary degrees: one Ph.D., three working on master's degrees, four more with bachelor's degrees, and one associate's degree. The careers of the Grasinski granddaughters include nursing, education, and retail, and almost all of them are mothers.

The Grasinski Girls are more likely to struggle against inequality as it operates in the lives of their daughters. While Caroline argued earlier for a gendered division of labor, when it came to her daughter she wanted what was a male-dominated profession to become more open to women. She said, "They should be treated equal, but they're not. You know, in jobs and stuff like that, men still have control of things. Like where [my daughter] works, as a chef, it's a man's world and they're not too eager to have women." Judith Lorber argues that, by caring for others, women become more selfless than selfish, they spend more time listening than speaking, and they become caretakers of others rather than themselves, so that motherhood transforms them into women less likely to fight for their own rights but more likely to fight for the rights of their children.[30]

The Grasinski Girls learned from their mother to value their selves and they taught their daughters to value their selves. Helen told her daughters they were beautiful, and her beautiful daughters told their daughters to go to college. What else do they want for their daughters? They want them to wait before they get married and start having children, they want them to develop their individual selves apart from a family. "If you could give any advice to young women today," I asked Caroline, and she finished my statement without pausing.

> Well, for one thing, I would not get involved with men. I would first find out about myself, and find out who I am, and what I am, and then take it from there. It's better when you get married to know who you are as a person, what you like. From the time you're eighteen, nineteen, twenty, maybe twenty-seven, you change a lot. I mean, you mature, you change. I think it's a good idea for women to know their self first. 'Cause, otherwise, you spend your whole life trying to find out, and you don't ever do that, and so that's what I would say.

I asked Angel what hopes and dreams she had for her daughters. She said, "I hoped that they would be happy, in whatever. I didn't hope that they would just marry and have babies or have a career, but I hoped that they would be content, maybe more than happy." And Nadine's hopes for Marie Chantal: "that she finds someone who looks and sings like Elvis and acts like Jesus."

> I would like her to get married, and have a family, when she's about twenty-seven years old. I don't want her to get married now. She's too young. I want her to have religion and have faith, a deep faith. And that's about it. And be able to, like I said, get married when she's older and have a child or two, and be able to work here [at the winery] and be successful and happy. That's about it. Those are my hopes and dreams for her. Religion, a man, and a place to work, what else is there? Money? [laughs]

They want their daughters to have it all—to have a marriage, to know motherhood, to develop their individual selves, to have careers outside the home, and to be happy. How is it that they can want more for their daughters than they had, and still be happy with what they have? They understand that "it was a different time" when they were young; they received strong directives to get married and have children early, and little encouragement to pursue an education. But that does not mean they cannot want something different for their daughters. We make our choices from the options available, and we can like the choices we made and still seek to expand the choices we give to our children.

The Grasinski Girls lived in female-dominant environments. Their woman's world—the kitchen, the convent, the obstetrics ward, and the secretarial pool—gave them the space to self-define. In the kitchen, talking to other women, their sentences loop and swirl and become connected with each other's, as they lose track of and then recapture fleeting topics. Conversation is not logical argument—it is connection. Life is not hierarchical ordering —but side-by-side connection. Their resistance is their refusal to believe this is wrong. Their resistance is to prefer to be women. Their resistance is more personal and private, but it is resistance. Kitchen table resistance. When I ask Mari to describe herself she does so without hesitating.

> I was somebody that was alive, enjoying life and everything. And it's weird, because you have this image of yourself, because of everything you've been through, and then [my daughter] suddenly says, "Well, you're so fluffy!" And I'm like, "God! What?" And she said, "Well, you know, you're not rough, and you don't talk loud." And that's true, I don't. In her eyes I'm just fluffy Mom, fat Mom, I guess. In my eyes, no! Well, maybe now I'm getting fluffier [laughs] but in my eyes, no-o! I did pretty much what I wanted to do, within a certain limit. That's how I see myself.

She defines herself. She does not let others, neither her daughter nor the sociologist niece, define who she is.

Being around women, they could more easily dismiss a male-centric set of values that devalued them. The kitchen is the space of feeling, connection, and relationships. Tears and laughter are more acceptable in the kitchen than in the boardroom. On the ball diamond, tears signal weakness, and you learn to despise them. Don't let them see you cry, learn to throw like a boy, learn to fight like a man—this is what you learn on the ball field, this is what you learn playing with men. But if you sit in the kitchen with the Grasinski Girls, you learn that tears flow as freely as laughter.

A Grasinski Granddaughter

ON A SNOWY WEDNESDAY evening in February, I walk uphill to the Hart Center and arrive just after the tip-off to the "best game in town"—Division I women's basketball at the College of the Holy Cross in Worcester. I plan to meet my colleague who has sat in the same seat for the last twenty years— front row, upper deck, center court. I don't look for him when I enter. Instead, I pause at the first wooden set of bleachers to give myself time to absorb the tears and swallow the sadness. The sadness makes me feel foolish, so I pretend the tears are not slipping from the corners of my eyes and rolling onto my cheeks, into the crevice of my closed lips, down the curve of my neck, under my shirt collar. It will pass, tears always do. The cheerleaders cheer, the crowd is standing and clapping now. As I watch the game come downcourt, the tall forward takes the pass, fakes to the outside, and then pivots inside under the basket and tucks it in. I would like to have done that, but didn't. Not couldn't, but didn't. No one forced me to stop playing basketball. I made that choice. But I made it, as Friedrich Engels said, under very definite assumptions and conditions. Nonetheless, I miss that person I might have been.

Had I been born twenty years later, there's a good chance I would have played college basketball. And Caroline, had she been born thirty years later, would probably have gone to college. We both miss the figment of the possible we can only now imagine. Caroline, describing her mother Helen, said, "I think that she maybe would've liked to have been in some kind of business, selling or doing something. She loved working with numbers. I think she would've made a good person selling real estate. And she raised her family, but I think that really, inside, that she would've just liked something else, that she would've been capable of something like that, *that she could've been, but she wasn't* [emphasis mine]." What we imagine and pursue as possible is influenced by our social locations within specific sociohistorical contexts. Where we came from, the settings of our childhood, carve the grooves of our life course. Sometimes the structures that shape the choices we are given are obvious, sometimes they are not.

I don't remember 3309 Boone Street being an easy house to read in. There were lamps by Mom's and Dad's chairs—his for the newspaper and cross-word puzzles, hers for the newspaper and sewing—but no reading lamps for us kids, no den, no study. A long desk was built into the wall when the base-ment was finished and made into a family room, but it was in the same room as the television so it wasn't useful for studying. The one bookcase in the house, four shelves, three feet long, was next to that desk, and it held a few hardcover books—*Gone with the Wind, To Kill a Mockingbird, Cardinal Sin*—along with a set of encyclopedias, bought in 1957, the result of an aggres-sive salesman finding eager young working-class parents who hadn't consid-ered that they would become dated by the time the children began to use them.

When I was in ninth grade I discovered an old desk in the basement of the house where I babysat. I bartered my time for it. My father helped me strip it and then we stained it antique blue. My freshman year, when I had the only single bedroom in the house, I remember how delicious it felt to be studying algebra in my own room at my own desk with my own lamp.

In the working-class schools in our neighborhood, the English teachers did not correct my papers—no red marks pointed out my split infinitives, misspellings, or misuse of words.[1] I guess simply being able to write coherent sentences counted for something in my high school. The teachers spent their time with students who had fewer skills. For example, in my tenth-grade his-tory class, only three students passed the first exam. The teacher sent the three of us down to the library for the next few weeks and retaught the material to the rest of the students. I didn't learn much history that year. No counselor, teacher, or parent encouraged me to take college preparatory courses, so in eleventh grade I stopped taking history, math, and science and signed up for woodshop, choir, art, gym, and family living (this course taught us that we shouldn't get married and have babies too soon because that cost a lot of money and we wouldn't have much). Many of my friends were in school only half of the day—in the afternoons they were at vo-tech jobs, doing clerical work at places like Montgomery Ward. Only about 10 percent of the graduating class went on to college, and most of them went to the local junior college.

I did not recognize any of these missing privileges—lamps, good teachers, active counselors—as problems, growing up. Back then, my voice as the daughter of a Thursday-night bowler was as soothing to me as a radio telecast of a Detroit Tigers game on a Sunday afternoon. Growing up in a working-class community, my reference group included the other working-class kids, and in comparison to them we were at the front of the assembly line—we were smart and beautiful, we played sports well, stood up straight, and the teachers liked us. Until I was eighteen, I was proud of my family, my neighborhood, my father and my mother.

My working-class limitations became apparent when I went to college. I attended a private, elite Catholic women's college by way of academic scholarships based on merit and federal grants based on need. It was at this college that I learned that the working class is not a desirable class.[2] I learned that good teeth, a quick mind, and a sly smile were of less importance than "Daddy's" profession and a good vocabulary. I experienced class shame for the first time. My freshman year, I came home for fall break and sewed myself a plaid wool skirt, had a sweater monogrammed, and permed my hair. My sisters made fun of me for affecting a New Jersey accent: "Why you talkin' like that? Come on, who do you think you are?" I didn't know.

Class shame is linked to a desire for class mobility. As I write this, I have just returned home from graduation ceremonies at another elite private Catholic college, where, this time, I am the professor. Yet, I am still uncomfortable. I still feel out of class bounds. I feel vulnerable and inadequate and worry that at any moment my language and anger will betray my class background and allegiance. Conversing with one parent whose eldest daughter works in upper management at General Motors corporate offices, I tell them, in a lowered voice, that my father also worked at General Motors. "He was a tool-and-die worker." And then I taste it, that slice of space between us that designates our class positions, and somehow I feel unworthy to have taught their daughter. Why, I imagine they are wondering, did we spend thirty thousand dollars a year to have our daughter taught by the daughter of a factory worker?

The working class lingers in my hair like smoke from Grandpa Joe's cigar. I remember my father arguing with my middle-class uncles at parties. My father would replay these arguments on our way home in the car, while my mother nodded and offered up murmurs of consolation. Mom had spent the party laughing with her sisters in the kitchen and hadn't heard the conversation. But I had, and I felt my father's injury, as if it pierced me too—and maybe it was because I wasn't in the kitchen laughing. I was in the room with the men who were drinking highballs, and I rooted for Dad, rooted for him as he stood facing those ten pins, the wrecking ball held aloft in the middle of his chest like one of my yoga mantra poses, rooted for him to knock down those pins of class arrogance. I wanted him to win one of those arguments in defense of the union, workers' wages, and decent benefits. After I started college, I entered the debate on the side of my father. I entered uninvited, of course, even by my father, because I was expected to be in the kitchen laughing with my aunts.

Structural inequalities are manifest in the absence of privilege as well as in acts of overt discrimination, though the latter are often more noticeable. We are more likely to see privileges (or lack thereof) when we cross borders. Living in Thailand, I saw my Americanism (and its cultural dominance); playing with boys, I saw my girlness (and its devaluation); and speaking with middle-class professionals, I am aware of my limited working-class vocabulary. Traversing boundaries (or jumping tracks) creates more potential for conflict, confusion, frustration, and shame than does staying inside our prescribed identity grooves. By staying in the house, cooking in the kitchen, and tending to their children, the Grasinski Girls compare themselves to other women doing the same things, and they come to value and appreciate those characteristics that make them good at mothering. Within more homogeneous identity communities, the Grasinski Girls were not ranked as "less than" anyone else: not in Hilliards, where they were all Polish Americans; not on working-class Boone Street, where "no one had more than the other so you can't be bragging about it"; not among secretaries, where "we were all on one level, I wasn't above no one"; and not around the kitchen table with their sisters, where their spoken words did not betray them. Within our own groups, understanding routines and sharing values provides relative feelings of security—it's at the borders that we become "the other," and where domination and subordination become visible.

When we migrate across borders—national borders, gender divisions, or class lines—we hear conflicting messages. Mari, the youngest, heard both the traditional gender expectations to stay home and raise children and the feminist directives to develop her self in a public-sphere career. Her husband's professional career gave her exposure to the values and expectations of educated professional women, at the same time that the feminist movement legitimated this groove. She struggled with her identity, and these struggles caused her heartaches that her more traditional sisters did not experience. Women in my generation who have been raised by mothers like Mari's sisters also hear conflicting messages as we struggle to construct identities outside the kitchen.

My mother was not taught the same set of values that I learned in the academy: that the world is dichotomized into public and private spheres; that the public sphere is more valuable; and that the more power one has, the better. Furthermore, she was not taught that the public sphere is the realm of power and that women should try to get into that sphere, to be the heads of state, industry, and the academy in order to make policy, money, and truth. The public sphere values competition, hierarchy, and objectification.[3] Socialized in this sphere, I have a harder time valuing a way of being that preferences connection over power, a way of understanding relationships as resource sharing rather than power struggles. I strongly believe that women should try to secure enough power to direct public policy, allocate public monies, and define public goods—and that this is a serious task to which my life should be devoted. Compared to this, the private sphere feels like a retreat or a cop-out; and the lives of the Grasinski Girls seem too easy, too frilly, too fluffy. If I gave myself over to the private sphere, I would spend more time playing with the neighborhood kids, making love to my partner, and hiking with my dog. But these activities are set in opposition to my need to prepare classes, grade papers, read academic journals, and publish my writing.

"Being educated" means more than simply learning a set of skills to get a better job that provides more economic security and higher social status. Education alters our set of values. It not only shapes the choices we are given, it shapes our perceptions and desires of the choices available. It was easier for Angel to sequence in and out of the public sphere as her mothering needs changed than for me to cycle in and out of being a college professor. I don't have the same freedom *nor the same disposition* to leave the labor market that my mother had. Education makes sacred the public sphere the way that motherhood makes sacred the private.

When Angel was in her fifties, she worked part-time, attended mass on

ιy mornings, took flute lessons, and studied Spanish with her handsome
̄ ̄ ̄ ̄ ̄munity education teacher. It would be equivalent to my reducing my
university obligations to twenty to thirty hours a week and spending the new
release time reading and hiking and playing basketball, or just taking off on a
Wednesday afternoon to go skiing because the snow is right and the sun not
too cold. Angel baked pies for her husband, babysat her grandchildren,
learned calligraphy, and took a basket-weaving class. She developed her skills
as ends in themselves, not as means toward an end.

It took me years to find my way back to the kitchen, and, ironically, it may
actually be in the kitchen that I find support for a revolutionary strand of
feminism. Reformist liberal feminism opened many doors to women. Once
women were included, however, many feminists unwittingly conformed to
and reproduced a system of inequality. In contrast, revolutionary feminists
challenge institutions predicated on hierarchy and inequality.[4] Returning to
the kitchen, then, means learning to take seriously a set of values that are
counterposed to competition and domination. What I see in the kitchen
when I watch the Grasinski Girls is how to create and preserve the self in relationships; how to live side-by-side instead of one in front of the other;
how to trust and to love even though it is a risk; and how to enjoy the day
that is given even while longing for the day that isn't there.

It is in the kitchen that I see the contrast between their relational selves
and my professionally driven instrumental self, and this makes evident the
limitations of the public sphere. I wonder why I define long afternoons at
the beach as "wasting time." From the window of my study I see days slipping by and worry that "much study is weariness for the flesh."[5] When I
email home to Mom, she tells me to go outside and appreciate the leaves'
burning autumn colors or pause by the trees flowering in spring, dripping
violet streams. I begin to notice clumps of pink tulips and yellow daffodils,
the fuzzy green growth on the tree limbs, bits of color being added so deli-
cately to the days, shards of forsythia yellow and bunches of azalea purple.
Although she does not say it, I understand from observing her life that it is
pleasurable to spend time engaged in activities that are ends in themselves, to
spend more time in the realm of freedom, to make my career work for me
rather than working for a career.[6]

Susan Krieger writes that what our mothers pass down is "a sense that

Fig. 32. Nadine and Angel at Nadine's home, 2001

women will improvise and find ways to do almost anything, a sense that we are, in fact, the invisible wealth we seek."[7] My Grandma Helen never did make it to New York, but she continued to wander her entire life. She was not a public accountant, but she did enjoy figuring out private budgets. She didn't become an opera singer, either, but that didn't stop her from singing. Her ability to "right herself" with the choices given, however, does not compensate for the choices not given. And yet, she learned to extend herself so that she was not trapped in her existence but grew beyond it.

Were these women privileged? Absolutely. Whiteness in a racist society and economic stability afforded them easy lives. As Angel said, "It's too easy for us. I think sometimes we'll have to be accountable for a lot." But subordination also circumscribed their life choices. Their class dispositions and gender expectations shaped their grooves and limited their possibilities. And yet, oppression is not depression, and happiness is not the absence of oppression. They laugh and cry and pray and sing, things they learned to do from within their gender and religious locations. They gather strength through their connections to Jesus and Mary, and create meaningful lives while caring for the family and carrying it through the generations.

Acknowledgments

I SINCERELY AND APOLOGETICALLY thank my aunts, the Grasinski Girls, for agreeing to do something that promised to be fun but turned out to be a rather skin-peeling experience. Despite my best humanist attempts, I could not eliminate completely the vulnerability that accompanies being the subject of an analysis. I owe them a great debt. Without their stories this manuscript is nothing. Thank you for allowing me to present you to readers as I do. And I want to thank my grandmother, Helen Frances Grasinski; I love her dearly, both her memory and the present-day guidance that her memory provides to stand up straight, to sing, and to roam. I would also like to thank Angel, my mom, for giving me the courage to write what I see, even if it differed from how others saw it. She is tolerant of new ideas while holding strong to her own convictions.

The people who read and commented on the entire manuscript include Celia Berdes, Tim Black, John Bukowczyk, Stephanie Gilmore, Carolyn Howe, Jean Malone, Nancy Slack Tester, as well as three anonymous reviewers for Ohio University Press. These readers challenged, encouraged, and polished the ideas presented here and in doing so made my analysis more complex and readable. Some requested more stories and less theory and others more theory and shorter stories; a few disputed and made more accurate my critique of feminism, while others helped me to better understand the nuances of social class; finally, several checked (and corrected) my understanding of Polish-American history and culture. Any errors that remain are mine.

I would also like to thank all of my women friends with whom I spent enjoyable hours on the porch laughing, discussing politics, analyzing our childhoods, and arguing theoretical points. We are indebted to the previous generation of women who stayed in the kitchen and taught us to laugh, as well as to those who entered the academy and taught us to argue.

Travel and research were supported with grants from the Women's Studies Program at the University of North Carolina, Greensboro, in 1999 and 2000, and the College of the Holy Cross in 2001. In addition, I received funds from both institutions to hire research assistants. I would like to thank Christine Culbreth at UNCG for her work in the incipient stage of this project, and Nicole Mortorano at Holy Cross, who helped me in the final stages. The College of the Arts and Sciences at Central Connecticut State University generously provided funds to complete the publication of the manuscript. Others who helped me to collect historical information in Grand Rapids and Hilliards include Jim Erdmans, Theresa Hartley, Helene Matecki, Walter and Marilynn Fifelski, and the staff at the Grand Rapids Public Library. I would also like to thank Gillian Berchowitz at Ohio University Press, for her gentle demeanor and thoughtful administration.

Finally, I am grateful for my companions Tim and Ernie, who walked beside me during these four long, somewhat tumultuous years of writing a sociological argument that explains the life choices of women who play a significant role in my emotional and psychological makeup. It has been excruciating at times, my humor not always a pretty sight. Throughout it all, Tim has provided a sensitive ear, 5:00 AM cups of coffee, Kris Kristofferson on his guitar, and fabulous slabs of smoked meat and habanero-heated sauces.

APPENDIX ⅠⅠⅠ
Description of Research Methods

I BEGAN COLLECTING their life stories on tape in December of 1997. I told them I wanted to write a book about them and gave them very general instructions: "Just tell me about your life, start from the beginning." I did not have a set of questions because I wanted them to construct their narratives in whatever form or direction they chose. Sometimes I would ask them to elaborate on a topic that I found interesting, but for the most part I wanted them to decide what to tell me. This open-ended invitation sometimes left them wondering what, exactly, they should be doing. Mari asked several times, "I don't know if this is boring, or should I go on?" And Fran said, "I don't know if you wanna listen to all of what I'm saying." Caroline and Angel also checked in with me, at times asking, "Is this what you want?"

What is it that I wanted? I wanted to know about the intersection of structure and agency. I chose life stories as a methodology because it fit with my epistemological assumptions regarding relational viewpoints and standpoint theory, which contends that knowledge is produced by the interaction between the knower with the world.[1] Their life stories showed me the process by which their lives unfolded, the historical context within which their lives and life decisions took place, and their interpretation of it all. For these reasons, the life story method helps me understand how the habitus mediates agency and structure, that is, how these women perceived and responded to the structural conditions of their lives. I was more interested in how they understood their role expectations than in how household chores were divided. The self-propelled feature of the life-story method allowed them to define what is meaningful and to emphasize life events they see as significant. This was especially true given their right to edit the life story that I culled from the transcripts.

I collected the first oral histories from Angel, Caroline, and Fran in 1998 and 1999. Some of them wanted more guidance than the open-ended directive, "Tell me about your life." One sister said, "I would have liked if we could have had an outline, so, start from birth and then go right down the line, so you aren't all screwed up with your answers and everything like that." After such requests, I developed a set of questions that emerged through collaboration with my students in a course I taught in spring 2000 at the College of the Holy Cross, "Oral Histories of Working-Class Women." I then interviewed Nadine and Mari, in long multiple sessions, eliciting first their self-narrated life history and then asking them the questions. I also went back to interview Angel, Caroline, and Fran with these questions which explored the areas of ethnicity and religion, generational differences, and their attitudes toward feminism and the feminist movement. Other questions at that session included: How would you describe yourself to yourself? What does it mean to be a woman? and What would you change about your life, or what is the thing you most regret?[2] Their answers were used in the chapters and not embedded into each sister's individual life story.

Almost all of the formal interviews were taped, as were the discussion sessions regarding the various drafts. Informal conversations and phone calls were not tape recorded but I did take notes. One sister was never comfortable with the tape recorder. On my second visit, I asked at the beginning if I could record her, and she said, "Not yet." After about ten minutes of seeing me scribble down everything I could, she said, "I guess you can turn it on now." But half an hour later she became conscious of it and, when talking about something she didn't want repeated, she asked, "Are you still recording?" I turned off the tape recorder. In the last session she did not allow me to tape her at all.

I transcribed all the material and then developed a coding scheme that emerged from a content analysis of their stories and my sociological agenda.[3] I developed the following categories: power and strength, ethnicity and race, religion (personal and institutional), finding voice and self-development, family (children and husbands), parents and background, feminism and inequality (denial of), body image, work and class, candy and clothes, music, death. I coded the material and began to write. As I wrote, I sent them snippets and then draft chapters for their comments. Our meetings during 2001 and 2003 were about the text, mostly about their objections to the text (they more often told me what they didn't like than what they did). Most of these discussions were face-to-face and most were taped; however, some also sent me written comments while others called me on the phone.

In the spring of 2001 we discussed more explicitly their rights as the owners of their life stories. I drew up a contract that explained those rights; it also served as a release form they needed to sign if Ohio University Press was going to publish this work using their real names. The relevant paragraph from this contract that detailed their rights read:

> I also understand that I will have the last word on anything that goes to publication. She [the author] will show me drafts of everything that she intends to publish from this material, and I will have the right to change and alter what goes to the publisher. *If there is something I do not want her to say about me I have the right to strike it from the manuscript.* She will show me the complete draft of the manuscript that she will finish in the summer of 2001, and then she will show me the revised manuscript. I have the right to read, to make comments on, and to delete anything in the manuscript that is made in reference to me and my life. [emphasis in original]

In the summer of 2002, all of them read the entire manuscript, after which several of them expressed a desire that this project not go forward.

There were three particular chapters they did not like, regarding their parents and sister Gene, so I deleted them. They asked me to change very little in the rest of the text—word usage (e.g., they didn't like the word "tit") and a sentence here and there. Even when they disagreed with my analyses, they did not ask that I delete them, but they argued their case for why they thought I was wrong. Only one of the sisters took out substantive parts of her narrative. In addition, we had a tug of war over the use of oral speech, and they expressed their feelings of betrayal about my agenda to show their social class. I made the changes they wanted and sent them the revised chapters. Only a few of the sisters responded this time. Most of the changes I could accommodate without altering the substance of the text, but I became obstinate when one of them asked me to eliminate references to religion being an opiate because she didn't want drugs mentioned in a book about her. To this request, I said no.

Notes

Introduction

1. Friedan [1963] 1983, 15–32.

2. Two of the sisters wanted it noted that they also give to nonreligious charities such as the Red Cross, the American Lung Association, the Special Olympics, and the American Cancer Society.

3. Early white feminist scholars were more often middle class, which may in part explain the class bias of their theories (Sidel [1978] 1995, 3). Today, many prominent black feminist scholars have working-class roots (e.g., bell hooks, Patricia Hill Collins, Audre Lorde), and they have only very recently made efforts to examine these roots (see, for example, bell hooks's slim book, *Where We Stand: Class Matters* [2000b]).

4. Hurtado does this "in order to understand women of Color and white women in general and feminists in particular" (1996, 5–6).

5. See Smith (1987).

6. Gabaccia (1991, 63–64); see also Collins (1991, 140–41). Working-class women appear in gender studies that focus on labor activism or labor market participation (e.g., Weiner 1985; Benson 1986; Cooper 1987; Gabin 1990; Norwood 1990; Cobble 1991; Faue 1991; Blum 1997; Glazer 1997; Roberts 1984; Cohen 1993).

7. See Smith (1987) and Faue (2001). When we do examine women's private lives, it is more often those of the middle class (e.g., Pleck 2000). For exceptions, see DeVault (1991) and Stacey (1998). For an excellent example of a complex analysis of the private world of one working-class woman, see Carolyn Steedman's *Landscape for a Good Woman* (1987), a psychological and emotional exploration of gender and class consciousness.

8. See, for example, Bourgois (1995). Even when social scientists write about the "good," they tend to write about extremes. For example, see Orsi (1996) on the cult of Mary in Chicago.

9. Doane (1999) shows how the dominant status hides ethnic identity of Yankees and the privileges of race.

10. Stone notes that family stories in general have a positive spin. To write unflattering stories would violate the norms of family stories, which are generally told to "provide the family with esteem. . . . Like all cultures, one of the family's first jobs is to persuade its members they are special, more wonderful than their neighboring barbarians" (1989, 5–7).

11. Laslett writes, "To call a personal narrative a story is not to call it fiction, although, like any other sociological source, it is constructed. Figuring out what it is constructed for is one task of sociological analysis" (1999, 392).

12. See also Kelley (1994), who discusses resistance in everyday activities of black working-class youth, and Bauer and Bauer (1971).

13. Genovese (1974, 597–98). The concept of accommodation is most often used to denote an acceptance of the system of oppression by subordinates, and the subsequent adjustments made by individuals to improve their comfort in the system. I do not intend this understanding in this book.

14. Collins (1991, 141). One reason it may not have been preferable for white women to confront the system was because of their intimate relations with the dominant members of this system. Accommodation as resistance grows from an intimate relation with the oppressor (Genovese 1974, 91–93, 597–98). Hurtado (1996, vii) argues that white women are seduced into compliance because of their intimate relations with the dominant group (white men).

15. This would mean to practice what Max Weber calls *verstehende Soziologie,* which is developed from a "system of sociological categories couched in terms of the subjective point of view, that is of the meaning of persons, things, ideas, normative patterns, and motives from the point of view of the persons whose action is being studied" (Parsons 1947, 10).

16. Mannheim wrote that "it is impossible to conceive of absolute truth existing independently of the values and position of the subject and unrelated to social context" (1936, 79).

17. Standpoint theory argues that "all knowledge about the world reflects the social position(s) of the knower, and therefore, at best can result in no more than a partial understanding of that world" (Chafetz 1997, 100). The subjectivity embedded in relative viewpoints is a critical component of the interactionist paradigm, often referred to as the "definition of the situation" (see Judith Wittner's discussion in Anderson et al. 1990, 106–9).

18. Clifford 1986, 7. Sociologist Dorothy Smith writes, "The 'one true story' is nothing more than a partial perspective claiming generality on the basis of social privilege and power" (1987, 121).

19. Krieger 1996, 3.

20. One of the benefits of examining people to whom you are close is that you know a lot about their lives. So, while "partial," you can be more sure than if studying strangers that there are not glaring oversights. Compare this to Stacey (1998) who was taken aback when she learned, years into the study, how much the "real story" of her respondents differed from what they initially revealed to her.

21. Merton 1972, 30–31.

22. Chafetz 1997; Anderson et al. 1990; Cook and Fonow 1990; Alpern et al. 1992.

Smith pointed out that "Established sociology is preoccupied with suppressing the presence of the sociological subject" (1987, 117). Reinharz argues that "not only is closeness necessary for understanding, but the case for respectful distance must be understood as a product of males' developmental history that requires distance from their mothers in order to produce male identity" (1992, 68). See Clifford's discussion of the traditional approach of anthropology in which the author's voice and presence are almost invisible in the final work, perpetuating the belief that there is a thick wall between the subject and the object of study (1986, 13). In contrast, see Liebow (1993) who asked several of the women included in his study to read and comment on the manuscript.

23. Reinharz 1992, 36–38.

24. L. Rubin 1994, 29. In the 1990s, only one in four Americans had a four-year college degree, seven in ten did not have professional or managerial jobs, and the median income was $39,000 (Rogers and Teixeira 2000, 66). Mantsios states that "class is not in the domain of public discourse" (1995, 131). Ellis refers to class as "America's dirty little secret" (1998, ch. 1, n. 3). For discussion of the forgotten working class, see Baca Zinn et al. (1986), Ehrenreich (1989), Garey (1999), Sacks and Remy (1984), and Sharlet (1999). Zweig (2000) argues that the majority of Americans do identify as being working class, and that the problem is not self-perception but the public's misperception. Vanneman and Cannon (1987) agree. They found that people misperceive that the working class has been subsumed into the middle class because of the low level of class conflict. But class conflict, they argue, is muted by a variety of factors (including the strength of the dominant class) and should be distinguished from class consciousness.

25. Some social scientists argue it is more useful to base social class on the status of the household rather than the individual worker (DeVault 1991; L. Rubin 1976, 1994).

26. Granting some gray area, the working and middle classes are nonetheless distinct in their labor market positions and educational levels. Differences in the labor market are defined by degree of autonomy and control, and differences in education reflected in speech. Vanneman and Cannon argue that the distinctions between the working and the middle class exist along three dimensions of control: economic (owning the means of production), political (supervising the behavior of workers), and ideological (defining the meaning of behavior, e.g., labeling manual work as bad and mental work as good) (1987, 46). See also Dahrendorf (1959), Ehrenreich and Ehrenreich (1979), Ehrenreich (1989), L. Rubin (1976), and Sennet and Cobb ([1972] 1993).

27. Steedman 1987, 13.

28. Stewart and Ostrove 1993, 476. See also Bourdieu (1977, 82–86), Brown (1997), and Vanneman and Cannon (1987, 46).

29. The feelings of betrayal could also have emerged from the nature of the oral history method, because there is "a particularly close proximity that involves trust and a sense of obligation" (Romero and Stewart 1999, xix). bell hooks also found that her family felt betrayed when she wrote about the negative parts of her working-class background (2000, 147).

30. "I Enjoy Being a Girl" (lyrics by Oscar Hammerstein II, music by Richard Rodgers), from the 1958 musical, *Flower Drum Song.*

Part 1 Introduction

1. Though we often conceive of immigration as an individual act, families commonly emigrated together, and women were active participants in the immigration and resettlement conversations (Anker 1988). I am indebted to Louise Fifelski Alflen and Marilynn Ciboch Fifelski, who compiled a history of the Fifelski family (n.d.). I also consulted a Fifelski family genealogy compiled by Theresa Loomis in 1981. I treat both of these as texts that represent the family stories we use to construct and interpret history (see Stone 1988; Rosenzweig and Thelen 1998).

In the preceding paragraph, the names were written as they appeared on the gravestones. While some stones had Polish words (e.g., *ojciec* and *matka*), for the most part their names were partially Americanized (e.g., Józef became Joseph) and in some cases Polonized (e.g., Johann became Jan). I use the Polish names of immigrants to stress their immigrant status. The gravestones, written at the end of their lives (and not by themselves), reflect their (and, more likely, their children's) assimilation. As for the name of Ladislaus Fifelski, it almost always appears as Ladislaus in other writings except when it is Americanized as Walter. According to Alflen and Fifelski (n.d.), Ladislaus was called Władziu, Walter, and Lonny. The only time I have seen his name as Ladislau (without the final "s") is on the gravestone. As for Johann, his gravestone reads Jan, but he is also referred to as John by his descendants.

2. Immigrant women, like their daughters and granddaughters to follow, worked at both paid and unpaid labor, inside and outside the home, contributing to the family income (Anker 1988; T. Radzilowski 1996, 1997). Young single women worked as domestics and in the factories. Mothers often worked at home, usually doing piecework, taking in boarders, or doing laundry.

3. By 1795, Poland was divided into three partitions: Prussia controlled the western regions and the northern Baltic provinces, Austria ruled the southeastern corner of Poland known as Galicia, and the Empress Catherine of Russia seized the largest area—the northeastern regions and the central basin of Poland. Poland did not reappear as a unified nation-state until after World War I.

4. Emigration from the Prussian partition peaked in the 1880s, when, on average,

thirty-seven thousand Poles emigrated annually (Greene 1961, 48; Michalski 1985, 14–15). Emigration from this region was motivated by economic factors (the need for land and money) and political factors, notably the Germanization programs known as the *Kulturkampf*, introduced by Otto von Bismarck in the 1870s as an attack on Catholics and Poles. Emigration subsequently slowed down in the 1890s, as developing mining and industrial districts in Silesia, Poznań, and the Ruhr basin absorbed surplus peasant labor and the Germanization programs abated (Kieniewicz 1969; Brozek 1985). While Prussian Poles represented 40 percent of the Poles in America in 1900, by the first World War they accounted for only 7.5 percent (Pinkowski 1978, 310–11). The Poles from the Prussian sectors were generally better educated and more skilled than the immigrants from the Austrian and Russian partitions, who arrived in large numbers between 1890 and 1920, and they were more likely to arrive with their families seeking permanent settlement (Bukowczyk 1984, 25; Golab 1977; Michalski 1985; Zubrzycki 1953; Kieniewicz 1969). According to the 1900 census, 71 percent of the 28,286 Poles living in Michigan were from the Prussian partition. The number of foreign-born Poles in Michigan rose to 62,419 in 1910 and peaked at 119,228 in 1930 (U.S. Census 1900, table LXXXII; 1910, table I; 1930, table 18). For a discussion of Prussian Poles in Michigan see Milostan (1977, 1984); Ziolkowski (1984); Skendzel (1999); Kolinski (1995); and Perkowski (1966).

5. Examples include Panna Maria, Texas (1854), St. Stanislaus Kostka Parish in Chicago (1867), and Parisville, Michigan (1852) (J. Radzilowski 1994; Lucille 1958; Kolinski 1995; Milostan 1977).

6. Most likely, his grammar school education in Prussia was conducted in German as a circumstance of von Bismarck's *Kulturkampf*, which defined Polish as an inferior language and barred it from use in all official forums (see Michalski 1985; Kieniewicz 1969).

7. While roughly three-quarters of the nine hundred Polish communities in the U.S. at the turn of the century were rural, the U.S. Immigration Commission reported that in 1910 only 10 percent of all Poles in the country worked in agriculture—but this added up to between five and seven hundred thousand Polish farm dwellers, two-thirds of whom lived in Wisconsin, Minnesota, and Michigan (Kolinski 1995, 22–51; Lucille 1958). Polish farmers were often from the Prussian-controlled sector, because they were more permanent immigrants than those from other sectors, and they generally arrived earlier, when land was more available and cheaper (J. Radzilowski 1994, 2002).

8. His brother Walter suggested this was because they had very little meat in Poland, and greater access in Chicago because they lived near the stockyards, "and they just gorged themselves on that, because they didn't have anything like that over there. A big thing in the old country for Christmas and Easter was a foot of a goose with a little piece of gut wrapped around it. That was a big treat. Do you know how much meat is on the bottom part of the foot?" The Dutch also noted the difference between

European and American fare in that, as one Dutch immigrant wrote, "Here meat and gravy are the main items and potatoes are only a side dish" (Brinks 1995, 248; see also 257, 324).

9. Kaszubi (Kashubians) lived near the Pomeranian region of West Prussia, and, although they are a Slavic group, for most of the nineteenth century they did not consider themselves Poles, but "Polish-speaking Prussians" (Davies 1982, 112; Perkowski 1966). Burchardt's gravestone is engraved "Michal Burchardt," without the Polish *ł*, but the stone does include several Polish words (e.g., *matka, ojciec,* names of months). His first name is spelled with the Polish "ł" on the stained-glass window at St. Stan's. In the 1880 census, his country of birth is listed as "Prussia" and the entry for his brother Jan is "Poland." In 1890, they both have "Poland (Ger)" as the country of birth. On the 1910 census, his birthplace is recorded as "Germany."

10. See Erdmans (1998) for a discussion of the sociological differences between immigrants and ethnics (i.e., native-born ethnic Americans).

11. In the Polish language, adjectives take on the gender of the nouns they modify, and they are spelled differently to reflect this. Surnames ending in -ski are regarded as adjectives, and thus vary by gender; for example, Pawel Zulawski but Frances Zulawska. Few Polish American women kept this gendered surname reflection even in the second generation. Frances used the surname Zulawski and later Fifelski, and others refer to her that way as well. Only once in Alflen and Fifelski's (n.d.) family history is she listed as Zulawska. Her mother, however, who was an immigrant, retained her maiden name of Chylewska in the family documents, but she became a Zulawski once married.

12. While the Zulawski name had an Americanized spelling, they pronounced it as if it had retained the Polish diacritic marks—Żuławski. His grandson Walter narrates, "My grandfather's father lost his farm. His wife supposedly died and he married a high-stepping gal that liked to spend money, and then they had some kind of a lawsuit over some hired guy that got gored by a bull." Many Polish families during that time lost land. Parot notes that in the Prussian partition "[r]evolts, poor harvests, and declining prices resulted in the wide-spread sale of gentry-owned lands," to Germans, mostly; between 1846 and 1855 more than a million acres of land changed hands from Poles to Germans (1981, 33).

13. In 1865, the stockyards were built, and the area around them soon became a settlement for Polish immigrants (Kantowicz 1975, 16–23).

14. This is the spelling of their surname on their gravestone. It is spelled differently on the stained-glass window they donated to St. Stanislaus Church—Gruszczyński.

15. This was the case for Polish farmers in the U.S. in general, and for Poles coming to both urban and rural centers in Michigan, who were likely to come from New York, Pennsylvania, Illinois, or Wisconsin (Anderson and Smith 1983, 220). In 1880, 40 percent of the native-born population in Michigan had been born out of state, with

New York, Ohio, and Pennsylvania providing the largest numbers of migrants (U.S. Census 1880, table XIV).

16. Unlike the Dutch community in the area, the Polish farming community was never large enough to provide jobs for farmhands. See Brinks (1995) for a discussion of Dutch farming in western Michigan. John Radzilowski also found that Polish farmers in Minnesota worked first in other cities (e.g., Chicago) for several years to earn money to buy land (1994, 52–53; see also Lucille 1958; Anderson and Smith 1983, 223; and Skendzel 1999, 149; 1981, 9).

17. Lopata (1976a) explicitly illustrates the importance of status in Poland and America. Status was determined vis-à-vis other families.

18. St. Stanislaus Parish 1992, 213.

19. Barth 1969, 9.

20. See Micaela di Leonardo (1987) for a discussion of "kinship work."

Chapter 1

1. Alflen and Fifelski n.d., 2.

2. It was a father's responsibility to find a spouse for his daughter. In Poland the father often arranged the marriage, but he took into consideration the desires of the child as well as the opinions of other family members (Thomas and Znaniecki [1918] 1958, 92). Admitting a member into the family through marriage was, in part, a group consideration. While marriages were not as much based on notions of romantic love as they are today, when they worked, the marriage was based on affection and mutual respect. "The marriage norm is not love, but 'respect,' as the relation which can be controlled and reinforced by the family. . . . The norm of respect from wife to husband includes obedience, fidelity, care for husband's comfort and health; from husband to wife, good treatment, fidelity, not letting the wife do hired work if it is not indispensable. . . . Affection is not explicitly included in the norm of respect, but it is desirable" (90). Lopata adds that "marriage was not a matter of love but an arrangement guaranteeing the best status and economic position for the new unit" (1976b, 22). This arrangement is well illustrated in the novel *Remember Me Dancing* by Ken Parejko (1996).

3. Thaddeus Radzilowski writes that, because of the shortage of female immigrants, many male immigrants married American-born Polish women (1996, 61). Not only did the woman's nativity (language skills, citizenship) provide her with more power, but new couples often lived with the woman's family because they were native born and so had more resources. Marilynn Ciboch Fifelski stated that Frances's landowning ancestry gave her a "better-than" attitude toward Ladislaus; it made her think "that she was going to get a better place in heaven."

4. Hilliards was named after David Hilliard, a wealthy landowner in the area who emigrated from Canada in the 1850s. In the early 1870s Kashubian and Poznanian immigrants built a small chapel in Hilliards, in 1885 they built a school, and in 1892 the church. The history of St. Stanislaus is taken from the centennial celebration book issued by St. Stanislaus in 1992, as well as work by Skendzel (1981, 1999). St. Stanislaus was the nineteenth rural Polish parish established in Michigan (Kolinski 1995, 53). The statues in the church reflect the Polishness of the parish: St. Stanislaus B.M., a former Bishop of Krakow; St. Stanislaus Kostka, patron saint of Poland; St. Hedwig from Silesia (in Prussia); and St. Casimir of Poland.

5. The area the Grasinski Girls come from has been referred to alternately as Wayland, Dorr, and Hopkins, which are all towns as well as townships. After consulting with the Grasinski Girls, I decided to use Hilliards as the spatial designation because it most signifies Polishness to them. Nadine said, "I think Hilliards is the best name for it because everybody says Hilliards is Polish. When you say Wayland, Dorr, or Hopkins you don't think Polish, but when anybody says Hilliards you think immediately Polish—Polish school, Polish parish, people around there are all Polish, all the farmers are Polish, all the drunks in the tavern are Polish." Caroline said, "There's not many Polish people in Wayland, that's where the Yankees live."

6. Polish ethnicity was identified by surnames, interviews, and personal knowledge. The information comes from township plat maps. Skendzel identified thirteen Polish families in the North Dorr church registries in 1868, and another nine in New Salem (1999, 146–47). Their names, however, do not appear on the Dorr or Hopkins plat maps, suggesting that they were not landowners, at least not in these townships.

7. Farmsteads increased by fifty-eight between 1895 and 1935; the number of surnames increased by thirty-six.

8. The first eighty acres Johann bought for $6,402 in 1892, with money the family had earned working in Chicago. They paid $5,180 in cash and assumed a mortgage for the remaining balance. On the deed, Johann is listed as John, and Mary's name is not listed at all. Nine years later, Johann Fifelski purchased an adjacent forty acres for $2,650. Like Johann, most of the farmers increased their acreage by buying nearby plots, making the farmstead more efficient than widely scattered farm holdings. As in Poland, Ladislaus became the manager of the farm after his father retired. Along with the farm came the responsibility of caring for the parents (Thomas and Znaniecki [1918] 1958, 92–128). In their case, they built a small cottage in the orchard for Ladislaus's parents.

9. Head cheese is a jellied loaf made from the edible parts of a pig's head, feet, and tongue.

10. At the turn of the century, the farms had an average of ten to fifteen cows that netted twenty-five to fifty dollars a month from milk sales (Alflen and Fifelski n.d.).

11. The pickling was a nasty job and afforded Nadine one of her first "acts of re-

sistance." Nadine explained, "We used to pick pickles. We'd plant them and pick them, and they had all these prickly needles. We'd have to get up early [to pick them] because they're so hot. And one day I just got so tired of doing that. I just got up real early and I took this poison and I killed them all. I smothered them! [laughs] And we didn't have any pickles, so we didn't have any money to buy ourselves clothes. But we didn't have to do all the crappy work."

12. Like their Minnesotan counterparts discussed by John Radzilowski (1994), the Polish farmers in Hilliards were "immigrant" farmers who wanted to create strong communities and viable farms that they could pass on to the next generation. But he found that Polish farmers in Minnesota also resembled "Yankee farmers," who had a more entrepreneurial model based often on a single cash crop, preferring "short-term profit over persistence on the land," and their farmsteads grew in size from an average eighty-acre to 160-acre holding between 1885 and 1905. This was not the case in Hilliards. By 1939, three-quarters of the farms were only eighty acres or smaller. The Polish farmers' patterns resembled those of the German farmers that Kathleen Neils Conzen (1990) studied. The farms grew slowly and the farmers avoided debt, which often meant they did not buy new machinery or build more comfortable houses as quickly as the Yankee entrepreneur farmers. Walter, the youngest son who inherited the Fifelski farm in the 1930s, said he had a difficult time convincing the family to buy a tractor, and when they finally did in the 1940s, it was a used, unreliable model. By 1913, only fourteen of eighty-eight Polish farmsteads had over a hundred acres; one was the Gruszczynski farm (140 acres) and another was Ladislaus Fifelski's farm (120 acres).

13. See also John Radzilowski (1994, 58), who found that Polish farmers migrated between urban and rural worksites, often working in factories to earn cash to buy additional land.

14. Three sons became tool-and-die makers who worked in wartime production plants in Lansing, and then later in Grand Rapids in the auto industry; a fourth son worked at American Motors (Kelvinator), but lived out in the country; a fifth worked at American Music Instruments, but when factory work slowed down he went back to work as a farmhand. His son Bill worked tool and die at a "job shop" (as-needed basis) with his brother during the Depression and then bought a farm across the street from his parents and worked it the rest of his life, at times hiring his brothers as farmhands.

15. Walter, the youngest, took over the farm and worked it until 1947, when he closed down the dairy business, auctioned off sixteen head of cattle, a team of horses, and some farm equipment, and, with his brothers, established the Fifelski Building Company, which built pole barns and other farm buildings in the area. None of the brothers or sisters received any inheritance from the sale of the farm; it went solely to Walter in exchange for his having cared for their parents in their old age. The last descendant of Ladislaus Fifelski to farm was Bill, who farmed his land until old age forced him to stop in the 1970s. None of Bill's three sons wanted to take over the farm

(they all chose to work in the auto industry), so he sold it. I received an inheritance from the sale of the farm: it was enough to buy a down coat and a mountain bike.

16. Alflen and Fifelski n.d., 7.

17. Large families were typical of Polish peasants in Poland (Thomas and Znaniecki [1918] 1958, 1516) as well as Polish-American families at the beginning of the twentieth century (Lopata 1976b, 29–30).

18. Conzen (1990) found this to be true of German immigrant farm women as well.

19. Marilynn Fifelski interview.

20. U.S. Census 1920, vol. III, table 6. By 1869 there were roughly a hundred Polish families in the city, many of them from the town of Trzemeszno near Poznań (Symanski 1964, 91; Skendzel 1999, 18, 26–28, 70–71). The Polish population increased steadily after 1890, as Poles from the Russian and Austrian partitions began arriving, yet by 1900, 63 percent of the 1,685 foreign-born Poles in Grand Rapids were from the Prussian partition (Jung n.d., 22; Skendzel 1999, 27, 70–71; 1981, 49; U.S. Census 1900, Michigan, table 34).

21. This was also true for the Dutch (Brinks 1995, 10; Bratt and Meehan 1993, 67, 92).

22. Bratt and Meehan 1993, 76; Skendzel 1999, 360.

23. In the 1922 city directory, his name is spelled Grucinski. The surname has been even more variably spelled: Gruscinski, Gracinski, Gruszczynski, and Grusczynski.

24. U.S. Census 1930, vol. III, part I, tables 18, 19.

25. By 1910, Dutch residents represented 42 percent of the foreign-born population in Grand Rapids, and Dutch foreign stock (28,341) represented a quarter of the total population (U.S. Census 1910, vol. II, table 15; 1930, vol. III, part I, tables 18, 19). For a discussion of Dutch settlements see Swierenga (1985).

26. Bratt and Meehan 1993, 92, 104–5.

27. Skendzel 1999, 10.

28. Even Eduard Skendzel, a Polish-American historian who more often positively embellishes the history of the Polish-American community, argues that their halls were "a scandal," with "numerous cases of over-indulgence and inebriation" (1993, 5).

29. Lydens 1976, 33–34.

30. Bratt and Meehan 1993, 80.

31. St. Adalbert was a German monk who brought Christianity to the Poles in the ninth century, and is especially revered by Poles from the Poznań province. The basilica of St. Adalbert was modeled after the Basilica of the Assumption in Trzemeszno (Skendzel 1999, 50).

32. Bishop Richter was against the naming of churches after national saints and proposed St. Isidore rather than the Polish-proposed St. Stanislaus (Ancona 2001, 50–51; Skendzel 1999, 26–51). These schisms and conflicts over the ethnic naming of new churches occurred in many parishes across the country (Meagher 2001, 29; Parot 1981; Bukowczyk 1980; 1985).

33. Skendzel 1999, 5, 72–77.

34. Skendzel 1981, 55, 215. The neighborhood was also called Krakowo (Kraków District) because, as one parishioner wrote, the church was built on a slight elevation and reminded them of Wawel Castle in Kraków (148).

35. Krakowski's mother emigrated from Poznań to Chicago before settling in Hilliards in the early 1870s. The family came to Grand Rapids in 1880 (Skendzel 1981, 100).

36. Symanski 1964, 93.

37. Eduard Skendzel writes that "upward bound Polish families" moved into the neighborhood, many of them from St. Adalbert's and St. Isidore's parishes (1999, 140; 1981, 56).

38. Skendzel 1981, 12. Grosse Point is a wealthy suburb of Detroit.

39. Skendzel 1981, 93, 141, 316–17.

40. City directories of Grand Rapids. Names are written as they appeared in the directories.

41. There were eighty-three family names listed on Muskegon Avenue between 9th and 12th Streets, and fifty-eight were recognizably Polish names (which makes it an underestimate, because it fails to count Poles with Americanized names).

42. Listed in the 1928 Polish Catholic Directory, reprinted in Milostan (1984, 12). The city directories for 1926, 1928, and 1929 list Gracinski as residing at 1014 Powers.

43. This is how their names were written on the mortgage papers.

44. Words like *grosernia* (grocery) or *buczernia* (butcher) represent hybrid Polish-English words, that is, English words given Polish pronunciations, spellings, and suffixes that take declensions.

45. While there was a Polish weekly, the *Echo Tygodniowe,* the older sisters have no memory of their father or mother reading Polish papers.

46. Skendzel 1981, 333.

47. Language retention declined after 1920, when 112,168 residents of Michigan reported Polish as their mother tongue; in 1930, this drops to 107,963, and by 1960 to 58,061 (U.S. Census 1960, Michigan, vol. 1, table 41).

48. Skendzel 1981, 293–300; see also Kuznicki 1978b, 442.

49. At the dedication of St. Isidore in 1897, Fr. Pulcher from the Irish St. James's Parish referred to the Poles as "good citizens and good church members. They are a credit to the city." He attributed their progress to their "thrift and steady living" (Skendzel 1999, 13). See also Bratt and Meehan (1993, 80).

50. Boarding was a very popular way for women to contribute income to the household, especially in rapidly industrializing urban centers (Modell and Hareven 1977; Anker 1988). The 1910 Immigration Commission report on furniture workers found that more than half of household income came from boarders for one-third of the Polish families, while another third supplemented their factory wages by letting out sleeping spaces (Kleiman 1985, 47).

51. T. Radzilowski 1996, 77.

52. In medium-sized industrial cities, immigrant home ownership often exceeded native-born home ownership, and this was true in Grand Rapids. However, these homes often carried a heavy debt. Houses averaging $3,325 in value carried a typical debt of $1,439 (Kleiman 1985, 48–49, 59, 178; Symanski 1964, 105).

53. The Polish American Bank was organized in 1919 by Stanley Jackowski and supported by Father Kaminski of Sacred Heart (Skendzel 1981, 130–31).

54. The $150,000 debt had an annual payment of $10,000 principal and another $9,000 in interest. The church defaulted on the semiannual interest payment in 1930, the diocese assumed the debt, and Kaminski was forced to resign (Skendzel 1981, 130–34).

55. Olson 1992, 147.

56. Lydens 1976, 81; Olson 1992, 155–57.

57. A narrow piece of cloth, cut on the bias, used to finish hems or decorate clothing.

58. They paid $4,400, Angel said. The down payment came from her father's wages.

59. See Chirot (1994) for a description of how the link developed between uncontrollable natural forces and farmers' conservative attitudes, in order to minimize the risk in their lives. Ken Parejko describes this attitude in his novel, *Remember Me Dancing* (1996).

Chapter 2

1. See Sollors (1986) for a discussion of consent and descent identities.

2. Waters (1990, ch. 3) shows that later-generation European Americans often define themselves predominantly by one ethnicity even when they descend from various ancestries. Factors influencing choice of ancestry include generation, knowledge of the ancestry, signifiers like surnames or physical appearance, and social desirability of the ethnic group. See also Sollors (1986, 232).

3. Three of their grandparents were born in Poland, but their maternal grandmother was born in the United States. Most fourth-generation Polish Americans do not marry other Polish Americans, worship in a Polish-American church, remember Polish-American customs, visit Poland or know much about Poland, speak Polish, read Polish newspapers or magazines (in Polish or English), belong to Polish organizations, or vote for Polish-American candidates (Obidinski 1985; Sandberg 1974). Other studies on third- and fourth-generation Polish Americans include Silverman (2000), Bukowczyk (1987, ch. 5–7), and Wrobel (1979).

4. Methodists (Yankees and Germans) were also leaders in industry (as furniture executives and financiers), politics, and social organizations (e.g., Rotary, Kiwanis, and Optimists). Catholics were absent from the rosters of prominent politicians, industrial leaders, and even police chiefs (Bratt and Meehan 1993, 32–33, 234–35).

5. Bratt and Meehan 1993; Kleiman 1985; Symanski 1964; Skendzel 1999, 5–10; Lydens 1976.

6. The literature on the construction of whiteness in the United States documents how eastern and southern Europeans, as well as the Catholic Irish, while originally discriminated against on the basis of national origins and religion, eventually lost their ethnic markers and became "white" (Roediger 1991, 1994; Ignatiev 1995; Jacobson 1995).

7. Chrobot (1973) and Lopata (1976b) demonstrate the overrepresentation of Polish Americans in the working class. In disagreement with them, Angela Pienkos argues that many Polish Americans were middle class (Taras, Pienkos, Radzilowski 1980). Sanders and Morawska (1975) give the most complete description of the structural location of Polish Americans in the early 1970s. They conclude that Polish Americans are found most often in semi-skilled and skilled labor positions and are underrepresented (as compared to the national average) in professional and managerial positions (1975, 28–36). The aggregate income levels for Polish Americans were high (among white ethnic groups they were second only to Russians), and they were even higher in industrial cities, especially in Detroit, where a large percentage were employed in the automobile industry. The salaries of these skilled laborers boosted the aggregate income level without raising the occupational class position. This was confirmed by lower levels of educational attainment. As a group, in the 1970s Polish Americans lagged behind the national average on years of education. Yet social mobility was evident, at this time, in the younger generation, which already had educational levels surpassing the national average (36–49).

8. Lieberson and Waters 1988; Alba 1990, 1995; Pula 1996, 89–91; Erdmans 2000.

9. Bukowczyk 1987, 107–10; Taras 1982, 52; Sanders and Morawska 1975; Napierkowski 1983; T. Radzilowski 1974; Lopata 1976a, 68–87. In the 1994 second edition of *Polish Americans*, Lopata continues to maintain that there is an underrepresentation of Polish Americans in the major institutions of America. Pula argues that while there have been "substantial economic and educational strides" among Polish Americans in the post-WWII era, placing them at parity or above the national averages on income and education, "full equality in hiring, promotion, and social acceptance remains to be achieved" (1996, 92).

10. Examining the portrayal of Polish Americans in literature, Napierkowski argues that one might conclude that Polishness is "a terrible heritage in which to be born" and that Polish life is debased, undemocratic, and impoverished (1983, 43–44). Bukowczyk, looking more specifically at the stereotypes of Polish women, found contradictory images: crude and uncouth, but also decent, wholesome, and virginal (2003, 195–201). Stereotypes of Polish-American men are also classed, as working-class men are often expected to be more brawny than brainy (Bukowczyk 1987, 113). Pula cites that 78 percent of Slavic characters on prime time television shows are portrayed as "muscular dimwits" or otherwise "socially dysfunctional" (1996, 76). And

yet, Bukowczyk shows that, on closer examination, the portrayal of Polish characters in film is not all derogatory (2002).

11. See Erdmans (1998, 224) and Bukowczyk (1996; 1986, 107–10).

12. Bukowczyk 1986; Erdmans 1998. For a contradictory view, see the work of Jim Pula, who argues that Polish jokes and other negative stereotypes of inferiority promoted "poor self-image and rejection of heritage" among many Polish Americans (1996, 92).

13. See Bukowczyk (2003, 198).

14. Mary Waters (1990) found that some European Americans equated their history of discrimination (and even present-day prejudice) with that of Mexican Americans and African Americans, claiming "we had it just as bad." Thomas Napierkowski, in an article about the defamation of the Polish character in literature, claims that "the situation of Polish Americans is probably even worse at present than that of blacks" (1983, 6). It is on the basis of this fictitious parity that whites both apply for and deny the resources meted out on the basis of historical and present-day discrimination. For example, Polish Americans actively fought against affirmative action in higher education by supporting the *Bakke v. Regents of University of California* case in 1976 (Erdmans 1998, 50). By invoking the history of discrimination toward Polish Americans, they can more easily dismiss the privileges of their white skin—and, in doing so, Lillian Rubin states, use that ethnicity as "a cover for 'white'" (1994, 195).

15. John Bukowczyk shows correctly that whites are not all privileged equally, that class does matter. For many Polish Americans, "the advantages conferred by their 'white' skin have been compromised by vestiges of their class backgrounds and by their unpronounceable names" (1996, 37). Many working-class Polish-American neighborhoods and labor sectors were devastated by the economic and urban transformations of the last forty years. The working class did not have the political or economic power to prevent newly constructed highways from slicing up their neighborhoods, to prevent Realtors from ravaging house prices through blockbusting, or to prevent the automobile and steel industries from closing factories (Bukowczyk 1987, ch. 5; Wrobel 1979; Pacyga 1996). The middle class is quick to blame the working class for being racist bigots, while their own neighborhoods, schools, and clubs remain predominantly white. Bukowczyk suggests that Polish Americans should claim their victimhood, their immigrant peasant, working-class roots so that they may enter into dialogue with other minorities and distance themselves from the privileges of white middle-class Protestants, and claim innocence in the construction of racist ideology in America (1996, 36–37).

16. Joanne Nagel (1994) theoretically defines the difference between ethnic identity and culture.

17. Between 1940 and 1950, the African American population in Grand Rapids grew from 2,600 to 6,813, and then more than doubled to 14,260 in the next decade,

until by 1970 African Americans were 14 percent of the city's population (Bratt and Meehan 1993, 157). The Latino population, mostly Mexicans who came to Michigan as seasonal farm workers and later Puerto Ricans migrating from Chicago, was at 10,588 in Kent County (where Grand Rapids is located) by 1970 (206).

18. This pattern has been repeated in Polonian neighborhoods across the United States. Obidinski (1985) documents the process of decline and demoralization in Buffalo; Bukowczyk (1987) and Wrobel (1979) look at the decline in Detroit; Pacyga (1996) examines it in Chicago.

19. Eduard Skendzel notes, "Today, Grand Rapid's citizens with Polish surnames are no longer 'Poles.' They are not even hyphenated 'Polish Americans.'" Instead, he says, that they are "Americans of Polish ancestry" (1983, 11). See also Obidinski (1985).

20. Bukowczyk 1987, 144–45.

21. Bukowczyk 1987, 110.

22. For Alba (1995), assimilation is an attainment of equality. He argues that assimilation represented a process of individuals choosing to change in order to take advantage of opportunities. Some Polish-American scholars argue that Poles exhibited an eagerness to assimilate (Gladsky and Gladsky 1997, 2). More often, scholars describe assimilation as a reaction to discrimination, pointing out the anti-immigration movement and other xenophobic practices directed at the large wave of Catholic and Jewish immigration from eastern and southern Europe at the turn of this century which led to self-negating practices such as abandoning native tongues, changing surnames, and moving away from ethnic neighborhoods (Bukowczyk 1996, 100; Lopata 1976a; Pula 1980, 1996).

23. Bukowczyk argues that Poles changed their names to avoid discrimination (1987, 106). Waters (1990) also links surnames to discrimination.

24. Bukowczyk 1987, 109–10; Glazer and Moynihan 1970; Sandberg 1974.

25. Galush (1990) shows how middle-class suburban residents maintain ethnicity through organizational participation, and Lopata refers to the "superterratorial ethnic community" of national organizations (1976a). But this community can exist even outside an organizational network. Silverman refers to "Polonia without walls"—Polish Americans attached to Polonia through participation in rituals (2000, 4). Micaela di Leonardo (studying Italian Americans in Northern California) also rejects the notion that ethnicity resides only in a geographic ethnic community or even an organizational community (1984, 25).

26. Savaglio 1997; Greene 1992; Silverman 2000, chapter 11.

27. For a mini-debate on the existence of a Polonian culture as distinct from American or Polish culture see Taras (1982) and Symmons-Symonolewicz (1983).

28. For a cataloguing of Polonian cultural traditions see Silverman, 2000; Taras, 1982; Zand 1958; and Obidinski and Zand, 1987. While it is commonly understood that Polish Catholicism is Marion based, Jesus also figures prominently as the crucified Christ, which the Sacred Heart wrapped in thorns signifies (Bukowczyk 1985, 21).

29. Chrobot, 1973, 2001; Napolska 1946.

30. It is rare that language is passed down into the third and fourth generations. In the 1940s and 1950s, only 20 percent of the children of prominent Polish American leaders spoke Polish (Bukowczyk 1987, 108).

31. Felician nuns staffed the grammar school at St. Stan's in Hilliards from 1937 to 1969 (Ziolkowski 1984, 69). The formal study of Polish language began to decline in 1930s, and was almost completely absent by the 1950s (Ziolkowski 1984, 272; Kuznicki 1978a, 110; 1978b, 451, 454; T. Radzilowski 1975, 25–26).

32. The correct spelling is *ryba*.

33. These same symbols of Polishness are salient in the short stories of Anthony Bukoski (1999) about a Polish-American town in rural Wisconsin. See also Bukowczyk (1985).

34. See Dennis L. Kolinski (1994), "Shines and Crosses in Rural Central Wisconsin."

35. Silverman (2000) discusses the authenticity argument debated in Polonia (174) and the split between high culture and low culture (ch. 15). Also see Thaddeus Radzilowski's defense of Wrobel's study in which he argues that Polonian scholars do not want to admit to a working-class Polonian culture (Taras, Pienkos, Radzilowski 1980, 45). The theoretical argument is discussed by Pierre Bourdieu (1984), who maintains that class culture is used to reproduce social rankings.

36. See di Leonardo (1987).

37. See Stone (1988) and Krieger (1996).

38. Immigrant women were arbiters of ethnicity. They "had to think consciously about what it meant to be Polish and how to translate that into the rituals of daily life. They had to decide what to keep, and what to abandon, and how to celebrate holidays and rites of passage in an unfamiliar environment" (T. Radzilowski 1996, 71). Women were responsible for defining and redefining the meaning of Polishness in America (Majewski 1997; see also Di Leonardo 1984). Pleck (2000) also shows how rituals are gendered routines enacted by women.

39. See Rosenzweig and Thelen (1998) who have documented the common practice of personalizing history and understanding national history as family narrative.

40. Gladsky 1997, 105.

41. Koloski 1997, 155.

42. Ethnic rituals "showcased gender ideals" (Pleck 2000, 15).

43. Wrobel 1979; T. Radzilowski 1996, 1997; Gladsky and Gladsky 1997; Chrobot 1973, 2001; Napolska 1946.

44. T. Radzilowski 1997, 21.

45. See Mary Waters (1990).

46. Bukowczyk talks about formal organizations, institutions and public spaces as expressions of ethnicity (1986, 96). Most historians of Polonia, including Don Pienkos, John and Thaddeus Radzilowski, Dominic Pacyga, Stan Blejwas, and Bill Galush

also focus on public ethnicity. In contrast, novelists Leslie Pietrzyk, Suzanne Strempek Shea, and Anthony Bukoski, and cultural studies scholars Karen Majewska and Thomas Gladsky provide more private-sphere and emotional expressions of ethnicity.

47. Short stories about Polish women often center on religious holidays (see Gladsky 1997). Silverman (2000) also notes the importance of Easter and Christmas traditions as the backbone of Polishness in America.

48. After her Dutch-American husband was killed in a car accident, my father's mother remarried a Polish American. The death weakened our ties to our Dutch relatives and severed our connection to Dutch culture.

49. Heinz 57, a brand of steak sauce, was a phrase we used on our street to refer to "mutts," that is, people whose ancestry was too muddied to have a clear picture of who they were. This term is different than calling someone an American or a "Yankee," which was an American of northwestern European ancestry, both of which connoted a higher status that transcended ethnicity.

50. Bukoski 1999, 179.

51. John Bukowczyk writes that Polish Americans in the later generations found ethnicity "appealing because it touched a sensitive psychological chord, which had little to do with ethnic background per se, but had a lot to do with the more general need for roots. Mass society in the 1970s was a rather faceless place, conducive to an assortment of psychological and personality disorders: rootlessness, alienation, anomie"(1987, 119). Silverman agrees that ethnic groups provide affective ties that help hold together splintered modern families. The folk culture "provides a sense of rootedness and stability in an era of economic and social uncertainty" (2000, 5). Chrobot (1973) also argued that the ethnic revival in the 1960s and 1970s was a response to commercialism. But Bukowczyk counters that the revival itself has become commercialized as the ethnic culture was mass produced in buttons and slogans and Bobby Vinton and the pope. "Ethnicity had become a purchasable and profitable commodity" to be bought and sold, made and eaten (1987, 119).

52. Elizabeth Pleck (2000) argues that the immigrants enact rituals from the old country to help themselves adjust to the new country; and the descendants of immigrants engage in rituals to connect them to their immigrant ancestors.

53. See also Edward Shils (1981) who uses the word "tradition" as a verb to refer to the process of passing down.

Part 2 Introduction

1. Friedan [1963] 1983, 67. In the 1920s, women's freedom and power were expanding in the public sphere as more women moved into the paid labor force, higher education, and political office. Women were marrying later and having fewer children,

which helped uncouple them from the domestic setting. These freedoms were eroded by midcentury as a result of a backlash against the previous gains, labor competition with men returning from the war, and a prosperous economy that allowed more women to stay home. See also Ferree and Hess (1994, ch. 1).

2. College attendance for women dropped from 47 to 35 percent between 1920 and 1958, and "by the mid-fifties, 60 percent dropped out of college to marry, or because they were afraid too much education would be a marriage bar" (Friedan [1963] 1983, 16). See also Ferree and Hess (1994, ch. 1).

3. Disposition implies it is "an organizing action" and a "way of being" and is similar to such concepts as predisposition, tendency, propensity, or inclination (Bourdieu 1977, 214, note 1).

4. Bourdieu 1977, 78.

5. Bourdieu 1977, 72. His theories better explain social reproduction than social revolution.

6. "Each agent, wittingly or unwittingly, willy nilly, is a producer and reproducer of objective meaning" (Bourdieu 1977, 79). Not being conscious of how and why we make choices increases the power of the social structure to slot us into life grooves. As Bourdieu states, "It is because subjects do not, strictly speaking, know what they are doing that what they do has more meaning than they know" (79).

7. Bourdieu 1977, 82.

8. See Collins (1991) for a discussion of this interlocking system, which she refers to as the "matrix of domination."

Nadine née Patricia

1. Convent law prohibited their going home for a wedding.

2. She later sent me the proposal in French: *Je vous aime chérie avec tout mon coeur. Je veux demeurer avec vous pour toute ma vie. Voulez-vous faire le même?* [I love you, dear, with all my heart. I want to live with you all my life. Would you like to do the same?]

Chapter 3

1. They are also known as the Felician Sisters of the Third Order of St. Francis, and as the Congregation of the Sisters of Saint Felix.

2. In addition to the Felician Sisters, there are at least sixteen other Polish-American religious orders. For a discussion of the Felicians see Amandine (1949), Betke (1946), Doman (1959), Hilburger (1946), Kuznicki (1978a, 1978b), T. Radzilowski (1975), Winowska (1972), Ziolkowski (1984).

3. Amandine 1949, 68.

4. Their first candidate presented herself only eighteen days after they had arrived (Winowska 1972, 196). Over the next twenty-five years, the order admitted 317 candidates, 90 of whom came from Michigan (Ziolkowski 1984, 103).

5. The number of candidates by decade were: 1920s: 186; 1930s: 168; 1940s: 121; 1950s: 149; 1960s: 192; 1970–1974: 11 (T. Radzilowski 1975, 21).

6. Doman 1959, 470–71.

7. Training for the convent took place in stages, and at each stage women were asked to make a deeper and longer commitment to religious life. Candidates as young as eleven years old came in through a preparatory stage known as aspirancy. They were sent to private schools that prepared them for the convent. They formally entered the convent and began the next stage, postulancy, when they came of age, which by the 1920s was after they completed high school. They were postulants for one year. After postulancy, candidates became novitiates and received a white veil and a sister name. As novitiates, they were not allowed to see their family or write or receive mail. After one year, they received their black veil and took temporary vows one year at a time for six years. After each year they could leave freely, until after the sixth year, when they took perpetual vows. In the 1950s, they started teaching as soon as they received their black veil. (This changed in the 1970s. Now they make two three-year commitments rather than one six-year commitment.)

8. Amandine 1949, 71. In 1882, the Felicians moved their Mother House from Wisconsin to Detroit and established the Seminary of the Felician Sisters and a teacher education program which offered courses in liberal arts, practical arts, and pedagogy (Ziolkowski 1984, 115–19). The sisters developed their own curricula and textbooks. By 1904, they had published forty-five Polish-language textbooks on Polish geography, history, and culture, Catholic history, and arithmetic, as well as workbooks and other readers. They also wrote course plans for parochial schools, the first in 1894 for elementary schools, and later, in 1932, for high schools (Hilburger 1946, 73–75).

9. Kuznicki 1978b, 436–37. See also Ziolkowski (1984, 237).

10. Kuznicki 1978a, 8.

11. Kuznicki 1978b, 439.

12. T. Radzilowski 1997, 18.

13. Kuznicki 1978a, 11.

14. Kuznicki 1978b, 451.

15. This refers to a 1970s television situation comedy, *The Mary Tyler Moore Show*, and a movie of the same era, *The Singing Nun.*

16. Ziolkowski 1984, 163.

17. T. Radzilowski 1975, 22. It is also important to remember that, as Lopata (1976a) argues, individual status was intertwined with family status, so that a son or daughter entering a religious order also raised the prestige of the family.

18. T. Radzilowski 1996, 73.

19. The one exception is always their Aunt Rose, who became a teacher before she married and returned to school to advance her degree after her husband died.

20. Taken from an autobiographical essay she wrote for Sister Evangeline in 1950.

21. Winowska 1972, 68–76.

22. Ziolkowski 1997, 77. Attitudes toward religious orders do vary across ethnic groups. See Daniels for a discussion of the different relations Irish and Italians had with the Roman Catholic Church, which led to the Irish community sending more young men and women to religious orders than the Italians (1997, 69–70).

23. Autobiographical essay.

24. Autobiographical essay.

25. See Bukowczyk for a discussion of the metaphor "brides of Christ" (1985, 10).

26. Winowska 1972, 60.

27. Evelyn Nakano Glenn defines social reproduction as "the array of activities and relationships involved in maintaining people both on a daily basis and intergenerationally" (1992, 1).

28. The patron saint of the Felicians, St. Felix of Cantalice, is also the patron saint of the sick and of children.

29. Similar to Bourdieu's notion of habitus as a durable, transposable set of dispositions.

30. See Getz, 1981.

31. Flinders 1999, 124.

32. Flinders 1999, 131.

33. Flinders 1999, 132–33. Today, feminism is doing for contemporary women what convents did for medieval women: "It insists upon women's right and capacity to choose, it celebrates the acts of courageous, decisive women, and it fosters feminine community" (135).

34. Flinders 1999, 191.

35. A more divine gender model is the Blessed Virgin Mary. The Marianism of Polish-American Catholicism, underscored in the Felician order, contributed to the advancement of women by elevating the adoration of the Virgin Mary. Like the woman mystics, their divine Mother is passionate and courageous and she teaches them how to be emotionally strong women. Mary is their intercessory to God, and, as such, Bukowczyk writes, Mary is "in some ways superior to both God the Son but especially God the Father in that, unlike them, she is fully tactile, available, accessible" (2003, 200). He also argues that the Felician Order, based on the Marian tradition, was liberating in that it presented a variation on the role of women, but the Catholic Church was still patriarchal and oppressive and the Felician Order was self-abnegating and repressive.

36. Women made up a third of PAHA's membership at that time (Bukowczyk 1996, 20–21).

37. Bukowczyk 1996, 20–21, 34.

Chapter 4

1. In the 1950s, roughly 40 percent of working white women were employed in sales and clerical positions, another 20 percent in the manufacturing sector, and another 18 percent were managers, administrators, and professionals (Hesse-Biber and Carter 2000, 41).

2. Everett Hughes ([1971] 1984, chs. 13, 14) defines a career as "the moving perspective in which the person sees his life as a whole and interprets the meaning of his various attributes, actions, and things which happen to him" (137), and he includes motherhood as a career (138). See also Becker (1952) for a discussion of the concept of career. Using Goffman's work on moral careers, Martha McMahon (1995) also makes use of the concept of motherhood as a moral career that transforms the identity and defines the self.

3. Bourdieu 1977, 77.

4. Office work was one of the main sectors open to women by the 1920s. Before then, men dominated the field. Women moved into this sector when the industry expanded, in part due to technological inventions such as the telephone and the typewriter, the latter of which was marketed specifically as a machine for women. Women were trained and recruited for these positions because they could be paid less than men. Soon, men occupied the managerial and professional strata of business and women became the support staff (Strom 1992). The number of workers in the sector doubled from 1940 to 1960, and then doubled again from 1960 to 1996. By 1996, there were 18.4 million clerical workers, most of them women, and roughly a quarter of all working women were employed in clerical positions (Hesse-Biber and Carter 2000, 114–17).

5. Most of the women doing office work in the first half of the twentieth century were white women. As late as 1960, only 8 percent of employed African-American women worked in clerical positions (compared to 35 percent of employed white women). By 1970, a fifth of all employed African-American women were clerical workers, and a quarter were for the next three decades (Hesse-Biber and Carter 2000, 117).

6. Ferree and Hess 1994, 12–13.

7. Most of the houses in the neighborhood were originally 900-square-foot, single-story, three-bedroom ranch homes with tornado shelters in the basements. The houses cost between $11,500 and $13,000 in the late 1950s and are worth at least $125,000 today. The FHA program made it easier and less expensive to own a home by extending the mortgage period and implementing practices that lowered the risk of lending, which in turn lowered interest rates. These practices favored loans for single-family homes in new developments in the suburbs (as opposed to multifamily dwellings in urban areas, or for the remodeling of older homes). It was difficult if not impossible to get loans to renovate or buy homes in urban neighborhoods that were more unstable,

especially in black or Hispanic neighborhoods. Real estate practices such as steering, along with violence and conflict, kept black families out of the suburbs until the late 1960s, and even then, the number of racial minorities moving into the white suburbs was small. This meant that government programs favored white homeowners who were able to buy homes in the suburbs. See Massey and Denton (1993, 51–54).

8. For a contrasting view of how a large segment of the working class and working poor were hurt by these economic changes see Newman (1993), L. Rubin (1994), B. Rubin (1996), Stacey (1998), as well as Michael Moore's documentary *Roger & Me* (1989), about the devastating effects of deindustrialization in Flint, Michigan. Since the 1970s, the bottom 60 percent of society has not shown a net income gain, and average wages for those without college degrees fell between 1979 and 1999 (Rogers and Teixeira 2000).

9. L. Rubin 1994, 4–6.

10. Brown (1997) found that six of the thirteen girls in her sample were physically abused at some point in their lives. In Lillian Rubin's sample of fifty working-class families, 40 percent had alcoholic parents and 40 percent came from divorced families (1976, ch. 3).

11. For example, Naples (1994, 113) refers to the working class on public assistance, while Cohen (1998, 355) lumps together those in her sample who come from "working-class and deprived backgrounds," and Brown (1997) defines the working class as the working poor. Steinberg, describing an email discussion list for academics from working-class backgrounds, refers to faculty whose family came from "the lowest sociological stratum" (2000, 10A).

12. "Cortez the Killer," *Zuma* (1975).

13. Master narratives provide direction about how we should act, what we are expected to do, and even how we ought to feel, and as such they invoke a moral authority (Romero and Stewart 1999). Scholars also construct theories through master narratives that are framed within epistemological and political agendas (e.g., feminism, liberalism, conservatism).

14. Massey and Denton 1993, 51–55; Newman 1993; B. Rubin 1996.

15. William Julius Wilson (1987) uses this phrase.

16. Lillian Rubin (1976) notes some of these same tensions, but the tone of her respondents (or at least the way she reports it) is much more depressing, as she focuses on the difficult emotional responsibilities and relationship adjustments working-class mothers have to make. She emphasizes the crying children and absent fathers; we don't hear about the corresponding joy of being a mother that is evident in Angel's narrative.

17. Bukowczyk (1987) also argues that postwar Polish-American men's decisions reproduced their own class positions: "Socialized to an ethnic, working-class way of life, they prized security, stability, and community over more individualistic goals

like money, power, and status" (107). But it is Bourdieu's notion of the habitus—our subjective dispositions grounded in objective conditions—that explains why they value security and stability.

18. Natalie Angier forcefully states, "Feminism had nothing to do with it. Women worked before and they're working now. Women have always worked" (2000, 393). Numerous scholars concur (Tilly and Scott 1978; Sapiro 1990, 402; Stewart and Ostrove 1993, 489; Garey, 1999; Newman 1993; Ferree and Hess 1994; Hesse-Biber and Carter 2000; T. Radzilowski 1996, 1997; Anker 1988; Ziolkowski 1997).

19. In 1960, only 19 percent of married women with children under the age of six were in the labor force, while by 1980, 45 percent of them were, along with 62 percent of mothers with children between the ages of six and seventeen (Hesse-Biber and Carter 2000, 17, 39). In 1960, roughly three-quarters of all single women aged twenty to twenty-four participated in the labor force, and this level remained constant through the 1990s. For married women in the same age group, however, less than a third were in the labor force in 1960; this increased to about half ten years later, and roughly two-thirds by 1985. When Angel returned to work in the early 1970s, roughly half of all married women in her age cohort participated in the labor force; by 1993, this rose to 75 percent (Statistical Abstracts 1994, 401).

20. In contrast, Lillian Rubin found that working-class men did not like their wives working, preferring women to be "more feminine" and to not act independent. "I like to feel I wear the pants in the house," one husband said (1976, 176–77). Some scholars argue that men's desire for women to stay home was more a part of middle-class culture, because men with professional occupations were more dependent on their wives as support staff than were laborers (Stewart and Ostrove 1993). In contrast, Rubin found that husbands who had more occupational prestige and larger salaries were less threatened by their wives working, because middle-class women seldom contributed more than 10 percent to the family budget, while working-class women contributed a greater portion. This contribution entitled working-class wives to a larger voice in the household than middle-class women (1976, 174–76). See also Astrachan (1994) and Hochschild and Machung (1990). The Grasinski Girls were also contributing only a small amount (and yet their income was critical to family comfort), and, perhaps because their husbands were the main breadwinners, they did not feel threatened by their wives working.

21. For a discussion of the cult of domesticity see Collins (1991) and Giddings (1984).

22. Newman 1993; L. Rubin 1994, 1976. None of the women in Ruth Sidel's study of immigrant and racial-minority working-class women in New York in the 1970s could afford to be stay-at-home moms ([1978] 1995, 157). Fox-Genovese (1997) also interviewed working mothers in the 1990s who wanted to stay home but could not.

23. Seifer 1976, 30. Sennet and Cobb also found that working-class women "feel a profound sympathy for their husbands' burdens" ([1972] 1993, 130).

24. Anita Ilta Garey (1999) outlines the strategies women use to weave together employment and motherhood, including part-time work, home work, and night shifts. Garey notes that a "working woman" is different from a "working mother." Working mothers must develop strategies that manage the competing mother and worker identities. Because the dominant paradigm in the United States defines women as either work oriented or family oriented, working mothers are in a compromised position—working mothers "are seen as less than fully committed mothers" and less committed workers, justifying their marginalized positions and low wages (7).

25. Garey 1999, 4–5.

26. Ferree 1984, 67. Garey also argues that social scientists too often conceptualize "working mothers" as "the professional or corporate woman, briefcase in hand." When we ignore working-class women, "the majority of employed mothers are missing from cultural images and social analysis" (1999, 4–5).

27. See Mansbridge (1986) and Ferree (1984, 67).

28. Hesse-Biber and Carter (2000) note that work provides women with a positive sense of well-being and feelings of self-fulfillment, competence, and assertiveness. Sidel ([1978] 1995) found that work was a source of self-esteem for the working-class women in her study, and that they felt more in control and more powerful when working. Garey (1999) noted that working-class hospital workers found their work rewarding, exciting, challenging, and enjoyable. See also Strom (1992) and Fox-Genovese (1997). Lillian Rubin (1976) found that, while at-home working-class women saw their possibilities of work outside the home as dull and oppressive, once they joined the labor force they had positive attitudes toward work.

29. Rosen 1987. Lillian Rubin argues that in the 1970s, working-class women defined their primary roles as wife and mother, maintaining that work was an "instrumental activity that served the economic needs of the family" (1994, 71). Ferree also found that women can place men's needs before their own "without thereby indicating that they subscribe to general principles about women's second-class status or place at home and hearth" (1984, 63). See also Tilly and Scott (1978), Newman (1993), and Fox-Genovese (1997).

30. Women themselves have at times defined women pursuing occupational careers as selfish because they placed individual needs above the family, and critically referred to careers as "yuppie things" (Fox-Genovese 1997, 218). This disdain for careers also surfaced in Garey's (1999) study of working-class mothers, who defined careers (but not jobs) as a source of tension between women and their families. See also L. Rubin (1994, 71) and Newman (1993).

31. See also Crittenden (2001, 153–61, 268–70).

32. See Ferree and Hess (1994) and Friedan ([1963] 1983).

33. Mansbridge 1986. See also Stacey (1998) and Fox-Genovese (1997).

34. Ferree and Hess 1994, 14–15.

Chapter 5

1. Marjorie DeVault (1991) writes about feeding the family as caring work. Micaela di Leonardo (1984) researches "kinship work" that keeps the family together. Evelyn Nakano Glenn (1992) describes the tasks of social reproduction.

2. See de Beauvoir [1952] 1989, 174–87. Many ethnic groups (e.g., Italians, Jews, Greeks) hold mothers in a special esteem, as do Polish Americans. Thaddeus Radzilowski attributes the stability and longevity of the Polish community to the "beloved mothers" who serve the community and hold it together (1996, 64–65). See also Bukowczyk (1987, 144–45).

3. McMahon 1995, 191–93; DeVault 1991, 29.

4. I would like to thank Carolyn Howe for pointing out these emotional tasks. See also Anderson et al., who found that in oral histories "it was easier to document activities than feelings and values" and that researchers often prefer to ask more neutral questions about activities than more emotionally-laden questions about feelings (1990, 95–98).

5. The General Social Survey (GSS) is a national survey that has been administered twenty-four times since its first survey in 1972. The survey is conducted by NORC, a national research center affiliated with the University of Chicago. The actual GSS statement was, "Yes, I think of myself as a feminist." The percentages reported held across age groups. Ellen Israel Rosen found that working-class women were resistant to feminism if it insults the dignity of their husbands or fathers (1987, viii). In the 1970s, Nancy Seifer found that working-class women saw feminists as "insensitive to their needs and values" (1976, 24). Many others agree; see Sidel [1978] 1995; L. Rubin 1976; Fox-Genovese 1997; Myaskovsky and Wittig 1997; and Bookman and Morgen 1988. Some evidence exists to contradict this argument. For example, researchers found that white working-class women attending an elite private women's college in the 1960s actually embraced the women's movement more eagerly and with less problems than did the middle-class women at the college (Stewart and Ostrove 1993). Lillian Rubin found that negative attitudes of working-class women toward feminism were changing by the late 1980s (1994, 71–72). Judith Stacey (1998) describes several working-class feminists and their participation in the movement.

6. Seifer 1976, 29. Other scholars found similar attitudes (Fox-Genovese 1997; Myaskovsky and Wittig 1997; L. Rubin 1994; 1976, 72–75; Sidel [1978] 1995; Ferree 1984; Ferree and Hess 1994).

7. L. Rubin 1994, 73.

8. White women tend to have more traditional definitions of womanhood than black women (Collins 1991; Giddings 1984). Dugger (1988) shows that women not in the labor force are more conservative than those in the labor force, so differences between black and white women may be more about labor force participation than

race. White women in the labor force are more likely to challenge traditional attitudes regarding pay equality, gender roles, abortion, and the culturally dominant views of gender. Black and white women's attitudes are converging, perhaps because white women are beginning to look more like black women in their productive and reproductive styles, that is, they are more likely to be working and raising children alone. Finally, white women are more likely to identify publicly as feminist than are black women (Myaskovsky and Wittig 1997).

9. L. Rubin, 1994, 72. See also Sidel ([1978] 1995, vii, 52, 157) and Fox-Genovese (1997).

10. Rymph 2000; Mansbridge, 1986, 104.

11. Mansbridge 1986, 112.

12. Fox-Genovese 1997, 28–29. See also Rowland (1986) and Kaminer (1993).

13. How do they reconcile being anti-abortion with using birth control? I asked one of the sisters, who said, "I thought and thought and the only answer I could come up with is this. If I had a small seed and threw it away and didn't plant it, nothing would happen. But if I took that same seed and planted it and it grew to become a beautiful plant and then I pulled it out and it died, the seed would have never reached its full potential. I don't know if this makes any sense, but to me it does."

14. Feminists can be both pro-choice and anti-abortion. The feminist organization Committee for Abortion Rights and Against Sterilization Abuse defines reproductive rights as the "right" to have children and the right to "resist pressures to have abortions" (Ferree and Hess 1994).

15. Crittenden 2001, 63.

16. In the 1960s and 1970s, middle-class women entered the labor force at a rate of two to one compared to working-class women (Mansbridge 1986, 106). However, this figure does not take into account that more working-class women were already in the labor force.

17. Mansbridge 1986, 100. See 99–113 for a description of the conflict between feminists and homemakers. See also Fox-Genovese (1997) and Crittenden (2001).

18. Crittenden 2001, 3.

19. Mansbridge 1986, 105. It is also the fact that, by the early 1970s, many middle-class lifestyles became dependent on the income of two wage earners, so the movement of middle-class women into the labor market was also a response to changing economic realities. Moreover, the value of "homemaking" rises and falls with capitalism's lesser or greater need for women in the workforce as wage earners or as a reserve army of labor. Both a push out of the kitchen (feminism) and a pull (capitalist needs) are at work here.

20. The women's movement called attention to the importance of the private domain, attempting to make domestic work visible and provide remuneration for it (Crittenden 2001; Nicholson 1986, 59). And yet I would agree with Barbara Ehrenreich (2000), who criticized Betty Friedan for implying that housework was lesser work.

Feminists wanted women out of the house but never had a plan for who should clean the house—thereby perpetuating a class-based assumption that others, in a lower class, could pick up the socks and scrub the toilets.

21. McMahon 1995, 10.

22. Crittenden (2001) argues that women should earn their own Social Security benefits while mothering, the government should provide universal preschool and affordable day care, and work sites should allow more flexible schedules.

23. In this way they were like "antifeminists," who "want to be 'equal but different' and see feminists as wanting to be the *same* as men, as forfeiting their uniqueness" (Rowland 1986, 686; italics in original). See Stacey (1998) for a discussion of antifeminists and postfeminists.

24. Many scholars have identified women's ways of thinking and acting (Gilligan 1982; Belenky et al. [1986] 1997; Lorber 1994, ch. 5; Collins 1991; Chodorow [1978] 1999).

25. Chodorow [1978] 1999, 93.

26. Chodorow [1978] 1999, 169.

27. Marxists argue that women's involvement in the reproductive work of maintaining the family is what allows men to be involved in productive work in the market arena. The caregiving that women provide helps develop the human capital necessary to sustain the workforce.

28. Gilman [1898] 1998, 120–39. Nancy Folbre (2001, 226–32) provides examples of less socialistic government programs to sustain families and children that bring women out of the home and men back into the home, including a progressive income tax, prekindergarten, and paid parental leaves. See also Crittenden (2001).

29. Folbre 2001, 231.

30. Collins 1991, 224.

Part 3 Introduction

1. See Anthony Giddens for a discussion of the process of "structuration," which represents the dynamic interplay and "mutual dependency" of agency and structure (1979, 69–71).

2. See Giddens (1979, 53–85). Symbolic interactionism also understands social actors as active constructors of the social worlds in which they live (Anderson et al. 1990, 108). The concept of agency stands as a corrective to Marxist economic determinism and Durkheimian structural determinism, as it acknowledges that social structures and institutions do not work independently of the people who produce and reproduce them. Resistance is possible because we all have human agency.

3. People often participate in their own destruction by engaging in behaviors that reproduce destructive structures. See Bourgois (1995) and Willis (1977).

4. Epstein 1997, 135.

5. Epstein 1997, 118.

6. Urzula Tempska points out that Suzanne Strempek Shea's fictional Polish-American women are too comfortable and apolitical, compared to the working-class militant women at the turn of the century who fought for family, church, and neighborhood. They are "comfortably American-with-Polish-roots, free from the internal conflicts of split ethnic identity, and from the engagement with feminist and nationalist causes which informed their lives. As hyphenated ethnics, they are cozier, but as (feminist) women they are more alone, less organized than their foremothers" (1997, 296).

7. Robin Kelley examines the non-collective resistance strategies of young black urban-poor boys, "from footdragging to sabotage, theft at the workplace to absenteeism, cursing to graffiti" (1994, 7). While different in tone and substance to how white women have resisted, their actions are similar, as forms of evasive resistance to structures of power.

8. Lemert 2002, 171.

Chapter 6

1. Norris 1993, 79.

2. Most scholars note the Marian-based nature of Polish and Polish-American Catholicism (Bukowczyk 1985; 2003). But the adoration of Jesus, especially as the suffering god-man represented often by the thorn and the bleeding heart, is also an integral component of Polish Catholicism (Thomas and Znaniecki [1918] 1958, 282–85). Silverman writes that the Blessed Virgin Mary "occupied a place second only to that of her son Jesus in the Polish peasant's hierarchy" (2000, 95). While the religious ceremonies of Poles and Polish Americans incorporate adoration of the Blessed Virgin, there are numerous Jesus-centered rituals, especially during the Lenten season (e.g., the Stations of the Cross and the Bitter Lamentations); Christmas and Easter, the two primary holidays, celebrate the birth and death of Jesus (see Parot 1981, 220–21).

3. The Grasinski Girls are not unique. Beverly Donofrio writes that religiously devout Catholics "believe your guardian angel leads you to the only empty parking place in the parking lot. And they believe the closer you get to God the more hotly the devil pursues you" (2000, 163). See Orsi (1996) for a description of women's concrete and personal prayers to St. Jude.

4. See Charles Lemert (2002) for an understanding of "mysterious" social structures.

5. Winowska 1972, 51–53.

6. Amandine 1949, 65. For a discussion of fate, see Kathleen Norris (1998, 139–43).

7. While good things are a result of God's compassion and their obedience, when bad things happen, they do not attribute this to God's being cruel, spiteful, or uncharitable, nor do they blame the individual for the misfortunes that have befallen them. Erich Fromm compares a patriarchal love of God that configures God as the punisher, the deliverer of justice, with a matriarchal love that understands God's unconditional love (1956, 67).

8. See also Thomas and Znaniecki ([1918] 1958, 252).

9. Bukoski 1999, 179.

10. Their prayers have none of the superstitious or magical qualities to them that Thomas and Znaniecki found in the beliefs of Polish peasants ([1918] 1958, 206–75). Nonetheless, their prayers did resemble in some ways the prayers of Polish peasants, which Bukowczyk described as "a mechanical means to influence practical affairs" (1985, 11). But their means of influence moved from the magical to the divine. Thomas and Znaniecki describe this as follows: "actions whose meaning in the magical system consisted in bringing immediately and mechanically a determined effect become now acts of worship, as conscious action of divinity moved by human worship. It is no longer the letter, but the meaning of the prayer and the religious feeling that accompanies it that influence God or the saint; it is the confidence in, and the love of, God . . . that compel God to grant men what they need" ([1918] 1958, 284–85).

11. "The Eucharist is bound with the passion, death and resurrection. . . . The Eucharist does not exist apart from the cross and only a share of the cross assures us of a share in the life of the risen Christ." To accept Mary, Mother of the Redeemer, means "that we are willing to accept, with her, a share in the atoning sacrifice of her son" (Winowska 1972, 38, 90–91).

12. Ahmad (1996) argues that prayer is a form of resistance.

13. Norris 1998, 350.

14. Thomas and Znaniecki argue that Jesus was more accessible to the Polish peasants than God because of the "half-human personality of Jesus" ([1918] 1958, 282).

15. Norris 1998, 351.

16. For example, the doctrine of Christianity and Southern black Baptist churches supported the civil rights movement in the United States, the Roman Catholic Church supported the Solidarity movement in Poland, and liberation theology supports populist movements in Central America.

Chapter 7

1. Joyce Antler refers to these types of personal attempts at social change as "feminism as life process," which is a "personal rather than a collective attempt by women to mold their destinies in the world and achieve autonomy" (1992, 110).

2. Simone de Beauvoir, a late bloomer as a feminist, also criticizes women for their own subjugation (see Deirdre Bair's 1998 introduction to de Beauvoir's *The Second Sex*). "For a great many women the roads to transcendence are blocked; because they *do* nothing, they fail to *make themselves* anything. They wonder indefinitely what they *could have* become" (de Beauvoir [1952] 1989, 258–59; italics in original). In contrast, Natalie Angier is critical of women who dismiss feminists as women whining. "Women have done much by pushing and whining," she writes, "but we're not there yet; we're still gripped with self-doubt, gynophobia, and cramps of spiritual autism" (2000, 395). See also Judith Stacey's (1998) discussion of postfeminism.

3. For a discussion of the stereotype of women as weak and submissive see Betty Friedan, who looks at the image of women portrayed in magazines in the early 1960s as "young and frivolous, almost childlike; fluffy and feminine; passive; gaily content in a world of bedroom and kitchen, sex, babies, and home" ([1963] 1983, 36). Simone de Beauvoir also notes that women are seen as weak, passive, futile, docile; their emotions are primitive and irrational ([1952] 1989, 7, 9, 336). Linda Nicholson shows that femininity connotes powerlessness, silliness, frivolity, dependency, decoration, and sentimentality (1986, 45).

4. I was introduced to these writers in a wonderful reading group I belonged to while at the University of North Carolina, Greensboro. I would like to thank Angela Rhone, Pat Bowden, Mary K. Wakeman, Lois Bailey, and the other members for this education.

5. It is important to add that I had not yet read about white working-class women. Writings on working-class women by white feminists such as Ruth Sidel, Karen Brodkin Sacks, Linda Frankel, and Louise Lamphere depict a tougher and rougher version of white women.

6. Hurtado 1996, 40. See also Dugger 1988, 428. This is certainly not true of all white feminists' analyses. In contrast to defining women as victims, some scholarship focuses on examining women's resistance (for example, Sheila Rowbotham's *Women, Resistance and Revolution: A History of Women and Revolution in the Modern World,* published in 1972). I would like to thank Carolyn Howe for this reference. Howe, a white feminist sociologist, argues in a personal communication that what is written and published about and by white feminists is not necessarily what white women who were activist feminists thought. Many white women did not think of themselves as victims as they marched down the streets demanding racial, class, and gender equality.

7. Just as the male-dominant ideology defined women as frail and weak, class and racial ideologies allowed white middle-class women to position themselves in leadership and advisory roles in order to "help out" working-class women and women of color. Constructing the racial and class "other" as a weak subordinate is a strategy (albeit at times unconscious) for claiming superiority and authority. This strategy for se-

curing a positive self-image through the denigration of the other can be implemented effectively by investing the other with the same characteristics that are most undesirable in the self. Thus, defining working-class women and women of color as in need of guidance was a way for white middle-class women to deny their own subordination. When white middle-class women define themselves as different from (better educated, more articulate, more conscious of gender inequality) working-class women and women of color, they recreate hierarchies of inequality and relations of domination.

8. Krieger 1996, 105.

9. Angier 2000, 315.

10. In fairness to earlier feminists, however, some of their structural analyses of gender inequality were so new and necessary for the more nuanced "structure and agency" analyses that followed. I would like to thank Carolyn Howe for pointing this out to me.

11. Lopata 1976b, 24–25.

12. Andre 1985, 112.

13. Sneakiness is not always seen as an inferior form of power. In fact, when attached to men's behavior, it is often portrayed as a keen, well-employed strategy. The "quarterback sneak" is designed to fool the opponent, as is a surprise attack from the flank in a military battle. Neither tactic has a negative value attached to it; attempts to fool the opponent do not represent weakness. It is as if, when men are sneaky, they are good strategists, while when women are sneaky, they are manipulators.

14. Tannen 1991, 225–26.

15. Hurtado 1996, vii; italics in original. She argues that women of color, because their oppression is based on rejection rather than seduction, can be more direct in their struggle for power because it is against the patriarchal white man and not men of color.

16. Collins 1991, 145–54.

17. Tannen states, "From childhood, girls criticize peers who try to stand out and appear better than others" (1991, 77). A woman who acts like she is better is considered to be bragging or showing off (158). Men can assert superiority because their mode of being in the world is to establish position. Women are in the world to establish connection, and one-upmanship goes against the value of connection.

18. Belenky et al. [1986] 1997, 47–48.

19. Collins 1991, 105.

20. Krieger 1996, 104.

21. See Bukowczyk (2003) on ways in which images of the suffering Blessed Virgin Mother helped construct an ideal type for Polish-American women.

22. Carol Lee Flinders found there is no going back to blindness after seeing systemic misogyny (1999, 214).

23. Wini Breines (1992) describes the anxiety of white middle-class women in the politically and culturally conservative postwar era that limited women's opportunities.

24. Angel made sure she told her male bosses about their errors in private. "This guy would give me these figures, and I'm looking, and it's, like, 'What?' And I would never, like, in public, like, 'What?' I would go into his office and say, [quiet tone] 'Do you really want this?' And he was, like, 'Oh, God, thank you for finding that.'"

25. L. Rubin 1994, 75.

26. Patricia Hill Collins argues that resistance begins with the reclaiming of self, by challenging the negative valuations that come from the dominant society (1991, 103, 142–43).

27. Natalie Angier suggests that this girl-bashing represents internalized oppression. Using Chrissie Hynde of the Pretenders as an example, she offers an adult version of the same process of women dismissing women "for not being serious enough about their work." In her own words, Hynde would rather "work with men. . . . They're single-minded, straight-forward, and they can rock. Most women can't" (2000, 395). However, Lyn Mikel Brown (1997) sees buffooning "the feminine" as a form of class and gender resistance. She found that rural working-class girls consciously reject dominant cultural ideologies found in middle-class gender-role expectations.

28. Working-class women resist in a variety of public arenas, most particularly the workplace, but also in the community, schools, the church, and in movements such as the pro-life movement (O'Farrell and Kornbluh 1996). The working class in general was not as much a part of the social movements of the 1960s (civil rights, women's, antiwar) as was the middle class (Sherkat and Blocker 1994; Seifer 1976). Seifer worked with working-class communities and found that "the Silent Majority was voiceless, but not out of choice" (12). It was voiceless because its members did not have the ability to make their voices heard, nor did they feel they were well-informed. Their activism was more local and personal. "They reacted less to abstract ideas about equality than to concrete problems related to their daily existence" (30).

29. Collins argues that black women have a long and powerful history of resisting oppression, but this culture of resistance has often been ignored by mainstream scholars because their acts are often on an individual level (1991, 10, 144). Ahmad (1996) identifies fasting, suicide, and praying as powerful reactions to powerlessness. Simone de Beauvoir identifies self-mutilation—burning oneself with a cigarette, cutting oneself with a hatchet in order to avoid tiresome garden parties—as acts of protest. "When she puts a snail on her breasts, swallows a bottle of aspirin tablets, wounds herself, the young girl is hurling defiance at her future lover" ([1952] 1989, 354). Bookman and Morgen (1988) argue, however, that a change in consciousness is empowering only when it leads to activism in the public sphere.

30. Lorber 1994, ch. 7.

Conclusion

1. During graduate school I pulled them out and, knowing a bit more about how to write by then, I could see that they were essentially uncorrected.

2. See bell hooks (2000) for a discussion of the class tensions, shame, and dis-ease she felt when she went to a private college. Louise DeSalvo (1996) writes in her memoir about the shame she felt over having neither money for the right clothes nor the cultural capital to know how to dress.

3. Assumptions common to science and the academy include (1) that the split between subject and object must be maintained; (2) that scientists should therefore keep a distance from the values, beliefs, and worldviews of the people they study, so as to not be biased by them; and (3) that truth is determined through adversarial debate (Collins 1991, 205).

4. See hooks (2000, ch. 9).

5. Ecclesiastes 12:12.

6. Of course, she does not make reference to Marx, but I do. See Karl Marx, *Capital,* vol. 3, "On the Realm of Necessity and the Realm of Freedom." The realm of necessity refers to our work life, where our labors are a means to an end (e.g., wages or status), whereas in the realm of freedom, our action is an end in itself.

7. Krieger 1996, 6.

Appendix A

1. Life stories, oral histories, and case studies have a deep history in sociology. One of the most famous and earliest examples of the use of life histories is William I. Thomas and Florian Znaniecki's now-classic *The Polish Peasant in Europe and America* (1918). In the 1920s and 1930s, Thomas and Znaniecki, along with Robert Park and Ernest Burgess, trained the next generation of sociologists to use these interpretative, qualitative methodologies. Toward the middle of the century, sociologists began to favor more quantitative methods (surveys, questionnaires, close-answered interviews), as well as historical, theoretical, and conceptual strategies. In the last few decades, however, qualitative methodologies, especially life stories and oral histories, have once again resurfaced as an important tool, coming back into favor through feminist studies, cultural studies, and postmodern theory. For discussion of the use of life stories, see Anderson et al. (1990), Alpern et al. (1992), Bertaux (1981), Denzin (1989), Dunaway and Baum (1996), Laslett (1999), Ritchie (1995), and Reinharz (1992).

2. These questions were patterned after those used by Belenky et al. ([1986] 1997), which we were reading in the course that semester.

3. Doing a content analysis of the transcripts places emphasis on the life stories when framing the interpretation. See Anderson et al. 1990, 103.

Bibliography

Ahmad, Aqueil. 1996. Powerful Reaction to Powerlessness. *Peace Review* 8 (3): 423–29.

Alba, Richard D. 1995. The Twilight of Ethnicity among American Catholics of European Ancestry. In *Majority and Minority: The Dynamics of Race and Ethnicity in American Life,* 5th ed., ed. Norman R. Yetman, 420–29. Boston: Allyn and Bacon.

———. 1990. *Ethnic Identity: The Transformation of White America.* New Haven: Yale University Press.

Alflen, Louise Fifelski, and Marilynn Ciboch Fifelski. n.d. *The Fifelski Family.* Unpublished manuscript.

Alpern, Sara, Joyce Antler, Elisabeth Israels Perry, and Ingrid Winther Scobie, eds. 1992. *The Challenge of Feminist Biography: Writing the Lives of Modern American Women.* Urbana: University of Illinois Press.

Amandine, Sr. Mary. 1949. Seventy-five Years of Felician Activity in America. *Polish American Studies* 6 (3–4): 65–79.

Ancona, Gaspar F. 2001. *Where the Star Came to Rest: Stories of the Catholic People in West Michigan.* Strasbourg: Editions du Signe.

Anderson, James M., and Iva A. Smith, eds. 1983. *Ethnic Groups in Michigan.* Detroit: Ethnos Press.

Anderson, Kathryn, Susan Armitage, Dana Jack, and Judith Wittner. 1990. Beginning Where We Are: Feminist Methodology in Oral History. In *Feminist Research Methods: Exemplary Readings in the Social Sciences,* ed. Joyce McCarl Nielsen, 94–112. Boulder: Westview Press.

Andes, Nancy. 1992. Social Class and Gender: An Empirical Evaluation of Occupational Stratification. *Gender and Society* 6 (2): 231–51.

Andre, Judith. 1985. Power, Oppression, and Gender. *Social Theory and Practice.* 11 (1): 107–22.

Angier, Natalie. 2000. *Woman: An Intimate Geography.* New York: Anchor Books.

Anker, Laura. 1988. Women, Work and Family: Polish, Italian and Eastern European Immigrants in Industrial Connecticut, 1890–1940. *Polish American Studies.* 45 (2): 23–49.

Antler, Joyce. 1992. Having it All, Almost: Confronting the Legacy of Lucy Sprague Mitchell. In *The Challenge of Feminist Biography: Writing the Lives of Modern American Women,* ed. Sara Alpern, Joyce Antler, Elisabeth Israels Perry, and Ingrid Winther Scobie, 97–115. Urbana: University of Illinois Press.

Astrachan, Anthony. 1993. Dividing Lines. In *Experiencing Race, Class, and Gender In the United States,* ed. Virginia Cyrus, 86–91. Mountain View, CA: Mayfield Publishing.

Baca Zinn, Maxine, Lynn Weber Cannon, Elizabeth Higginbotham, and Bonnie Thornton Dill. 1986. The Costs of Exclusionary Practices in Women's Studies. *Signs: Journal of Women in Culture and Society* 11 (2): 290–303.

Barth, Fredrik. 1969. Introduction. In *Ethnic Groups and Boundaries: The Social Organization of Culture Difference,* ed. Frederick Barth, 9–38. Boston: Little, Brown and Company.

Bauer, Raymond, and Alice Bauer. 1971. Day to Day Resistance to Slavery. In *American Slavery: The Question of Resistance,* ed. John H. Bracey Jr., August Meier, and Elliott Rudwick. Belmont, CA: Wadsworth Publishing Company, Inc.

Becker, Howard. 1952. The Career of the Chicago Public School Teacher. *American Journal of Sociology* 57 (March): 470–77.

Belenky, Mary Field, Blythe McVicker Clinchy, Nancy Rule Goldberger, and Jill Mattuck Tarule. [1986] 1997. *Women's Ways of Knowing: The Development of Self, Voice, and Mind.* New York: Basic Books.

Bertaux, Daniel, ed. 1981. *Biography and Society: The Life History Approach in the Social Sciences.* Beverly Hills, CA: Sage Publications.

Betke, Sr. M. Angela. 1946. The Felician Sisters and Social Service. *Polish American Studies* 3 (1–2): 21–29.

Blum, Linda M. 1997. Possibilities and Limits of the Comparable Worth Movement. *Workplace / Women's Place,* ed. Dana Dunn, 88–100. Los Angeles: Roxbury Publishing Company.

Bookman, Ann, and Sandra Morgen, ed. 1988. *Women and the Politics of Empowerment.* Philadelphia: Temple University Press.

Bourdieu, Pierre. 1977. *Outline of a Theory of Practice.* Trans. Richard Nice. New York: Cambridge University Press.

———. 1984. *Distinction: A Social Critique of the Judgement of Taste.* Trans. Richard Nice. Cambridge, MA: Harvard University Press.

Bourdieu, Pierre, and Jean-Claude Passeron. 1977. *Reproduction in Education, Society and Culture.* Trans. Richard Nice. Beverly Hills, CA: Sage Publications.

Bourgois, Philippe. 1995. *In Search of Respect: Selling Crack in El Barrio.* Cambridge: Cambridge University Press.

Bratt, James D., and Christopher H. Meehan. 1993. *Gathered at the River: Grand Rapids, Michigan and Its People of Faith.* Grand Rapids: William B. Eerdmans Publishing Co.

Breines, Wini. 1992. *Young, White, and Miserable: Growing Up Female in the 1950s.* Boston: Beacon Press.

Brinks, Herbert J., ed. 1995. *Dutch American Voices: Letters from the United States, 1850–1930.* Ithaca: Cornell University Press.

Brown, Lyn Mikel. 1997. Performing Femininities: Listening to White Working-Class Girls in Rural Maine. *Journal of Social Issues.* 53 (4): 683–701.

Brozek, Andrzej. 1985. *Polish Americans, 1854–1939.* Trans. Wojciech Worsztynowicz. Warsaw: Interpress.

Bukoski, Anthony. 1999. *Polonaise.* Dallas: Southern Methodist University Press.

Bukowczyk, John. 1980. The Immigrant "Community" Re-examined: Political and Economic Tensions in a Brooklyn Polish Settlement, 1888–1894. *Polish American Studies* 37 (2): 5–16.

———. 1984. Polish Rural Culture and Immigrant Working Class Formation, 1880–1914. *Polish American Studies* 41 (2): 23–44.

———. 1985. Mary the Messiah: Polish Immigrant Heresy and the Malleable Ideology of the Roman Catholic Church, 1880–1930. *Journal of American Ethnic History* 4 (Spring): 5–32.

———. 1987. *And My Children Did Not Know Me: A History of the Polish-Americans.* Bloomington: Indiana University Press.

———. 1996. Polish Americans, History Writing, and the Organization of Memory. In *Polish Americans and Their History: Community, Culture, and Politics,* ed. John J. Bukowczyk, 1–38. Pittsburgh: University of Pittsburgh Press.

———. 1998. Polish Americans, Ethnicity, and Otherness. *Polish Review* 43 (3): 299–313.

———. 2002. The Big Lebowski Goes to the Polish Wedding: Polish Americans—Hollywood Style. *Polish Review* 47 (2): 211–30.

———. 2003. Holy Mary, Other of God: Sacred and Profane Constructions of Polish-American Womanhood. *Polish Review* 48 (2): 195–203.

Chafetz, Janet Saltzman. 1997. Feminist Theory and Sociology: Underutilized Contributions for Mainstream Theory. *Annual Review of Sociology* 23: 97–120.

Chirot, Daniel. 1994. *How Societies Change.* Thousand Oaks, CA: Pine Forge Press.

Chodorow, Nancy J. [1978] 1999. *The Reproduction of Mothering: Psychoanalysis and the Sociology of Gender.* Berkeley: University of California Press.

Chrobot, Rev. Leonard. 1973. The Elusive Polish American. *Polish American Studies* 30 (1): 45–53.

———. 2001. Typologies of Polish American Parishes: Changing Pastoral Structures and Methods. *Polish American Studies* 58 (2): 83–94.

Clifford, James. 1993. Introduction: Partial Truths. In *Writing Culture: The Poetics and Politics of Ethnography,* ed. James Clifford and George E. Marcus, 1–26. Berkeley: University of California Press.

Cohen, Rosetta Marantz. 1998. Class Consciousness and Its Consequences: The

Impact of an Elite Education on Mature, Working-Class Women. *American Educational Research Journal* 35, no. 3 (Fall): 353–75.

Collins, Patricia Hill. 1991. *Black Feminist Thought: Knowledge, Consciousness, and the Politics of Empowerment.* Boston: Unwin Hyman.

Conzen, Kathleen Neils. 1990. *Making Their Own America: Assimilation Theory and the German Peasant Pioneer.* Oxford: Berg Publishers.

Cook, Judith A., and Mary Margaret Fonow. 1990. Knowledge and Women's Interests: Issues of Epistemology and Methodology in Feminist Sociological Research. In *Feminist Research Methods: Exemplary Readings in the Social Sciences,* ed. Joyce McCarl Nielsen, 69–93. Boulder: Westview Press.

Crittenden, Ann. 2001. *The Price of Motherhood: Why the Most Important Job in the World is Still the Least Valued.* New York: Henry Holt and Company.

Dahrendorf, Ralf. 1959. *Class and Class Conflict in Industrial Society.* Stanford: Stanford University Press.

Daniels, Roger. 1997. *Not Like Us: Immigrants and Minorities in America, 1890–1924.* Chicago: Ivan R. Dee.

Davies, Norman. 1982. *God's Playground: A History of Poland,* vol. 2. New York: Columbia University Press.

de Beauvoir, Simone. [1952] 1989. *The Second Sex.* Trans. H. M. Parshley. New York: Vintage Books.

Denzin, Norman. 1989. *Interpretive Biography.* Newbury Park, CA: Sage Publications.

DeSalvo, Louise. 1996. *Vertigo: A Memoir.* New York: Dutton.

DeVault, Marjorie L. 1991. *Feeding the Family: The Social Organization of Caring as Gendered Work.* Chicago: University of Chicago Press.

di Leonardo, Micaela. 1984. *The Varieties of Ethnic Experience: Kinship, Class, and Gender among California Italian-Americans.* Ithaca: Cornell University Press.

———. 1987. The Female World of Cards and Holidays: Women, Families, and the Work of Kinship. *Signs: Journal of Women in Culture and Society* 12 (3): 440–53.

Doane, Ashley W., Jr. 1999. Dominant Group Ethnic Identity in the United States: The Role of "Hidden" Ethnicity in Intergroup Relations. In *Majority and Minority: The Dynamics of Race and Ethnicity in American Life,* 6th ed., ed. Norman R. Yetman. 72–85. Boston: Allyn and Bacon.

Doman, Sr. M. Tullia. 1959. Polish American Sisterhoods and Their Contributions to the Catholic Church in the U.S. *Sacrum Poloniae Millennium* (Rome, Italy) 6: 371–622.

Donofrio, Beverly. 2000. *Looking for Mary, or, The Blessed Mother and Me.* New York: Viking Compass.

Dugger, Karen. 1988. Social Location and Gender-Role Attitudes: A Comparison of Black and White Women. *Gender & Society* 2 (4): 425–88.

Dunaway, David, and Willa Baum, eds. 1996. *Oral History: An Interdisciplinary Anthology,* 2d ed. London: AltaMira Press.

Ehrenreich, Barbara. 1989. The Silenced Majority: Why the Average Working Person has Disappeared from American Media and Culture. *Zeta Magazine* 2: 22.

———. 2000. Maid to Order: The Politics of Other Women's Work. *Harper's Magazine* 300, no. 1799 (April): 59–70.

Ehrenreich, Barbara, and John Ehrenreich. 1979. The Professional-Managerial Class. In *Between Labor and Capital,* ed. Pat Walker, 5–45. Boston: South End Press.

Ellis, Jacqueline. 1998. *Silent Witnesses: Representations of Working-Class Women in the United States, 1933–1945.* Bowling Green, OH: Bowling Green State University Popular Press.

Epstein, Helen. 1997. *Where She Came From: A Daughter's Search for Her Mother's History.* Boston: Little, Brown and Company.

Erdmans, Mary. 1998. *Opposite Poles: Immigrants and Ethnics in Polish Chicago, 1976–1990.* University Park: Pennsylvania State University Press.

———. 2000. Polonia in the New Century: We Will Not Fade Away. *Polish American Studies* 57 (1): 5–24.

Faue, Elizabeth. 2001. Reproducing Class Struggle: Class, Gender and Social Reproduction in U.S. Labor History. In *Labor History and the Labor Movement: Recent Trends in the United States and Canada,* ed. Irmgard Steinisch, 47–66. Ruhr-Universitaet, Germany: Bochum Institute.

Ferree, Myra Marx. 1984. Sacrifice, Satisfaction, and Social Change: Employment and the Family. In *My Troubles Are Going to Have Trouble with Me: Everyday Trials and Triumphs of Women Workers,* ed. Karen Brodkin Sacks and Dorothy Remy, 61–79. New Brunswick, NJ: Rutgers University Press.

Ferree, Myra Marx, and Beth B. Hess. 1994. *Controversy and Coalition: The New Feminist Movement across Three Decades of Change,* 2d ed. New York: Twayne.

Flinders, Carol Lee. 1999. *At the Root of This Longing: Reconciling a Spiritual Hunger and a Feminist Thirst.* San Francisco: HarperSanFrancisco.

Folbre, Nancy. 2001. *The Invisible Heart: Economics and Family Values.* New York: New Press.

Fox-Genovese, Elizabeth. 1997. *"Feminism Is Not the Story of My Life": How Today's Feminist Elite Has Lost Touch with the Real Concerns of Women.* New York: Anchor Books.

Frankenberg, Ruth. 1993. *White Women, Race Matters: The Social Construction of Whiteness.* Minneapolis: University of Minnesota Press.

Friedan, Betty. [1963] 1983. *The Feminine Mystique.* New York: Dell Publishing.

Fromm, Erich. 1956. *The Art of Loving: An Inquiry into the Nature of Love.* New York: Harper.

Gabaccia, Donna. 1991. Immigrant Women: Nowhere at Home? *Journal of American Ethnic History* 10 (4): 61–87.

Galush, William J. 1990. Purity and Power: Chicago Polonia Feminists, 1880–1914. *Polish American Studies* 47 (1): 5–24.

Garey, Anita Ilta. 1999. *Weaving Work and Motherhood.* Philadelphia: Temple University Press.

Genovese, Eugene D. 1974. *Roll, Jordan, Roll: The World the Slaves Made.* New York: Pantheon Books.

Getz, Lorine M. 1981. Women Struggle for an American Catholic Identity. In *Women and Religion in America.* Vol. 3, *1900–1968,* ed. Rosemary Radford Ruether and Rosemary Skinner Keller, 175–223. San Francisco: Harper & Row.

Giddens, Anthony. 1979. *Central Problems in Social Theory: Action, Structure, and Contradiction in Social Analysis.* Berkeley: University of California Press.

Giddings, Paula. 1984. *When and Where I Enter: The Impact of Black Women on Race and Sex in America.* New York: Bantam Books.

Gilligan, Carol. 1982. *In a Different Voice: Psychological Theory and Women's Development.* Cambridge, MA: Harvard University Press.

Gilman, Charlotte Perkins. [1898] 1998. *Women and Economics: A Study of the Economic Relation between Men and Women as a Factor in Social Evolution.* Mineola, NY: Dover Publications, Inc.

Gladsky, Thomas S. 1992. *Princes, Peasants, and Other Polish Selves: Ethnicity in American Literature.* Amherst: University of Massachusetts Press.

———. 1997. Monika Krawczyk, Victoria Janda, and the Polonie Club. In *Something of My Very Own to Say: American Women Writers of Polish Descent,* ed. Thomas S. Gladsky and Rita Holmes Gladsky, 101–11. Boulder: East European Monographs.

Gladsky, Thomas S., and Rita Holmes Gladsky, eds. 1997. *Something of My Very Own to Say: American Women Writers of Polish Descent.* Boulder: East European Monographs.

Glazer, Nona Y. 1997. "Between a Rock and a Hard Place": Racial, Ethnic, and Class Inequalities in Women's Professional Nursing Organizations. In *Workplace / Women's Place,* ed. Dana Dunn, 300–314. Los Angeles: Roxbury Publishing Company.

Glenn, Evelyn Nakano. 1992. From Servitude to Service Work: Historical Continuities in the Racial Division of Paid Reproductive Labor. *Signs: Journal of Women in Culture and Society* 18 (1): 1–43.

Gordon, Linda. 1999. *The Great Arizona Orphan Abduction.* Cambridge, MA: Harvard University Press.

Greene, Victor. 1992. *A Passion for Polka: Old-Time Ethnic Music in America.* Berkeley: University of California Press.

Gromada, Thaddeus V. 1997. Polish Americans and Multiculturalism. *Polish American Studies* 54 (2): 5–8.

Hesse-Biber, Sharlene, and Gregg Lee Carter. 2000. *Working Women in America: Split Dreams.* New York: Oxford University Press.

Hilburger, Sr. M. Charitina. 1946. Writings of the Felician Sisters in the United States. *Polish American Studies* 3 (3–4): 65–97.

Hochschild, Arlie, and Anne Machung. 1990. *The Second Shift.* New York: Avon Books.

hooks, bell. 1989. *Talking Back: Thinking Feminist, Thinking Black.* Boston: South End Press.

———. 1993. *Sisters of the Yam: Black Women and Self-Recovery.* Boston: South End Press.

———. 2000a. *Feminism is for Everybody: Passionate Politics.* Boston: South End Press.

———. 2000b. *Where We Stand: Class Matters.* New York: Routledge.

Howell, Joseph T. [1972] 1991. *Hard Living on Clay Street: Portraits of Blue Collar Families.* Prospect Heights, IL: Waveland Press, Inc.

Hughes, Everett C. [1971] 1984. *The Sociological Eye: Selected Papers.* New Brunswick, NJ: Transaction Books.

Hurtado, Aida. 1996. *The Color of Privilege: Three Blasphemies on Race and Feminism.* Ann Arbor: University of Michigan Press.

Ignatiev, Noel. 1995. *How the Irish Became White.* New York: Routledge.

Jacobson, Matthew Frye. 1995. *Special Sorrows: The Diasporic Imagination of Irish, Polish, and Jewish Immigrants in the United States.* Cambridge: Harvard University Press.

Jung, Philip. n.d. *The First 100 Years: Basilica of St. Adalbert, 1881–1981.* Greenville, MI: Greenville Printing Co.

Kaminer, Wendy. 1993. Feminism's Identity Crisis. *Atlantic Monthly,* October, 51–68.

Kantowicz, Edward. 1975. *Polish-American Politics in Chicago, 1888–1940.* Chicago: University of Chicago Press.

Kelley, Robin D. G. 1994. *Race Rebels: Culture, Politics, and the Black Working Class.* New York: Free Press.

Kieniewicz, Stefan. 1969. *The Emancipation of the Polish Peasantry.* Chicago: University of Chicago Press.

Kleiman, Jeffrey D. 1985. The Great Strike: Religion, Labor, and Reform in Grand Rapids, Michigan, 1890–1916. Ph.D. diss., Michigan State University.

Kolinski, Dennis L. 1994. Shrines and Crosses in Rural Central Wisconsin. *Polish American Studies* 51 (2): 33–47.

———. 1995. Polish Rural Settlement in America. *Polish American Studies* 52 (2): 21–55.

Koloski, Bernard. 1997. Children's Books: Lois Lenski, Maia Wojciechowska, Anne Pellowski. In *Something of My Very Own to Say: American Women Writers of Polish Descent*, ed. Thomas S. Gladsky and Rita Holmes Gladsky, 147–57. Boulder: East European Monographs.

Krieger, Susan. 1996. *The Family Silver: Essays on Relationships among Women.* Berkeley: University of California Press.

Kuznicki, Ellen Marie. 1978a. A Historical Perspective on the Polish American Parochial School. *Polish American Studies* 35 (1–2): 13–22.

———. 1978b. The Polish American Parochial School. In *Poles In America*, ed. Frank Mocha, 435–60. Stevens Point, WI: Worzalla Publishing Company.

Laslett, Barbara. 1999. Personal Narratives as Sociology. *Contemporary Sociology* 28 (4): 391–401.

Lemert, Charles. 2002. *Social Things: An Introduction to the Sociological Life,* 2d ed. Lanham, MD: Rowman and Littlefield Publishers.

Lieberson, Stanley, and Mary C. Waters. 1988. *From Many Strands: Ethnic and Racial Groups in Contemporary America.* New York: Russell Sage Foundation.

Liebow, Elliot. 1995. *Tell Them Who I Am: The Lives of Homeless Women.* New York: Penguin Books.

Lopata, Helena. 1976a. *Polish Americans: Status Competition in an Ethnic Community.* Englewood Cliffs, NJ: Prentice Hall Inc.

———. 1976b. The Polish American Family. In *Ethnic Families in America: Patterns and Variations,* eds. C. H. Mindel and R. W. Habenstein, 15–40. New York: Elsevier.

Lorber, Judith. 1994. *Paradoxes of Gender.* New Haven: Yale University Press.

Lorde, Audre. 1982. *ZAMI: A New Spelling of My Name.* Freedom, CA: Crossing Press.

Lucille, Sister, C.R. 1958. Polish Farmers and Workers in the United States to 1914. *Polish American Studies* 15 (1–2): 1–9.

Luttrell, Wendy. 1997. *Schoolsmart and Motherwise: Working-Class Women's Identity and Schooling.* New York: Routledge.

Lydens, Z. Z. 1976. *A Look at Early Grand Rapids.* Grand Rapids, MI: Kregel Publications.

Majewska, Karen. 1997. Toward "a Pedagogical Goal": Family, Nation, and Ethnicity in the Fiction of Polonia's First Women Writers. In *Something of My Very Own to Say: American Women Writers of Polish Descent,* ed. Thomas S. Gladsky and Rita Holmes Gladsky, 54–66. Boulder: East European Monographs.

Mannheim, Karl. 1936. *Ideology and Utopia: An Introduction to the Sociology of Knowledge.* New York: Harcourt Brace Jovanovich.

Mansbridge, Jane. 1986. *Why We Lost the ERA.* Chicago: University of Chicago Press.

Mantsios, Gregory. 1995. Class in America: Myths and Realities. In *Race, Class, and*

Gender in the United States: An Integrated Study, 3rd ed., ed. Paula Rothenberg, 131–43. New York: St. Martin's Press.

Marx, Karl, and Friedrich Engels. 1959. *Basic Writings on Politics and Philosophy*, ed. Lewis Feuer. Garden City, NY: Anchor Books.

Massey, Douglas S., and Nancy A. Denton. 1993. *American Apartheid: Segregation and the Making of the Underclass.* Cambridge, MA: Harvard University Press.

McMahon, Martha. 1995. *Engendering Motherhood: Identity and Self-Transformation in Women's Lives.* New York: Guilford Press.

Meagher, Timothy J. 2001. *Inventing Irish America: Generation, Class, and Ethnic Identity in a New England City, 1880–1928.* Notre Dame, IN: University of Notre Dame Press.

Merton, Robert K. 1972. Insiders and Outsiders: A Chapter in the Sociology of Knowledge. *American Journal of Sociology* 77 (July): 9–47.

Michalski, Thomas A. 1985. The Prussian Crucible: Some Items in the Cultural Baggage of Prussian Polish Immigrants. *Polish American Studies* 42 (2): 5–17.

Milostan, Harry. 1977. *Parisville Poles: First Polish Settlers in U.S.A.?* Mt. Clemens, MI: MASSPAC Publishing Co.

——— [Natsolim, pseud.]. 1984. *Gniezniks: Pioneer Polonians, Facts & Fables.* Mt. Clemens, MI: MASSPAC Publishing Co.

Modell, John, and Tamara K. Hareven. 1977. Urbanization and the Malleable Household: An Examination of Boarding and Lodging in American Families. In *Family and Kin in Urban Communities, 1700–1930*, ed. Tamara K. Hareven, 164–86. New York: New Viewpoints.

Moody, Ann. 1976. *Coming of Age in Mississippi.* New York: Laurel.

Myaskovsky, Larissa, and Michele Andrisin Wittig. 1997. Predictors of Feminist Social Identity Among College Women. *Sex Roles: A Journal of Research* 37 (11–12): 861–83.

Nagel, Joanne. 1994. Constructing Ethnicity: Creating and Recreating Ethnic Identity and Culture. *Social Problems* 41 (1): 152–76.

Napierkowski, Thomas J. 1983. The Image of Polish Americans in American Literature. *Polish American Studies* 40 (1): 5–44.

Naples, Nancy A. 1994. Contradictions in Agrarian Ideology: Restructuring Gender, Race-Ethnicity, and Class. *Rural Sociology* 59 (1): 110–35.

Napolska, Sr. M. Remigia, CSSF. 1946. The Polish Immigrant in Detroit to 1914. In *Something of My Very Own to Say: American Women Writers of Polish Descent*, ed. Thomas S. Gladsky and Rita Holmes Gladsky, 87–99. Boulder: East European Monographs.

Newman, Katherine S. 1993. *Declining Fortunes: The Withering of the American Dream.* New York: Basic Books.

Nicholson, Linda J. 1986. *Gender and History: The Limits of Social Theory in the Age of the Family.* New York: Columbia University Press.

Norris, Kathleen. 1993. *Dakota: A Spiritual Geography.* New York: Houghton Mifflin Company.

———. 1998. *Amazing Grace: A Vocabulary of Faith.* New York: Riverhead Books.

Obidinski, Eugene. 1985. Beyond Hansen's Law: Fourth Generation Polonian Identity. *Polish American Studies* 42 (1): 27–42.

Obidinski, Eugene, and Helen Stankiewicz Zand. 1987. *Polish Folkways in America: Community and Family.* New York: University Press of America.

O'Farrell, Brigid, and Joyce L. Kornbluh, eds. 1996. *Rocking the Boat: Union Women's Voices, 1915–1975.* New Brunswick, NJ: Rutgers University Press.

Olson, Gordon L. 1992. *A Grand Rapids Sampler.* Grand Rapids, MI: Grand Rapids Historical Commission.

Orsi, Robert A. 1996. *Thank You, St. Jude: Women's Devotion to the Patron Saint of Hopeless Causes.* New Haven: Yale University Press.

Pacyga, Dominic. 1996. To Live Amongst Others: Poles and Their Neighbors in Industrial Chicago, 1865–1930. *Journal of American Ethnic History* 16 (1): 55–73.

Parejko, Ken. 1996. *Remember Me Dancing.* Oregon, WI: Badger Books, Inc.

Parot, Joseph John. 1975. The Racial Dilemma in Chicago's Polish Neighborhoods, 1920–1970. *Polish American Studies* 32 (2): 27–38.

———. 1981. *Polish Catholics in Chicago, 1850–1920: A Religious History.* DeKalb: Northern Illinois University Press.

Parsons, Talcott. 1947. Weber's Methodology of Social Science. In *The Theory of Social and Economic Organization,* by Max Weber, trans. A. M. Henderson and Talcott Parsons, 8–29. Glencoe, IL: Free Press.

Patai, Daphne, and Sherna Berger Gluck, eds. 1991. *Women's Words: The Feminist Practice of Oral History.* New York: Routledge.

Perkowski, Jan. L. 1966. The Kashubs—Origins and Emigration to the U.S. *Polish American Studies* 23 (1): 1–7.

Pinkowski, Edward. 1978. The Great Influx of Polish Immigrants and the Industries They Entered. In *Poles in America: Bicentennial Essays,* ed. Frank Mocha, 303–70. Stevens Point, WI: Worzalla Publishing Company.

Pleck, Elizabeth H. 2000. *Celebrating the Family: Ethnicity, Consumer Culture, and Family Rituals.* Cambridge, MA: Harvard University Press.

Pula, James. 1980. American Immigration and the Dillingham Commission. *Polish American Studies* 37 (1): 5–31.

———. 1995. *Polish Americans: An Ethnic Community.* New York: Twayne Publishers.

———. 1996. Image, Status, Mobility and Integration in American Society: The Polish Experience. *Journal of American Ethnic History* 16 (1): 74–95.

Radzialowski, Thaddeus. 1974. A View from the Polish Ghetto: Some Observations of the First Hundred Years in Detroit. *Ethnicity* 1 (2): 125–50.

———. 1975. Reflections on the History of Felicians in America. *Polish American Studies* 32 (1): 19–28.

Radzilowski, John. 1994. Family Labor and Immigrant Success in a Polish American Rural Community, 1883–1905. *Polish American Studies* 51 (2): 49–66.

———. 2002. A New Poland in the Old Northwest: Polish Farming Communities on the Northern Great Plains. *Polish American Studies* 59 (2): 79–96.

Radzilowski, Thaddeus. 1996. Family, Women, and Gender: The Polish Experience. In *Polish Americans and Their History: Community, Culture, and Politics*, ed. John J. Bukowczyk, 58–79. Pittsburgh: University of Pittsburgh Press.

———. 1997. Reinventing the Center: Polish Immigrant Women in the New World. In *Something of My Very Own to Say: American Women Writers of Polish Descent*, ed. Thomas S. Gladsky and Rita Holmes Gladsky, 11–24. Boulder: East European Monographs.

Reinharz, Shulamit. 1992. *Feminist Methods in Social Research.* New York: Oxford University Press.

Ritchie, Donald. 1995. *Doing Oral History.* New York: Twayne Publishers.

Roberts, Elizabeth. 1984. *A Woman's Place: An Oral History of Working-Class Women 1890–1940.* Oxford: Basil Blackwell Publisher.

Roediger, David R. 1991. *The Wages of Whiteness: Race and the Making of the American Working Class.* New York: Verso.

———. 1994. Whiteness and Ethnicity in the History of "White Ethnics" in the United States. In *Towards the Abolition of Whiteness: Essays on Race, Politics, and Working Class History.* New York: Verso.

Rogers, Joel, and Ruy Teixeira. 2000. America's Forgotten Majority. *Atlantic Monthly* 285 (June): 66–75.

Romero, Mary, and Abigail J. Stewart, eds. 1999. *Women's Untold Stories: Breaking Silence, Talking Back, Voicing Complexity.* New York: Routledge.

Rooney, Elizabeth. 1957. Polish Americans and Family Disorganization. *American Catholic Sociological Review* 18 (March): 47–51.

Rosen, Ellen Israel. 1987. *Bitter Choices: Blue-Collar Women in and out of Work.* Chicago: University of Chicago Press.

Rosenzweig, Roy, and David Thelen. 1998. *The Presence of the Past: Popular Uses of History in American Life.* New York: Columbia University Press.

Rothenberg, Paula S., ed. 1995. *Race, Class, and Gender in the United States: An Integrated Study,* 3d ed. New York: St. Martin's Press.

Rowland, Robyn. 1986. Women Who Do and Women Who Don't, Join the Women's Movement: Issues For Conflict and Collaboration. *Sex Roles* 14 (November 12): 679–92.

Rubin, Beth A. 1996. *Shifts in the Social Contract: Understanding Change in American Society.* Thousand Oaks, CA: Pine Forge Press.

Rubin, Lillian Breslow. 1976. *Worlds of Pain: Life in the Working Class Family.* New York: Basic Books, Inc.

———. 1994. *Families on the Fault Line: America's Working Class Speaks about the Family, the Economy, Race, and Ethnicity.* New York: HarperCollins.

Rudnick, Lois. 1992. The Life of Mabel Dodge Luhan. In *The Challenge of Feminist Biography: Writing the Lives of Modern American Women,* ed. Sara Alpern, Joyce Antler, Elisabeth Israels Perry, and Ingrid Winther Scobie, 116–38. Chicago: University of Illinois Press.

Rymph, Catherine E. 2000. Neither Neutral nor Neutralized: Phyllis Schlafly's Battle against Sexism. In *Women's America,* ed. Linda K. Kerber and Jane Sherron De Hart, 501–7. New York: Oxford University Press.

Sacks, Karen Brodkin. 1984. Introduction; Generations of Working-Class Families. In *My Troubles Are Going to Have Trouble with Me: Everyday Trials and Triumphs of Women Workers,* ed. Karen Brodkin Sacks and Dorothy Remy, 1–12, 15–38. New Brunswick, NJ: Rutgers University Press.

Sandberg, Neil C. 1974. The Changing Polish American. *Polish American Studies* 31 (1): 5–14.

Sanders, Irwin, and Ewa Morawska. 1975. *Polish-American Community Life: A Survey of Research.* New York: Polish Institute of Arts and Sciences.

Sapiro, Virginia. 1990. *Women in American Society,* 2d ed. Mountain View, CA: Mayfield Publishing.

Savaglio, Paula. 1997. Big-Band, Slovenian-American, Rock, and Country Music: Cross-Cultural Influences in the Detroit Polonia. *Polish American Studies* 54 (2): 23–44.

Seifer, Nancy. 1976. *Nobody Speaks For Me!: Self-Portraits of American Working Class Women.* New York: Simon and Schuster.

Sennet, Richard, and Jonathan Cobb. [1972] 1993. *The Hidden Injuries of Class.* New York: W.W. Norton and Company, Inc.

Sharlet, Jeff. 1999. Seeking Solidarity in the Culture of the Working Class. *The Chronicle of Higher Education,* July 23, A19–20.

Sherkat, Darren, and T. Jean Blocker. 1994. The Political Development of Sixties Activists: Identifying the Influences of Class, Gender, and Socialization on Protest Participation. *Social Forces* 72 (3): 821–42.

Shils, Edward. 1981. *Tradition.* Chicago: University of Chicago Press.

Sidel, Ruth. [1978] 1995. *Urban Survival: The World of Working-Class Women.* Lincoln: University of Nebraska Press.

Silverman, Deborah Anders. 2000. *Polish-American Folklore.* Chicago: University of Illinois Press.

Skendzel, Eduard Adam. 1981. *The Sacred Heart Story: A History of Sacred Heart Parish in Grand Rapids, Michigan, on the Occasion of its Diamond Jubilee, 1904–1979*. Grand Rapids, MI: Foremost Press, Inc.

———. 1983. The Polanders. *Grand River Valley Review* 4 (2): 2–11.

———. 1993. The Rise and Fall of the Grand Rapids Polonia. Presented at the Association for the Advancement of Dutch American Studies Conference, Grand Rapids, Michigan, October 8–9.

———. 1999. *A Book of Remembrance: The Grand Rapids St. Isidore's Story, A History within a History, Centennial 1897–1997*. Grand Rapids, MI: Littleshield Press.

———. n.d. *Polonian Musings*. Two-volume manuscript in the Local Historical Collections of the Grand Rapids Public Library.

Smith, Dorothy. 1987. *The Everyday World as Problematic: A Feminist Sociology*. Boston: Northeastern University Press.

Sollors, Werner. 1986. *Beyond Ethnicity: Consent and Descent in American Culture*. New York: Oxford University Press.

Stacey, Judith. 1998. *Brave New Families: Stories of Domestic Upheaval in Late-Twentieth-Century America*. Berkeley: University of California Press.

Steedman, Carolyn Kay. 1987. *Landscape for a Good Woman: A Story of Two Lives*. New Brunswick, NJ: Rutgers University Press.

Steinberg, Jacques. 2000. Working-Class Origins Unite Educators Group. *New York Times*, 27 November, A10.

Stewart, Abigail J., and Joan M. Ostrove. 1993. Social Class, Social Change, and Gender: Working-Class Women at Radcliffe and After. *Psychology of Women Quarterly* 17: 475–97.

Stone, Elizabeth. 1989. *Black Sheep and Kissing Cousins: How Our Family Stories Shape Us*. New York: Penguin Books.

Strom, Sharon Hartman. 1992. *Beyond the Typewriter: Gender, Class, and the Origins of Modern American Office Work, 1900–1930*. Chicago: University of Illinois Press.

St. Stanislaus Parish, 1892–1992. 1992. Centennial Committee, Hilliards, Michigan.

Swierenga, Robert P. 1985. *The Dutch in America: Immigration, Settlement, and Cultural Change*. New Brunswick, NJ: Rutgers University Press.

Symanski, Edward. 1964. Polish Settlers in Grand Rapids, Michigan. *Polish American Studies* 21 (2): 91–106.

Symmons-Symonolewicz, Konstantin. 1983. Is There a Polonian Culture? *Polish American Studies* 40 (1): 88–90.

Tannen, Deborah. 1991. *You Just Don't Understand: Women and Men in Conversation*. New York: Ballantine Books.

Taras, Piotr A. 1982. The Dispute over Polonian Culture. *Polish American Studies* 39 (1): 38–54.

Taras, Piotr, Angela T. Pienkos, and Thaddeus Radzilowski. 1980. Paul Wrobel's *Our Way*—Three Views. *Polish American Studies* 37 (1): 32–51.

Tempska, Urzula. 1997. From (Ethnic) Mama's Girl to Her Own (New Ethnic) Woman: Gender and Ethnicity in Suzanne Strempek Shea's *Selling the Lite of Heaven.* In *Something of My Very Own to Say: American Women Writers of Polish Descent,* ed. Thomas S. Gladsky and Rita Holmes Gladsky, 287–303. Boulder: East European Monographs.

Tester, Nancy. 2001. Missing Person. *Notre Dame Magazine* 30, no. 3 (Autumn): 84–85.

Thomas, William, and Florian Znaniecki. [1918] 1958. *The Polish Peasant in Europe and America.* Chicago: University of Chicago Press.

Tilly, Louise A., and Joan W. Scott. 1978. *Women, Work and Family.* New York: Holt, Rinehart and Winston.

U.S. Census. 1880. *Statistics of the Population of the United States.* Washington, D.C.: U.S. Government Printing Office.

U.S. Census. 1900. *Population, Part I.* Washington, D.C.: U.S. Government Printing Office.

U.S. Census. 1910. *Population, Alabama-Montana.* Washington, D.C.: U.S. Government Printing Office.

U.S. Census. 1920. *Population, Composition and Characteristics of the Population by State.* Washington, D.C.: U.S. Government Printing Office.

U.S. Census. 1930. *Population, Alabama-Missouri.* Washington, D.C.: U.S. Government Printing Office.

U.S. Census. 1950. *Characteristics of the Population, Michigan.* Washington, D.C.: U.S. Government Printing Office.

U.S. Census. 1960. *Characteristics of the Population, Michigan.* Washington, D.C.: U.S. Government Printing Office.

Vanneman, Reeve, and Lynn Weber Cannon. 1987. *The American Perception of Class.* Philadelphia: Temple University Press.

Waters, Mary. 1990. *Ethnic Options: Choosing Ethnic Identities in America.* Berkeley: University of California Press.

Wax, Rosalie. 1971. *Doing Fieldwork: Warnings and Advice.* Chicago: University of Chicago Press.

Willis, Paul. 1977. *Learning to Labor: How Working Class Kids Get Working Class Jobs.* New York: Columbia University Press.

Wilson, William Julius. 1987. *The Truly Disadvantaged: The Inner City, the Underclass, and Public Policy.* Chicago: University of Chicago Press.

Winowska, Maria. 1972. *Go Repair My House.* Lodi, NJ: Congregation of the Sisters of Saint Felix.

Wrobel, Paul. 1979. *Our Way: Family, Parish, and Neighborhood in a Polish-American Community.* Notre Dame, IN: University of Notre Dame Press.

Zaborowska, Magdalena. 1995. *How We Found America: Reading Gender Through East European Immigrant Narratives.* Chapel Hill: The University of North Carolina Press.

Zand, Helen Stankiewicz. 1958. Polish American Holiday Customs. *Polish American Studies* 15 (3-4): 81-90.

Ziolkowski, Sr. Mary Janice, CSSF. 1984. *The Felician Sisters of Livonia, Michigan: First Province in America.* Detroit: Harlo Press.

———. 1997. Spiritual Voice, Social Conscience. In *Something of My Very Own to Say: American Women Writers of Polish Descent,* ed. Thomas S. Gladsky and Rita Holmes Gladsky, 77-86. Boulder: East European Monographs.

Zweig, Michael. 2000. *The Working Class Majority: America's Best Kept Secret.* Ithaca, NY: Cornell University Press.

Index